Telling Performances

Marie Maclean

Telling Performances

Essays on Gender,
Narrative, and Performance

Edited by
Brian Nelson, Anne Freadman,
and Philip Anderson

DELAWARE

Newark: University of Delaware Press
London: Associated University Presses

Associated University Presses
440 Forsgate Drive
Cranbury, NJ 08512

Associated University Presses
16 Barter Street
London WC1A 2AH, England

Associated University Presses
P.O. Box 338, Port Credit
Mississauga, Ontario
Canada L5G 4L8

The paper used in this publication meets the requirements of the American National Standard for Permanence of Paper for Printed Library Materials Z39.48-1984.

Library of Congress Cataloging-in-Publication Data

Telling performances : essays on gender, narrative, and performance / edited by Brian Nelson, Anne Freadman, and Philip Anderson.
    p. cm.
    Includes bibliographical references and index.
    ISBN 0-87413-707-1 (alk. paper)
    1. Gender identity in literature. 2. Narration (Rhetoric) 3. Literature, Modern—History and criticism. I. Nelson, Brian, 1946– II. Freadman, Anne, 1944– III. Anderson, Philip, 1949–

PN56.G45 T45 2001
809'.93353—dc21

          2001027012

PRINTED IN THE UNITED STATES OF AMERICA

In Memoriam
Marie Maclean
1928–1994

Contents

Introduction

LITERARY THEORY FINDS IN ITS CLASSICAL CANON TWO PRESTIGIOUS models for an act of mourning: one is Aristotelian catharsis—vexed though the interpretation of this topic continues to be[1]—and the other is the funeral oration. In the first, an audience seeks "in one short sorrowing the remedy of a long and grievous sorrow"; in the second, a community comes together to praise a life, in the narrative of a person's works and days. Only on rare occasions, says Quintilian, do we enjoy the privilege of giving a posthumous vote of thanks, and of taking as the theme of our panegyric a moment of genius that has stood the test of time.[2] This book is not cathartic in its inspiration, but panegyric. It seeks not to purge—how could we?—the pain of Marie Maclean's passing but (in the Renaissance sense) to illustrate—would that our unworthy powers could rise so high!—the teaching of her work.

Nevertheless, it is a book about performance—the telling of performance, the performance of telling—and it is a book that supposes that some performances are particularly telling and that they matter through their art. This supposition rests on what is common to the lore of the ancient orators and the art of the dramatists and actors. The stakes are high: no pity, shame, or fear, no moving of the passions, no catharsis, can take place in the absence of a telling performance. No knowledge, either, no act of informing or understanding or invention, no inspiration by a teacher or scholar, no homage, mourning, or celebration by her students and colleagues. The prestige of the theater has all too often been invoked to contrast, or even to oppose, the performance arts with those, such as fictional or historical narrative, that "report" and do not mime their events: theater and narrative, mimesis and diegesis, performance and text, the body and the word—as if the one would purge the other the better to colonize an exclusive domain. Yet this opposition always fails, whether we find narrative on stage in the recitations of a Greek chorus, a Shakespearean prologue or epilogue, or the reported climax of French classical conventions, or whether, with the bards, we find performance in the telling of the tale. As Marie Maclean herself puts it, narrative and theater are more like "fraternal enemies" than

9

mutually exclusive opposites; it is, she writes, a prerequisite to understanding the performativity even of written narrative, to recognize that they have common roots in oral performance.[3]

The significance of folklore studies to Marie Maclean's work on narrative cannot be overestimated, yet, as she is careful to point out, the issue she pursues is the mediation of the relations between teller and audience, showing, in the course of her abundant research, the way the models of oral performance can be modified to suit the demands of the written form and the modalities of reading that it imposes. This relation between teller and audience is the subject of an instructive series of essays by the folklorist Richard Bauman on the performance of storytelling in oral settings in contemporary America.[4] The capacity of the telling to interpret both the context of the telling and the reported events, and its mediating powers in the social environment, are constitutive of the power of storytelling and indeed of its point. This is also the focus of Maclean's work. It would be all too easy to restrict findings such as these to the eventfulness of an oral culture or, worse, to a naive metaphysics committed to presence. If, as Jacques Derrida has argued so persuasively,[5] speech events are constitutively written in the sense that no sign is a sign if it is absolutely confined to the context of its original utterance, then "oral performance" is not the opposite of "written" or printed "texts." This is not to say, writes Derrida in a careful qualification, that there is no "relative specific effect" of the spoken word as distinct from the written "in the traditional sense,"[6] but that speech is posited in the "graphematic" as the condition of its possibility. Derrida argues that this relation is asymmetrical, yet it would be a mistake to think of writing as confined to the transcendental condition of all language. Writing, too, has specific material effectivity that emerges in the paradoxical relation of the contemplative solitary activity of reading with the rhetorical performativity of the writing. It was Barthes, first, who reminded us that the solitary reader is more like a musician than a cerebral scholar or a passive consumer, in the well-known analogy of reading with the performance of a musical score.

Maclean's work on this issue counts among the most illuminating of recent contributions to narratology. In *Narrative as Performance* she makes two crucial moves. The first is the issue of "narrative space" (*NP*, 100).[7] Written narratives are read for traces of performance, often thematized emblematically in metaphors and analogies associated with the storytelling act itself, or in representations *en abyme* of the narration as theater or oratorical display. While in traditional forms of storytelling, audiences are selected by diverse performance spaces, from the relative inclusiveness of the "mat laid on the street corner"

(*NP,* 1) to the relative exclusiveness of the "temple sanctuary" (ibid.), the "open performance" (*NP,* 133) of the published text intervenes actively in these processes, making and breaking conventionalized systems of referentiality and material space to create the conditions for a diversity of readerly performances. Maclean elaborates the complexity of these theses in her reading of Baudelaire's *Choses parisiennes:* the artist is *satimbanque,* storytelling may resemble a rhetorical joust (*NP,* 141–60). The role of the reader is inflected accordingly, and the space of narration opened into the history of its readings.

The figure of space is also evident in the second major move for which Maclean's work is known, which is to practice a dialectic between theories of the solitary reader—as played out in theories of subjectivity and desire, for example—and theories of the audience. Here the energies unleashed by focusing on the performance of writing and reading act to challenge the very scope of the questions raised in narrative theory. Maclean interrogates the territorial control implied in the Freudian account of desire through her reading of Deleuze and Guattari's articulation of theories of desire with theories of power. In a significant feminist modification of the agenda for analyzing autobiography and other genres of personal life-writing, Maclean's last book, *The Name of the Mother,* works through the problematic of the family romance in relation to authorship and the matter of the name. With an analysis of illegitimacy and "delegitimation," the loss and the rejection of the name of the father, Maclean uses this work to deconstruct the terms of a whole generation of literary theory, and thus, to displace its "fathers."[8]

We cannot—and neither did Marie Maclean—stop there. The history of narrotology has, in some sense, brought us to this place, where literary theory accepts and explores the constitutive paradox according to which performance inhabits the word itself and makes it act. The scope of its acts is demonstrated by the significance of the general theoretical issues raised through Marie Maclean's apparently modest proposals, her readings, her minute attention to the detail of texts. Yet the important question is the one that is posed next: what is the upshot of this move—the upshot in terms of the sense and direction of theoretical reflection, and the upshot in terms of what it reveals about the literature we read? *Telling Performances* collects eleven essays that read printed narratives according to the imperative we find in Maclean's work, and that, in a variety of ways, explore the upshot of the move to performativity.

The first five essays explore what has happened to the issue of plot in this move. What are the properties of a good story? asks Gerald Prince. Is it all in the telling, or was there a baby in the bathtub

somewhere? The very business of telling is incited by some events and
not by others, and Prince wonders if we can discern the properties of
tellable plots. We have placed Prince's essay at the head of this collection in order to make it stand both as a reminder of the history that
locates Maclean's work, and as the insistent question of that history.[9]
Only by indulging in a naive modernism could we believe we had left
it behind: the move to performativity in narrative does not eliminate
the issue of plot, but reconstrues it, and it does so in a variety of ways.
The challenge Prince issues is taken up in practice by considering
what kinds of plots have in fact pervaded Western writing. Gale Mac-
Lachlan studies the quintessentially modern genre of the detective
novel, showing how the very formation of the plot, and its plausibility,
are secured through performance. The theatrical model is central to
her reading of the issue of "textual success" where, as she puts it,
histoire gives way to histrionics. MacLachlan's study of this genre
shows that it depends on a reconstruction of the relation between
histoire and *discours,* but in no way does this imply the subsumption,
let alone the obliteration, of plot. On the contrary, she demonstrates
that performance itself is the climax of the story, and the crucial
topos of the genre. Indeed, we could suggest, more generally, that
the relation between the telling and the topoi of the told is the
question of genre, and that genre is the performative dimension of
narrative. The performativity issue retrieves the teachings of rhetoric
and deploys them anew.

It is in this way that the apparently formalist and certainly technical
issues of narratology emerge as instruments for investigating the insistent preoccupations of postmodern cultures: what is "a place in
the library," what the relation with language and culture, with the
normativities of family and profession and stories themselves, for
"the women and children first?" Marie Maclean's work on excluded,
enforced, and occluded readers is of signal importance in these questions (see *NP,* 38–41, 100–101, 107–9, 171–72). Naomi Segal inflects
for gender the triangles that form the story of adultery; in her essay,
the insistence on the gender of point of view functions to enact
narrative outcomes, and readerly engagements, beyond the general-
izations offered by standard treatments of the genre. Chris Worth
considers the patriarchal plot, showing the law of the father to be
subverted by competing narratives, as intertextuality subverts the law
of the author. His is an explicit uptake of Maclean's project for a
gendered criticism, interrogating the legitimacy of meaning by un-
dermining the name of the father, as she examines delegitimation
through the name of the mother. Philip Anderson studies a modern
bildungsroman in which the constitution of subjectivity occurs in a

postcolonial setting. Here too, the telling itself enters into active conflict with what we might call the authorized version, the subject of the *énonciation* with the subject of the *énoncé*. The business of storytelling itself, and of readerly performance, brings us close to the issue of the relation of the subject with cultural codifications, and hence to issues of identity.

A special sense of "performance" is played out in erotic fiction, the subject of essays by Peter Cryle and Rosemary Sorensen. Cryle studies the history of his genre through the telling of sexual performance itself, the reduction of plot to the exclamation that signals climax, the discursive and the bodily coming together in "ejaculation." Sorensen matches his focus on telling with her own, on reading; she takes up Maclean's question of the excluded or enforced-upon reading in relation with "sex texts," and asks what it would be to develop feminist reading strategies of the special kind of textual bullying she discerns. This is gendered reading of normatively heterosexual encounters. It is followed by another essay on erotic performance, this one by Nathaniel Wing, who explores the full import of queer theory's uptake of "performativity" in a reading of that canonical object of perennial fascination, Gautier's *Mademoiselle de Maupin:* cross-dressing, the performance of cross-gendering, and the ultimate undecidability of both genre and gender, lead in this case to the impossibility of narrative closure. Does the plot thicken or thin here? Does it dissolve together, taking on the status of a mirage, like the impossibility of firm sexual identity in the desired other?

The theatricality of sex and gender has become one of the signs of modernism, famously explored by Colette, who is the subject of two essays in the collection, by Julie Solomon and Anne Freadman. Solomon explores the theater as site and as metaphor for the issue of self-representation and, through that, the performance of feminine identity. Freadman's essay, which uses both fiction and pictorial material as well as some documentary genres, describes the rupture brought about by the fashions of modernity as they provoked crises in sexual identity and drama in gender roles. It tells a story of the history of butch.

As we open the volume with the trace of oral performance in all narrative, with its representation in narrative as theater, so we close it with the radical necessity of writing as it displaces and replaces the ephemerality of the oral, the last gesture of the tongue, the death of the author. Ross Chambers pursues a different upshot of the question that informs this collection. This is the performance of writing itself. Chamber's texts are AIDS diaries, first person narratives of the unbecoming of the first person, and they perform an act of survival.

What is it to read these texts, to be positioned as the one for whom death and survival, both, are the messages that cancel each other out? What is it to survive both the reading and the writing of the trauma of AIDS? Shadowing his reading is the pain of the friend, writing what it is to read and write in the absence of Marie Maclean. The friendship that linked Ross Chambers and Marie Maclean took its place in "a communion of minds and a dialogue between a family of friends."[10] The rhizomic structure of this "indirect discourse" may be a form of "influence," but this influence was utterly mutual and hence devoid of the anxiety that comes of "authority and hierarchy" associated with the "rigidity of the father's line (p. 214). If Ross Chambers's text, like all the texts published here, is an expression of grief, it, like them, is also marked by the kind of celebration that can be read through Marie Maclean's "Many hearts will understand me," itself a kind of eulogy for what she knew she was about to lose, a text of implicit sadness, courage and joy that looks not at what is lost but what has been gained.

"Literature alone can provide true solace in adversity." Thus writes Quintilian, in his poignant and moving tribute to his son, who had died during the course of composition of the *Institutio,* thus robbing his father, who "survives only to weep," of his chosen interlocutor. "I thought," he writes, "that this work would be the most precious part of the inheritance that would fall to my son. . . ." This moment of intense personal grief comes from the Preface to Book VI, and forms a pendant to the preface to the whole work. There, at the outset of his teaching, Quintilian offers a model of the genre of deliberative rhetoric, in which he considers the arguments for and against public instruction by a teacher such as himself, as against instruction by private tutors. He concludes—predictably—in favor of the former, which alone can justify the writing and publishing of a codified art such as he envisages. The writing of a work on the art of speaking is a bequest; it enacts the paradox of the writtenness of speech, which it passes on to succeeding generations, and of the codification of an art of invention. Even if he does not have anything original to add to the debates of his predecessors, he writes, thus inserting the issue of originality into the problem of traditional teaching, at least his work will perform the rhetoric of deliberation as it weighs up the points at issue in these debates. But even as he abjures originality, Quintilian states what he believes to be special and different about his pedagogy: unlike his predecessors, "I hold that the art of oratory includes all that is essential for the training of an orator. . . . I propose to mould the studies of my orator from infancy. . . ." This is the place of his son, whom he has instructed from a very young age, and who had already been promised to "all the high offices of state" and given signs of "rivalling in eloquence [his] grandsire." It is as if, not only in his learning, but in his promised practice, "my little Quintilian" was destined not only to receive, but to pass on to future generations, the great traditions of public speech. Quintilian is concerned, however, to assure his dedicatee (Marcellus Victorius) that he is not merely indulging in an unseemly public display of private grief, for this preface is also the very model of the panegyric, offered to exemplify the second of the recognized genres.[11] Speech, for the orators and rhetors, was by definition a public matter, something to be learned and practiced with care, something to be inherited and passed on. Taught from its exemplary models, it was to be imitated and adapted to changed needs and different contexts; speech was everything that we must say about writing. The performativity of language is written, its writing is performed.

Some years have now passed since the death of Marie Maclean; it is a long sorrow that brooks no sudden purging, but yet too short for the scale Quintilian envisaged for his perdurable monuments to genius. Besides, the idea of treating Marie's work as a monument, heaven forfend. Quintilian's funeral oration tells us that writing is constitutively bereaved. Would that we could write back to Marie Maclean to have her know that her teaching is the stuff of our work! But bereft of our chosen interlocutor, we must—as she always did— accept Quintilian's wisdom: published writing goes in search of its reader, and the stake of its performance is to secure in that place a reading (equally bereft, no doubt)—another performance of our thanks for her works and for her days.

January 2001

NOTES

1. For an interesting collection of readings of Aristotle on catharsis, see Andrew Ford, "*Katharsis:* The Ancient Problem," Stephen Orgel, "The Play of Conscience," and Elin Diamond, "The Shudder of Catharsis in Twentieth-Century Performance," in *Performativity and Performance,* ed. Andrew Parker and Eve Kosofsky Sedgwick (New York: Routledge, 1995).

2. *The Institutio Oratoria of Quintilian,* trans. H. E. Butler (1920; reprint, Cambridge and London: Harvard University Press, 1989, III: vii, 17–18.

3. Marie Maclean, *Narrative as Performance: The Baudelairean Experiment* (London and New York: Routledge, 1988), ch. 1, passim.

4. Richard Bauman, *Verbal Arts as Performance* (Prospect Heights, Ill.: Waveland Press, 1977); Idem, *Story, Performance, and Event* (Cambridge: Cambridge University

Press, 1986); Idem, "Ed Bell, Texas Storyteller: The Framing and Reframing of Life Experience," *Journal of Folklore Research* 24, no. 3 (1987): 197–221; Richard Bauman and Charles L. Briggs, "Poetics and Performance as Critical Perspectives on Language and Social Life," *Annual Review of Anthropology* 19 (1990): 59–88.

5. Jacques Derrida, "Signature Événement Context," in *Marges de la philosophie* (Paris: Minuit, 1972).

6. Ibid., 390.

7. *Narrative as Performance* will be abbreviated to *NP* and page references given in parentheses in the text.

8. On the publication of *The Name of the Mother,* Marie sent a copy of the book to one of those fathers, Jacques Derrida, to whom a section of the chapter on "Delegitimation by proxy" was devoted. Derrida replied as follows:

le 22 juillet 1994

Chère Marie Maclean,

J'avais reçu votre livre et commenencé à le lire avec reconnaissance et admiration. Je m'apprêtais même à vous écrire pour vous remercier au moment où m'arrive, ce matin même, votre lettre si amicale. Elle me bouleverse, bien sûr, et j'espère encore que vous gagnerez le combat que vous me dites avoir perdu, je l'espère du fond du coeur.

Votre livre est remarquable à beaucoup d'égards. Bien au-delà des signes généreux qu'il fait dans ma direction, je le trouve fort, lucide et original. Il traverse un corpus très riche et très différencié en suivant de façon cohérente, à travers des abîmes et des labyrinthes, cette vertigineuse question de la légitimation ou de l'illégitimité. (Connaissez-vous cet autre texte de Freud, une note de *L'homme aux rats,* où, citant Lichtenberg, il dit d'une autre façon ce que vous citez de lui p. 37, et lie tout cela à la supériorité du patriarcat dans la civilisation: phallologocentrisme où l'incertitude quant au père va de pair avec le progrès de la raison! J'avise Joyce's *Ulysses*—le père est une "legal fiction"—et *Tristram Shandy!*)

J'ai été particulièrement passionné, m'intéressant en ce moment à la structure méthodique, par le chapitre sur Flora Tristan. Comme dans tout votre livre, j'y apprends beaucoup, et après les lectures et relectures nécessaires, je m'y référerai nécessairement dans l'avenir . . .

Je n'ose pas commenter, surtout pas de façon définitive, les lucides et généreuses pages que vous me consacrez, avec ici ou là quelques pointes ou épines. Elles sont justes mais si je voulais à tout prix "me" justifier, j'invoquerais le statut instable de ces textes, notamment de *Glas,* qui joue, ironiquement souvent—avec des rêves, des fantasmes, des hantises, comme vous le dites vous-même, plutôt qu'il ne pose des "statements," "assertions" et . . . Et oui, ambivalence, je l'avoue "In the name of the mother." Je me permets de vous renvoyer ici à *Circonfession* . . .

Mais je voulais surtout vous dire avec quelle joie j'ai découvert ce livre magnifique, un livre de référence, désormais, et non seulement pour moi . . .

Je vous relirai, j'espère avoir la chance de lire d'autres textes de vous et de vous rencontrer un jour. Ma pensée vous accompagne et je vous dis encore, de tout mon coeur, mon admirative amitié.

Votre

Jacques Derrida

22 July 1994

Dear Marie Maclean

I received your book and started reading it with gratitude and admiration, and I was on the very point of writing to thank you when, this morning, your generous letter reached me. It touched me deeply, and I still hope you will win the fight you say you have lost. My hope comes from the bottom of my heart.

Your book is remarkable in many ways. Quite apart from its kind gestures toward me, I find it powerful, lucid, and original. It covers a very rich and varied corpus, pursuing in a coherent manner, across abysses and through labyrinths, the dizzying question of legitimation or illegitimacy. (Do you know the other text of Freud, a note to *The Rat Man*, where, quoting Lichtenberg, he says in another way what you quote from him on p. 37, and ties it all to the superiority of patriarchy in civilization: a phallologocentrism in which the uncertainty about the father is linked with the progress of reason! I am reminded of Joyce's *Ulysses*—the father is a "legal fiction"—and *Tristram Shandy!*

I was particularly excited, since I am interested at present in methodical structure, by the chapter on Flora Tristan. As throughout your book, I am learning a great deal from it; and after the necessary readings and rereadings, it will be an essential reference for me in the future.

I don't dare to comment, especially not in any definitive way, on the lucid and generous pages you devote to me, with a few barbs here and there—they are fair but if I really wanted to justify my "self," I would appeal to the unstable status of these texts, particularly *Glas*, which plays—often ironically—with dreams, phantasms, obsessions, as you say yourself, rather than making "statements," "assertions," and . . . And yes, I admit ambivalence "In the name of the mother." Allow me to refer you here to *Circonfession* . . .

But most of all I wanted to tell you the joy with which I discovered your magnificent book, which is already a work of reference from now on, and not just for me . . .

I will reread your book. I hope to have the good fortune to read further texts by you and to meet you one day. My thoughts are with you.

With admiration and my very warmest regards,

Yours

Jacques Derrida

9. Marie Mclean traces that history as "waves . . . roughly divided into those concerned with narrative *structure*, those concerned with narrative *authority* and those concerned with narrative *interaction*" (*NP*, 14).

10. Marie Maclean, "Many Hearts Will Understand Me: Ross Chambers, Nerval and Rhizomatic Criticism," *Canadian Review of Comparative Literature* 22, no. 2 (June 1995): 213.

11. The third, forensic rhetoric, is pervasive throughout the *Institutio,* providing most of the problems and most of the exemplary material of the work.

Bibliography of the Work of Marie Maclean (not including short reviews)

Books

Le Jeu suprême: Structure et thèmes dans "Le Grand Meaulnes." Paris: Corti, 1973. 185pp.

Narrative as Performance: The Baudelairean Experiment. London and New York: Routledge, 1988. xiii + 220pp.

(ed. with John Hay) *Narrative Issues.* Special issue of *AUMLA* (Journal of the Australasian Universities Language and Literature Association) 74 (1990). 223pp.

The Name of the Mother: Writing Illegitimacy. London and New York: Routledge, 1994. ix + 269pp.

Articles, Chapters in Books

"Jean Giraudoux and Frank Wedekind." *Australian Journal of French Studies* 4 (1967): 97–105.

"*Keir Vardo* ou la maison qui voyage." *Romantisme* 4 (1972): 45–53.

"The Artificial Paradise and the Lost Paradise: Baudelairean Themes in Cocteau's *Les Enfants terribles,*" *Australian Journal of French Studies* 12 (1975): 57–58.

"Structural Narcissism in *Le Grand Meaulnes.*" *Australian Journal of French Studies* 14 (1977): 152–62.

(With Eunice Leong) "Baudelaire's *Les Phares* as Master-Class in the Uses of Artistic Analogy." *Australian Journal of French Studies* 15 (1978): 125–32.

"*Lorenzaccio* and 'le revers de la médaille.'" *AULLA: Papers and Proceedings of the 19th Congress,* Brisbane (1978): 228–37.

"The Sword and the Flower: Sexual Symbolism in *Lorenzaccio.*" *Australian Journal of French Studies* 16 (1979) 166–81.

"Baudelaire and the Paradox of Procreation." *Studi francesi* 76 (1982): 87–98.

"Recent Approaches to Speculative Fiction." *AUMLA* 59 (1983): 118–25.

"Cellini and Musset: The 'reverse of the medal' in *Lorenzaccio.*" *Rivista di letterature moderne e comparate* 37 (1984): 41–52.

"Metamorphoses of the Signifier in 'Unnatural Languages.'" *Science Fiction Studies* 11 (1984): 166–74.

"Spécularité et inversion transformationnelle chez Baudelaire: *Un Fantôme.*" *Australian Journal of French Studies* 21 (1984): 58–69.

"True Coin and False Coin: The Implications of the Narrative 'Act.'" In *Not the Whole Story.* Edited by S. Gunew and I. Reid. Sydney, 1984, 161–68.

"The Private Stage in Baudelaire's Poetry: The Implied and the Excluded Audience in 'La Fememme sauvage et la petite-maîtresse.'" *Australian Journal of French Studies* 23 (1986): 234–47.

"Speaking in the Other's Voice: Women and Metalanguage." *Australian Journal of Cultural Studies* 4 (1986): 93–102.

"Oppositional Practice in Women's Traditional Narrative." *New Literary History* 19, no. 1 (autumn 1987): 375–51.

"The Signifier as Token: The Textual Riddles of Russell Hoban." *AUMLA* 70 (1988): 211–19.

"Revolution and Opposition: Olympe de Gouges and the *Déclaration des droits de la femme.*" In *Literature and Revolution.* Edited by David Bevan. Amsterdam and Atlanta, Ga.: Rodopi, 1989, 171–82.

"Revolution and Exclusion: The Other Voice." In *Discourse and Difference.* Edited by A. Milner and C. Worth. Clayton, Melbourne: Monash University (Centre for General and Comparative Literature), 1990, 127–40.

"Narrative and the Gender Gap." In *Narrative Issues, AUMLA* (1990), 69–84.

"Pretexts and Paratexts: The Art of the Peripheral." *New Literary History* 22 (1990–91): 273–79.

"Do-It-Yourself, B.Y.O. and Australian Science Fiction." *Journal of Narrative Technique* 21 (winter 1991): 136–42.

"Gendered Language, Gendered Criticism." *Australian Book Review* 131 (June 1991): 32–39.

"Such Stuff as Dreams Are Made On: The Dream Work in the Parnassian and Anti-Parnassian Poetry of Baudelaire and Rimbaud." *Revista di letterature moderne e comparate* 44, no. 4 (1991): 335–48.

"Generic Narrative." *Papers of the Greenmill Project.* Canberra: Ausdance, 1994, 7–11.

"Monstre et signature: Mary Shelley et le pouvoir procréateur." *Romantisme* 85 (1994): 27–36.

"The Performance of Illegitimacy: Signing the Matronym." *New Literary History* 25 (1994): 95–109.

"Performances of Exclusion." In *Literature and Opposition.* Edited by C. Worth, P. Nestor, and M. Pavlyshyn. Clayton, Melbourne: Monash University (Centre for Comparative Literature and Cultural Studies), 1994, 29–44.

"The Heirs of Amphitryon: Social Fathers and Natural Fathers." *New Literary History* 26 (1995): 787–807. Reprinted in *Scarlet Letters: Fictions of Adultery from Antiquity to the 1990s.* Edited by Nicholas White and Naomi Segal. London: Macmillan, 1997, 13–33.

"Many Hearts Will Understand Me: Ross Chambers, Nerval and Rhizomatic Criticism." *Canadian Review of Comparative Literature/Revue canadienne de littérature comparée* 22 (1995): 213–21.

"Narrative Involution: The Gendered Voices of the Text." *Rivista di letterature moderne e comparate* 48 (1995): 113–25.

"Shape-Shifting, Sound-Shifting: *Oneirocritie* and the Dream Work." *French Forum* 20 (1995): 45–63.

"The Role of Structural Analysis: 'Les Sept vieillards.'" In *Understanding "Les Fleurs du mal": Critical Readings.* Edited by William J. Thompson. Nashville and London: Vanderbilt University Press, 1997, 133–44.

Translations

Baudrillard, Jean. "The Masses: The Implosion of the Social in the Media." *New Literary History* 16 (1984–85): 577–89.

Cixous, Hélène. "Introduction to Lewis Carroll's *Through the Looking-Glass* and *The Hunting of the Snark*." *New Literary History* 13 (1981–82): 231–51.

Deleuze, Gilles, and Felix Guattari. "Kafka: Toward a Minor Literature: The Components of Expression." *New Literary History* 16 (1984–85: 591–608.

Genette, Gérard. "Introduction to the Paratext." *New Literary History* 22 (1990–91): 261–72.

Marin, Louis. "The Figurability of th Visual: The Veronica or the Question of the Portrait at Port-Royal." *New Literary History* 22 (1990–91): 281–96.

Marini, Marcelle. "From Minority Creation to Universal Creation." *New Literary History* 24 (1992–93): 225–41.

Robbe-Grillet, Alain. "Autobiography and the New Novel." *Scripsi* 4, no. 4 (1987): 165–78.

Telling Performances

From
Narrative . . .

Revisiting Narrativity

GERALD PRINCE

NARRATIVE HAS BEEN MINIMALLY DEFINED AS THE REPRESENTATION of at least one event, one change in a state of affairs.[1] If, according to E. M. Forster,[2] "The king died and then the queen died" contitutes a narrative, so does "The king died" according to the minimal definition (it could even be a news story). Indeed, texts like "The boy came" would also constitute narratives. Granted, they may not be interesting; but not every narrative is necessarily interesting.

The minimal definition captures an important difference between narrative and non-narrative texts: on the one hand, "Mary drank a glass of apple juice and then she drank a glass of beer" or the news story "The king died"; on the other hand, "Marcello is Milanese and therefore he is Italian" or "Elephants are large herbivorous animals." What the definition does not capture is that certain texts that satisfy it are not always taken to be narratives. I am thinking not only of "The boy came," which is formally equivalent to "The king died," but also of more complicated texts like "Janet closed the window," many a recipe, or countless lyric poems that depict actions and happenings. More generally, what the definition does not specify (nor does it attempt to) and what more constraining definitions (which specify, for instance, that narrative represents at least one event and one resulting state of affairs not logically entailed by that event) likewise do not capture is that different narrative texts exhibit different kinds or different degrees of narrativity (with some being more narrative than others, as it were) and that, even among persons of widely different backgrounds, there is considerable agreement about their comparative narrativity. Few people, if any, would think that *Nausea*, for example, "tells a better story" than *The Three Musketeers* (though, given that there is much more than narrative in a narrative, many people may prefer Sartre's novel to Dumas's) and even fewer would consider that a text like "Mary drank a glass of apple juice and then she drank a glass of beer" has a particularly high degree of narrativity. In other words, the definition does not (try to) distinguish between narrativeness (what makes a text narrative, what all and only narratives have in common) and narrativity (what in a text underlines its narrative nature, what emphasizes the presence and semiotic role of narrative structures in a textual economy, what makes a given narrative more or less narrative).

Now, narratologists have long made (implicit) distinctions between different narrativities. Aristotle, not surprisingly, provides a kind of early example. His consideration of *mythos* leads him to a number of judgments about various plot types and, by extension, various types of narrativity: the imitated action must be complete and whole just as it must be of a certain magnitude (neither too small nor too big!); dramatic rather than episodic plots ought to be devised; complex plots are preferable to simple ones; sameness of incidents should be avoided; and so on. Similarly, in our own century, E. M. Forster, in his *Aspects of the Novel,* contrasted what he called stories ("The king died and then the queen died") with what he called plots ("The king died and then the queen died of grief"). Among the great French structuralists, Barthes broached the subject with his discussion of the *post hoc ergo propter hoc* confusion, Genette addressed it in his studies of the boundaries of narrative or the notion of motivational cost, and Greimas adumbrated it through his insistence on structural closure and internally governed predictability of denouement. William Labov, in his influential examination of oral narratives of personal experience and tellability, compared not only pointed and pointless stories but, more specifically, narratives that "are complete in the sense that they have a beginning, a middle, and an end" (362) and "more fully developed types" (363) that include their own evaluation and indicate their point: why they are told and "what the narrator is getting at" (366). In his exploration of the difference between annals, chronicles, and histories, Hayden White made a fundamental distinction between narrating (reporting a series of events in a chronological order) and narrativizing (imposing "story form" on events or making the world speak itself as a story). And Paul Ricoeur was led, through his analysis of time and historical knowledge, to distinguish between the plots of (fictional) narratives and the quasi-plots of (modern) historiography as well as between the characters of the former (individual human agents, say) and the quasi-characters of the latter (entities like nations or cultures). Numerous other names could, of course, be mentioned: Brooks (the prospective/retrospective movement of narrative), Chatman (the nature of textual and, in particular, narrative service), Culler (the conveying of a human project or a human engagement in the world), Shen (the kind of connections between events), Wilensky (external and internal, static and dynamic plots), and so forth.[3]

Indeed, despite a general reluctance to engage universals (they smack of imperialism) and despite a strong tendency to shy away from possibly value-laden problems, the past dozen years have seen the interest in (factors universally affecting) narrativity assert itself in increasingly explicit ways, partly—no doubt—because of the so-called narrativist turn (the reliance on the category "narrative" to describe, discuss, and account for indefinitely many activities, fields, and texts, from political speeches, legal briefs, or philosophical arguments to scientific proofs, psychoanalytic sessions, and L. L. Bean catalogues). By the end of the 1960s the very word "narrative" (or "story") begins to invade a multitude of (discursive) terrains. One says "narrative" instead of "explanation" or "argumentation" (because it is more tentative); one prefers "narrative" to "theory," "hypothesis," or "evidence" (because it is less scientistic); one speaks of "narrative" rather than "ideology" (because it is less judgmental); one substitutes "narrative" for "message" (because it is more indeterminate). The notion of narrative is repeatedly called upon to characterize this or that domain, practice, or object and—with the spread of anti-foundationalism, post-structuralism, and postmodernism—narrative becomes one of the most common hermeneutic grids of our time. But even if it is true that "everything" is narrative, perhaps it is also true that "everything" is not equally narrative. More pointedly, if *Nausea, The Three Musketeers,* "Janet closed the window," a supermarket ad, and even my wanting to have a drink all constitute narratives, don't they exemplify different kinds of narrativity? In fact, aren't some of them more narrative than others?

In order to start answering such questions (and also in the hope of devising a more "realist" grammar of narrative that would adequately characterize not merely narratives like "Janet closed the window" or "The boy came" but also more "narrative" narratives), I have attempted, in my own work, to isolate some of the factors affecting narrativity. I have argued, for instance, that the narrativity of a text depends on the extent to which that text constitutes a doubly oriented autonomous whole (with a well-defined—and interacting—beginning, middle, and end) that involves some kind of conflict (consider "The cat sat on the mat" versus "The cat sat on the dog's mat"), that is made up of discrete, particular, positive, and temporally distinct actions having logically unpredictable antecedents or consequences, and that avoids inordinate amounts of commentary about them, their representation, or the latter's context. I have also contended that, all other things being equal, the presence of disnarrated elements (representing what did not happen but could have) affected narrativity in a positive manner.[4]

In *Narrative as Communication,* Didier Coste too presented what can be called a scalar view of narrativity.[5] Besides maintaining that narrativity varies with the degree of narrative dominance in a semiotic act and that this dominance can be quantitative (out of twenty predicates, say, fifteen are narratemes, three are descriptemes, and two are ontemes) or that it can be hierarchic (the most important predicates are narratemes; the act makes the most sense if it is viewed as narrative; the text is interpretable [only] if a narrative grid is invoked), Coste specified several elements positively affecting narrativity: transactiveness rather than non-transactiveness (in other words, actions as opposed to mere happenings); transitiveness rather than intransitiveness (events involving an agent and a patient, as in "Peter insulted Paul," instead of an agent only, as in "Mary smiled"); deep or remote causality as opposed to a lack of it (so that the first events, chronologically speaking, are linked to the last ones in significant ways); specificity instead of generality (rather than sequences fitting any or indefinitely many sets of circumstances like "Countless people were born and died," the narrative act would figure sequences contingent on specific sets like "Wellington was born in 1769 and died in 1852); singularity instead of banality (with the consequent avoidance of repetitiveness and merely superficial diversity); and, finally, the presence as opposed to the absence of alternative courses of action for the narrative participants.

But it is perhaps Marie-Laure Ryan who has done the most systematic and promising work on narrativity.[6] According to her, narrative texts create a world by depicting particular entities and events and they make that world coherent and intelligible by evoking a network of relations—causal links, psychological motivations, goals, plans— among the entities and events. Their narrativity (and, in particular, what Ryan called plot tellability) varies with the way they realize these definitional traits. In *Possible Worlds, Artificial Intelligence, and Narrative Theory,* Ryan not only showed that an adequate model of plot must represent the relational changes obtaining between the constituents of the actual narrative world (what is true in the story) and the constituents of the characters' private worlds (the virtual embedded narratives fashioned in terms of their knowledge, wishes, obligations, simulations, intentions, or fantasies); she also insisted that "not all plots are created equal" and that narrativity is rooted in the configuration of the relational changes as well as "in the richness and variety of the domain of the virtual." More recently, Ryan sketched an open-ended taxonomy of different modes of narrativity, including the *simple narrativity* of fairy tales or urban legends (where the semantic dimension of the text primarily springs from a linear plot revolving around a single problem), the *complex narrativity* of Balzac, Dickens, or Dumas (where narrative structures appear on both the macro- and the microtextual level and where semantic integration obtains between the main plot lines and the subordinate ones), the *figural narrativity* of lyric, historiographic, or philosophic texts (in this case, the sender or the receiver constructs a story by reshaping universal claims, collective entities, and abstract concepts into particular characters and events), and the *instrumental narrativity* of sermons and debates (where narrative structures appearing on the microtextual level function merely as illustrations or clarifications of a nonnarrative macrotextual level).

If, as my remarks have more than suggested, narrativity is not to be confused with textual value (one can find in a narrative much more than narrative or narrativity: wit, imagery, psychological insight, philosophical vision, documentary information), it is also not to be conflated with the category of narrative appeal or narrative interest and, in particular, with a notion that pertains to that category and that has evoked a good deal of discussion. I am speaking of the notion "point" (and the class of pointed—as opposed to pointless—narratives). William Labov is surely correct when he writes: "Pointless stories are met (in English) with the withering rejoinder, 'So what?' Every good narrator is continually warding off this question: when his narrative is over, it should be unthinkable for a bystander to say 'So what?' Instead, the appropriate remark would be 'He did?' or similar means of registering the reportable character of the events of the narration."[7] But what Labov says of narratives and narrators can, mutatis mutandis, be said of any utterance and speaker. Indeed, the point(edness) of a narrative or any other kind of text depends not only on the constituent features of those texts but also on the context. Different persons (or the same person on different occasions) can greet the same story with a "So what?" or a "He did?" whether or not that story is an instance of a "more fully developed" type of narrative, comprising its own evaluation and explicitly indicating its raison d'être. I may have heard this or that tale a dozen times or not even once; I may long to hear it anew, but then again, I may not; I may want to learn what happened and why but you couldn't care less; I may admire a certain metaphysical vision or find an account of what took place fascinating and you may disagree. In other words, narrativity should be distinguished from what is sometimes called reportability or tellability (what makes a narrative worth telling, interesting, appealing in a given context).[8]

Just as narrativity is not a function of context (and, I think, partly because of that), it is not a function of the specific subjects addressed by a narrative. In fact, though there is a good deal of convergence among the various discussions of narrativity (several of them stress the importance of such features as specificity or virtuality, for instance), none of them links narrativity to particular topics or themes. Even such specifications as the importance of human projects or conflicts can be seen as deriving from more general or formal imperatives. Thus, the presence of anthropomorphic beings allows for that of private worlds and for virtual embedded narratives (wishes, obligations, fantasies, etc.); their projects imply an orientation, an end, a closure; and conflicts involve relational changes between the different worlds making up a narrative universe. Granted, "great topics" and "surefire themes" have long been thought or claimed to awaken narrative desire and have long drawn the attention of best-seller seekers. A sexist French formula for successful narratives valorizes the elements of mystery, religion, sex, and aristocracy ("'My God,' said the duchess, 'I am pregnant. Who done it?'");[9] and an old *Readers' Digest* recipe is said to stress—along with sex and religion—personal experience, foreign travel, money, and the animal kingdom ("How I Made Love to a Rich Bear in the Alps and Found God"). But money, sex, or religion are not topics specific to or characteristic of narrative and its structures, and their force varies considerably with circumstance.

What narrativity seems primarily linked to is general narrative configuration (as opposed to specific thematic traits, contextual appeal, or textual value). More particularly, it seems linked to the nature of the narrated (e.g., structural autonomy or presence of alternative courses of action), that of the narrating (e.g., foregrounding of event discreteness), and the relations between the two (e.g., avoidance of inordinate amounts of commentary). But that characterization— which takes into account the set of narrativity-affecting features mentioned in my exposition—conceals the problematic nature of that set. For one thing, the latter is not free of various redundancies: "wholeness," for instance, implies "internally governed predictability of denouement," and "human engagement in the world" implies "transactiveness." For another, it may well be incomplete: I more than suspect a link between the hermeneutic arrangement of a narrative (in the Barthesian sense of the term) and its narrativity; and I believe, along with Ryan and others, that the representation of external events ("She walked across the United States") rather than internal ones ("She thought about the United States") increases narrativity. Furthermore, the set includes (possibly) incompatible elements or elements whose interaction has unclear effects. Specifically, narrativity is said to depend on the extent to which a text involves a hierarchical organization as opposed to a mere temporal concatenation of events (some of the latter should be of greater moment than others); and such a hierarchical organization can be brought about by commentary, by evaluative statements like "This was really surprising" or "That was really fabulous." On the other hand, narrativity is also said to be affected negatively by inordinate amounts of commentary (of non-narratemes). In other words, the link between commentary and narrativity is far from evident. Indeed, and more generally, the set of narrativity-affecting features assigns them no comparative weight and gives no indication of their relative importance. Would a narrative exhibiting every single feature save x have a higher or lower degree of narrativity than one with every pertinent feature save y? Or, to put it differently, how distinct in terms of narrativity would a narrative displaying x and one displaying y turn out to be? I happen to think that the positiveness of event representation is more important than its transactiveness. I also think that structural autonomy or wholeness is more important than conflict. But I am not clear about, say, the significance of singularity; and I have even weaker intuitions about the extent of the weight difference between the various features (how much more important than conflict is structural autonomy? how much more significant than transactiveness is positiveness?). Of course, even if the various features were ranked according to weight, there would still remain a sizable area of indeterminacy, given that some of them are "precise" or "absolute" whereas others are "fuzzy" or "relative": compare, for example, "no inordinate amounts of commentary" or "specificity instead of generality" with transitiveness or transactiveness.

Rather than attempting to eliminate this indeterminacy, perhaps one should view it as an integral and irreducible feature of narrativity. On the one hand, its existence does not represent a counter to the argument that different people often (but not always) agree on the comparative narrativity of different texts. On the other hand, it can help to explain in part disagreements in narrativity judgments. I find text A more narrative than you do because I do not take it to involve inordinate amounts of commentary, for instance; and you consider text B more narrative than I do because you think it favors specificity rather than generality. In effect, rather than saying that, if a text exhibits features x, y, and/or z, it is endowed with a certain kind (or degree) of narrativity, one should perhaps say that if a text is thought to have a certain kind (or degree) of narrativity, it is because it is taken to involve x, y, and/or z (and because the latter are assigned a certain weight).

Of course, only extensive empirical study and (cross-cultural) testing can determine the adequacy of these (or other) claims about narrativity. And such testing itself presents a number of difficulties: it is not easy to invent or discover laboratory specimens free of the crippling disease of clumsiness, nor is it easy to devise protocols for a sound assessment of responses. Still, it seems to me that further study of narrativity constitutes perhaps the most significant task of narratology today. In the first place, it can help provide answers to problems transcending the domain of narrative proper, such as that of the expressiveness of different media. Consider painting or sculpture, for example. If they have not proven particularly fertile ground for narrative representation, it may be due not so much or not only to their affinities for the spatial instead of the temporal but, rather, to their limited ability to convey differences between actuality and virtuality, existence and nonexistence, presence and absence. The study of narrativity also generates a wide range of other questions worth exploring. What kind of narrativity-pertinent features do different groups favor? What stages do we go through in acquiring the capacity to manipulate narrativity? Do "emotionally challenged" persons consistently privilege certain features that other persons would not? And so on and so forth. Above all, by shedding light on what in a text foregrounds its narrative potential, dimension, or thrust, the study of narrativity can clarify the nature and specificity of narrative semiosis, the functioning and meaning of the narrative moment.

NOTES

1. See Gérard Genette, *Narrative Discourse Revisited*, trans. Jane E. Lewin (Ithaca: Cornell University Press, 1983).

2. *Aspects of the Novel* (London: Methuen, 1927).

3. Works referred to in this paragraph are as follows: Aristotle, *Poetics: A Translation and Commentary for Students of Literature*, trans. Leon Golden, commentary by O. B. Hardison (Englewood Cliffs, N.J.: Prentice Hall, 1968); Roland Barthes, "An Introduction to the Structural Analysis of Narrative," *New Literary History* 6 (1975): 237–62; Peter Brooks, *Reading for the Plot: Design and Intention in Narrative* (New York: Knopf, 1984); Seymour Chatman, *Coming to Terms: The Rhetoric of Narrative in Fiction and Film* (Ithaca: Cornell University Press, 1990); Jonathan Culler, *Structuralist Poetics: Structuralism, Linguistics, and the Study of Literature* (Ithaca: Cornell University Press, 1975); Gérard Genette, "Vraisemblable et motivation," *Communications* 11 (1968): 5–21 and "Boundaries of Narrative," *New Literary History* 8 (1976): 1–15; A. J. Greimas, *Structural Semantics: An Attempt at a Method*, trans. Daniele McDowell, Ronald Schleifer, and Alan Velie (Lincoln: University of Nebraska Press, 1983); William Labov, *Language in the Inner City* (Philadelphia: University of Pennsylvania Press, 1972); Paul Ricoeur, *Time and Narrative*, vol. 1, trans. Kathleen McLaughlin and David Pellauer (Chicago: University of Chicago Press, 1984); Yeshayahu Shen, "The X-Bar Grammar for Stories: Story-Grammar Revisited," *Text* 9 (1989): 415–67; Hayden White, "The Value of Narrativity in the Representation of Reality," in *On Narrative*,

ed. W. J. T. Mitchell (Chicago: University of Chicago Press, 1980), 1–24; Robert Wilensky, "Story Grammars versus Story Points," *Behavioral and Brain Sciences* 6 (1983): 579–623.

4. See Gerald Prince, *Narratology: The Form and Functioning of Narrative* (Berlin: Mouton, 1982) and "The Disnarrated," *Style* 22 (1988): 1–8.

5. Didier Coste, *Narrative as Communication* (Minneapolis: University of Minnesota Press, 1989).

6. Marie-Laure Ryan, *Possible Worlds, Artificial Intelligence, and Narrative Theory* (Bloomington: Indiana University Press, 1991) and "The Modes of Narrativity and Their Visual Metaphors," *Style* 26 (1992): 368–87.

7. Labov, *Language in the Inner City*, 366.

8. In *Narratology* I considered narrative pointedness to be relevant to narrativity (pp.158–60).

9. This is the English rendition of "'Mon Dieu,' dit la Marquise, 'je suis enceinte et ne sais pas de qui.'" See Margaret Boden, *Artificial Intelligence and Natural Man* (New York: Basic Books, 1977).

through
The Performance of Telling

Detectives and Criminals as Players in "Le Théâtre du crime": A Reading of Emile Gaboriau's *Le Crime d'Orcival*

GALE MacLACHLAN

— Il est des gens, continua-t-il, qui ont la rage du théâtre. Cette rage est un peu la mienne. Seulement, je ne comprends pas qu'on puisse prendre plaisir au misérable étalage des fictions qui sont à la vie ce que le quinquet de la rampe est au soleil. S'intéresser à des sentiments plus ou moins bien exprimés, mais fictifs, me paraît une monstrueuse convention . . .

— Fermons les théâtres! murmura le docteur Gendron.

— Plus difficile ou plus blasé que le public, continua M. Lecoq, il me faut à moi, des comédies véritables ou des drames réels. La société, voilà mon théâtre. Mes acteurs, à moi, ont le rire franc ou pleurent de vraies larmes.[1]

["There are people," he continued, "who are mad about the theater. I am, myself, to some extent. All the same, I can't understand how people can enjoy a wretched parade of fictions that are in the same relation to life as the footlight to the sun. To be interested in feelings that are more or less well expressed but remain fictional, seems to me a monstrous convention . . .

"Let's close the theaters!" murmured Dr. Gendron.

"Being more demanding or more blasé than the public," Lecoq went on, "I need real-life comedies or dramas. Society is my theater. My actors' laughter is genuine and their tears are real."

The irony of this little exchange about the "monstrous" conventions associated with theatrical representations—occurring as it does within a popular nineteenth-century *roman-feuilleton*—is obvious enough.[2] Similar in function to the play within a play, such self-reflexive moves serve to establish, among other things, what Marie Maclean calls "the truth of the virtual world of fiction as opposed to its reality."[3] That is to say, they remind readers that their reference point is not so much the real world of crime and detection but a fictional world whose truth is related to narrative conventions of *vraisemblance.* By suggesting in this way the norms appropriate to their own reception, popular novels like *Le Crime d'Orcival* seek to woo the "difficult" or "blasé" reader (Lecoq's terms) into accepting their more outrageously implausible revelations.

The exchange quoted above is not, however, the first or the last allusion to the theater as model (or apparent anti-model) in this early *roman policier.* Indeed, references to the theatre saturate the narrative from its beginning at the scene of the crime (referred to throughout as "le théâtre du crime") to its melodramatic end, a "scene of justice" staged by the detective that produces a second murder. Masks and disguise,[4] role-playing, references to the staging and scripting of particular scenes and the obvious manipulation of audience response at both textual and narratorial levels are recurring features throughout. It will be argued that allusions to the theater as generic point of reference, commonplace in detective fiction from its inception down to the present day, represent more than a simple gesture of literary filiation or ironic self-designation.[5] Taking Emile Gaboriau's *Le Crime d'Orcival* as exemplary, given its status as one of the first detective novels ever written, this essay aims to show that the detective novel is a particularly self-conscious genre, displaying through allusion to its theatrical cousins an almost obsessive concern with the issue of its own reception and performance as text. This is evident both at the level of story, where the detective must pit his wits against the murderer and other competitors in a bid for narratorial authority, and at the level of discourse where it is the "textual" performance that ensures the success or failure of the enterprise. The reasons for this concern may be traced to the particular sociohistoric conditions of the genre's emergence in the middle of the nineteenth century; these are discussed below.

In the scene referred to above, other ironies come into play as we read on, but this is not initially clear either to the reader or to the textually embedded audience. For what immediately follows is a rather long, autobiographically inflected disquisition by the detective M. Lecoq on the analogy between the judicial processes set in train by the commission of a crime and the writing and production of a play: "Un crime se commet, c'est le prologue. J'arrive, le premier acte commence . . ." (130) [A crime is committed, that's the prologue. I arrive and the first act begins . . .]. Drawing attention to the similarities between the stages in a police investigation and the structure of a classical play, Lecoq's speech can be read as a kind of aesthetic manifesto sketching the plot outline for a new genre that will deviate significantly in narrative organization from its fictional competitors, the crime novel and the mystery novel.

Dominated by the figure of the detective ("J'arrive, *le premier acte commence*") and the story of the investigation rather than by the criminal, the crime necessarily remains "off-stage," part of the "prologue" rather than the main action, an antecedent act forever absent from the event-structure of the novel.[6] "Voici l'exposition," continues Lecoq. "Bientôt l'action se corse, le fil de mes inductions me conduit au coupable; je le devine, je l'arrête, je le livre" (130) [Soon the plot thickens, inductive reasoning leads me to the criminal; I guess his identity, I arrest him, I hand him over]. As Lecoq's insistence on the *je* as instigator of the action at every stage in the process suggests, interest focuses in these *romans judiciaires* (or *romans policiers* as they were later called)[7] on the detective's attempts to discover the author of the crime under investigation. Using both his powers of induction ("le fil de mes inductions") and his imagination ("je le devine"), the detective works backwards from crime to criminal, from present traces to past origins. As several theorists of the genre have pointed out, two different chronologies are superimposed here: one representing the (forward) story of the investigation and the other the (backward) reconstruction of the crime.[8] Stories that focus on detection are therefore structurally different from the crime and mystery stories popular at this time. Instead of simply juxtaposing two narratives of approximately equal length—the mystery and its resolution—in this new genre it is the story of the investigation that is the longer narrative and main focus of interest as the detective progressively reconstructs the events leading up to the crime. Given the principle of gradual disclosure, the climax of such novels must occur towards the end with the final resolution of the mystery being presented to the reader in an often dramatically staged scene of revelation or reenactment of the crime.

But the detective is not the only major player in the "théâtre du crime." In the French judicial system the detective's role is subordinated to that of the investigating magistrate, the person who, unlike the police in the Westminster system, directs and controls the conduct of criminal investigations in France. Confined to the role of scriptwriter of the "grande scène" of revelation, the detective may be upstaged by the investigating magistrate at this point in the investigative process, since it is the latter who confronts the suspect with evidence of his guilt in an attempt to secure a confession. The detective's reconstruction of the crime—normally presented in the form of a written report—is thus subject to a highly critical reading by the investigating magistrate, for whom in the first instance it has been produced. The reception of the detective's "script" can thus be enacted in the text itself, and indeed this is what happens in *Le Crime d'Orcival.* In a highly dramatic scene, the investigating magistrate, after some hesitation over the issue of judicial precedents and protocols, agrees to abrogate his usual responsibilities and to allow the detective both to present his controversial account of the crime and to interrogate the suspects in his presence. Before an audience of interested parties, two competing narratives—the investigating magistrate's and Lecoq's—vie with each other for plausibility. The success of Lecoq's performance is amply demonstrated not only by the enthusiastic response of the various assembled auditors, but by the investigating magistrate's capitulation in the face of Lecoq's persuasive oratory. The falsely accused are released from custody and Lecoq vows to track down the real murderer.

Lecoq concludes his elaborate theatrical metaphor by referring to the trial as the final "tableau" in the judicial drama. Staged in the *Cour d'Assises,* the detective's reconstruction of events is once again submitted to the critical scrutiny of an audience, this time to a group of his peers, the assembled jurors. As he develops the analogy, Lecoq, in what seems like a gesture of megalomanic excess, arrogates to himself the multiple roles of chief actor, scriptwriter, stage manager and director of the whole production, the success or failure of which it is ultimately the jury's role to decide: "L'accusation parle, mais c'est moi qui ai fourni les idées; les phrases sont les broderies jetées sur le canevas de mon rapport. Le président pose les questions aux jurés; quelle émotion! C'est le sort de mon drame qui se décide. Le jury répond: Non. C'en est fait, ma pièce était mauvaise, je suis sifflé. Est-ce oui, au contraire, c'est que ma pièce était bonne; on m'applaudit, je triomphe" (131) [The prosecution speaks, but I am the one who has supplied the ideas; his words simply embroider the framework provided by my report. The presiding judge asks the jurors for their verdict; how exciting! It's the fate of my drama that's being decided. The jury replies: Not guilty. It's all over, my play was a failure, I am booed off the stage. If, on the other hand, the answer is "guilty," then my play is a success; they applaud me, I win].

Significantly, what Lecoq emphasizes here is not the "historic" truth or falsity of the case presented to the jury, but the success or failure of his own performance in persuading first the investigating magistrate, and then the jury, of the plausibility of his account. From this perspective, it is not so much the fate of the accused that hangs in the balance, but rather, as Lecoq stresses, "le sort de mon drame" and, of course, the detective himself as its scriptwriter/producer.

As Marie Maclean observes in her introduction to *Narrative as Performance:* "Performance always implies submitting to the gaze and measurement of others. . . . [P]erformance is not subjected to the criterion of truth or falsehood, but judged on success or failure."[9] This is precisely the emphasis in Lecoq's theatrical analogy, and it has implications for the reader's response to the text.[10] Although, in a sense, all written texts constitute performances when actualized by acts of reading, not all betray anxiety about control of reader reception by embedding theatrical models (or anti-models) of their performance as texts. Scenes like the one discussed above imply that readers should not be sidetracked by considerations of the "truth-value" of the story produced by the detective, the quest for historical truth being subsumed by the quest for fictional plausibility or "narrative fit" between a set of events (or traces of events) and the narrative produced by the detective to make sense of them. The protocols of a certain kind of realism, it is implied, are inappropriate in a popular genre whose success or failure should be judged on performance criteria alone.[11] In the case of serialized popular novels like the *roman judiciaire*, newspaper sales provide an instant barometer of success.

Thus, at the metacommunicative level of the text, several things seem to be accomplished by Lecoq's long speech: first, it serves the function of a kind of aesthetic manifesto whose purpose is to foreshadow the distinctive narrative trajectory of a new genre, the *roman judiciaire*, and second, it can be viewed as an attempt to set and control the terms of its reception as a particular kind of text. A closer examination of the context of its utterance in the diegesis brings other issues into play. Lecoq's recital is directed to specific narratees at a crucial point in the investigation and bears a significant relation to the rest of the scene. Gathered together in the library after dinner to discuss the Orcival murder case, Lecoq's audience, le père Plantat (the *juge de paix*) and Dr. Gendron (the local doctor-cum-eccentric man of science), are clearly bemused by this seemingly gratuitous digression. Alert to incongruities of tone and occasion, they ponder the point of Lecoq's recital, rather than engage with the content of the speech: "M. Lecoq, en ce moment même, était-il de bonne foi, ou jouait-il une comédie! Quel était le but de cette autobiographie?" (131) [Was M. Lecoq being sincere right now or was he playing a part! What was the aim of this autobiographical sketch?].

Lecoq sweeps relentlessly on, seemingly unaware of the puzzlement of his audience. Finally, after what appears to be a fatuous piece of self-congratulation, he introduces a note of modesty. His weakness, he confides, is "la femme," or, more precisely, a particular woman. This revelation is accompanied by a sly bit of stage-management on his part. Moving the table lamp so that it dramatically spotlights the face of le père Plantat (whose sentimental connection with the more sinister players in the "théâtre du crime" Lecoq is anxious to discover), the detective, now masked in shadow, is at liberty to read the other man's reactions. Warming to the role of the lover hopelessly enamoured of a much younger woman, Lecoq breaks off his speech, seemingly overcome with emotion. The ruse succeeds: Plantat is taken in by the policeman's performance, his face revealing "une indéfinissable expression de souffrance" [an indefinable expression of suffering]. At this point, as he observes both actor and audience, "le sens de cette scène éclatait enfin dans l'esprit de M. Gendron" (132) [the meaning of this scene finally dawned on M. Gendron].

Whether or not the doctor is also struck by the irony of this bit of playacting, given Lecoq's earlier comments, is not clear. From the reader's point of view, however, reframing Lecoq's original condemnation of the "monstrous conventions" underwriting our response to stage dramas, in the light of the knowledge that the whole scene is *itself* a staged performance within the fictional frame of a novel, multiplies the ironies in play here. For such a scene positions us not only, like Gendron, as the audience of Lecoq's cunning role-playing within the diegetic space of the story, but also as the more knowing audience of what we might call the "textual" performance of the novel itself, a performance whose virtuosity we are presumably invited to applaud.[12] At the same time scenes like this draw our attention to the performative aspects of language, reminding us of the rhetorical as well as the mimetic power of the text.

It is hardly surprising that models for textual performance and reader reception are frequently embedded in these early detective novels, given the particular socioeconomic conditions of their production in the latter half of the nineteenth century. Published in serial form in the popular press, *Le Crime d'Orcival* and novels like it had to secure and maintain a readership over a long period of time to ensure a financial return to the journal. With "performance indicators" in the material form of fluctuating daily sales, seduction of the public was an on-going concern. Artistic control of the *roman judiciaire* was thus subject both to the pressures of the marketplace and to editorial constraints. Such pressures readily translate into anxieties expressed at the story level about performance, notably, as we have seen, in the "scene of instruction" (where the investigating magistrate may be viewed as a figure of editorial acceptance and control) and in the (foreshadowed) courtroom scene before a jury of critics, a prefiguration of the popular audience for whom the novel is intended. Significantly, though, the judicial process that should have culminated in the trial of the murderer is short-circuited in *Le Crime d'Orcival* through the direct intervention of the detective figure. Presumably the only jury that really matters is that constituted by the community of readers following the story in its daily installments.

Evidence that market concerns lie close to the surface of the *roman judiciaire* is clear from statements like the following: "Décidément, l'agent de la sûreté était 'empoigné.' L'artiste en lui se réveillait; il se trouvait en face d'un beau crime, d'un de ces crimes *qui triplent la vente de la «Gazette des Tribunaux»*" (121, italics added) [There was no doubt about it, the detective's interest was 'captured.' The artist in him was awakening; he was faced with a beautiful crime, the kind of crime *that trebles the sales of the "Gazette des tribunaux"*]. The comparison here between the aesthetic appeal of Lecoq's (fictive) "beau crime" and the popularity of actual criminal cases that "treble" the sales of publications like the *Gazette des tribunaux* is a revealing one, for the second half of the nineteenth century saw major changes in the distribution of the popular press, changes that posed a threat to the survival of the *roman-feuilleton*. The increasing tendency toward single issue rather than subscription-based sales signaled the arrival of a press able to report the events of the day, among which the criminal *faits divers* were a strong drawing card. As Jacques Goimard notes, while the most popular novels by such writers as Gaboriau and Ponson du Terrail increased the sale of *Le Petit Journal* by about 20 percent, the Troppman Affair in 1868 doubled its sales.[13] Clearly the public had a taste for the real thing, and writers like Gaboriau were quick to exploit this in ways that shaped both the structure and subject matter of the emerging *roman judiciaire:* "Le détrônement du roman-feuilleton par le fait divers, qui s'achèvera sous la IIIe République, obligera le vaincu, pour se maintenir, à se modeler sur son rival; de là une tendance au raccourcissement, déjà sensible chez Gaboriau (dont les romans «judiciaires» ne sont pas autre chose que des faits divers fictifs), et surtout une recherche de ce qu'il est convenu d'appeler la vraisemblance"[14] [The dethroning of the serialized novel by the *fait divers,* a process that was completed during the Third Republic, forced the loser, in order to hold its own, to imitate its rival; hence a tendency, already discernible in Gaboriau, toward a reduction in length (the latter's "judicial" novels are no more than fictional *fait divers*) and hence, more especially, the quest for what is conventionally called verisimilitude].

Competing for space in a daily newspaper, the *roman judiciaire* had clearly to target not only its fictional rivals in the marketplace, but also its factual competitors closer to home. (This rivalry often leads to the emergence of a new kind of hero subsuming the roles of both journalist and detective, such as the figure of Rouletabille in the later detective novels of Gaston Leroux.) In *Le Crime d'Orcival* the challenge is met indirectly, through a concern with issues of *vraisemblance* and audience reception, and more directly toward the end of the novel in the form of an exchange between Lecoq and Plantat. The latter condemns journalists as ethically irresponsible scandalmongers exploiting the private lives of victims and criminals alike in an attempt to pander to "la malsaine curiosité de la foule" (353) [the unhealthy curiosity of the mob]. But in fact (as the subtext of Plantat's ironic outburst and subsequent revelations imply), such prurient interest is more likely to be merely titillated than fully satisfied, given the particular conventions governing the reporting of crimes and court cases and the limited investigative powers of the journalists concerned. By contrast, what its fictional rival has to offer is a more binding generic contract, a guarantee of reader satisfaction through full disclosure of events seldom revealed to the general public in the reporting of the real thing. As readers of detective fiction we can thus safely indulge our curiosity about a crime and its players in the sure knowledge that all will be revealed, while at the same time distancing ourselves from the vulgar curiosity of the crowd.[15] In the closing pages of *Le Crime d'Orcival,* our attention is drawn once again to the fact that the details of the crime to which we have just been privy remained "fort obscure" as far as the general public were concerned.[16]

Given the relative lack of control exercised by the detective figure over the course of the investigation in the French legal system ("Je suis aux ordres de monsieur le juge d'instruction" [64] [I am at the command of your honor, the investigating magistrate], remarks Lecoq laconically at the scene of the crime), it is perhaps hardly surprising that the dynamics of the investigative process itself should be represented in more agonistic terms than in the early Anglo-American versions of this genre. Securing and maintaining credibility through virtuoso performance is Lecoq's primary concern, the issue of interpretative authority being played out in numerous scenes as rival players compete for dominance. For unlike Lecoq's immediate predecessor, Edgar Allan Poe's detective the chevalier Dupin, or his British successor, the amateur detective Sherlock Holmes, both of whose authority is simply assumed on the basis of class membership and independence from any state apparatus of control, Lecoq enjoys no such unconditional respect. A mere functionary in a society where the police are more often reviled than admired, Lecoq has to work hard to establish his authority.[17] One of several "délégués de la justice" [representatives of justice], he seems at first an unprepossessing member of the small professional community summoned to the scene of the crime. Each being aware of the experience and perspicacity of the other, no one appears willing to take the initiative by exposing his particular view of the crime to the critical scrutiny of the group: "Tout en dissimulant son intime pensée, chacun cherche à pénétrer celle du voisin, et s'efforce, si elle est opposée, de ramener cet adversaire à son opinion, non en la lui découvrant franchement et sans ambages, mais en appelant son attention sur les mots graves et futiles qui l'ont fixée." (73) While concealing their personal views, at the same time they each try to intuit those of their neighbor, making an effort, if these run counter to their own, to bring their opponent around to their opinion, not by frank and direct self-revelation, but by drawing attention to both the serious and trivial words that have determined their point of view.]

It is finally Lecoq, prompted by Plantat, who takes the plunge. He reveals a view of the crime that is close to that of the latter, but widely divergent from the conclusions of the investigating magistrate, for whom the material facts of the case point overwhelmingly to the guilt of a servant at the castle. A short synopsis of the story may be helpful here: In the little village of Orcival, two poachers have discovered the half-submerged body of the Countess of Trémoral on the banks of the Seine not far from the château, which has been ransacked, presumably by the perpetrators of the crime in a desperate search for a large sum of money received by the count the day before. It is assumed that the count's body has been washed downstream. Suspicion focuses on one of the servants and on the poachers, since their knowledge of the money and of the absence at a wedding of the castle staff on the night of the crime provides both motive and opportunity. (A distracting event in the form of a suicide note received by the mayor called in to assist the inquiry and written by his daughter Laurence, apparently in an access of shame at falling pregnant to a man who has abandoned her, does not appear initially to have any bearing on the events at the castle, but later proves to be significant.)

Entering the interpretive fray with a dazzling display of professional acumen, Lecoq establishes his ascendancy over the investigating magistrate as a subtle and canny reader. Trained by that master-detective Tabaret (the hero of the first detective novel, *L'Affaire Lerouge*), Lecoq is practiced in reading against the grain, in assuming, as he puts it, "le contrepied des apparences" (84) [that appearances are always deceptive]. He is thus able to offer a triumphant deconstruction of evidence left behind at the castle and grounds, which he considers to be a botched "mise en scène" staged by the murderer (the count himself) to suggest the motive of robbery. Lecoq's performance excites admiration from an astonished audience. Plantat, "visiblement charmé," applauds: "Bravo! oui, bravo!" (85). In a final gesture of competitive one-upmanship, this time vis-à-vis the murderer himself, Lecoq delivers a withering critique of his handiwork from the position of a fellow, superior artist: "M. Lecoq, lui, paraissait indigné, exaspéré comme peut l'être un véritable artiste devant l'oeuvre grossière, prétentieuse et ridicule de quelque écolier poseur" (88) [M. Lecoq appeared indignant, exasperated, as a true artist might be faced with the crude, pretentious, ludicrous handiwork of some posturing schoolboy].

If the detective can be interpreted as an image of the (resistant) reader who produces an interpretation of the crime by reading against the grain of appearances, the criminal must necessarily double as his Other, the elusive, unidentified author of a sometimes duplicitous and always fragmentary "text." At the same time, given the degree of imaginative reconstruction such readings demand, these distinctions tend to dissolve, since detectives also necessarily figure as the criminal's double, the coauthor or coproducer of the story of the crime. In fact, Lecoq's "authorial" status is alluded to on several occasions, specifically when he has terminated his investigations at the scene of the crime. In a typically provocative overstatement (since a key document remains purely hypothetical at this stage of the investigation), Lecoq asserts: "Je tiens mon affaire, mon *roman*, si vous voulez, et sans la moindre lacune" [I have the whole case, my *novel*, if you like, worked out, and there's not a single msising piece]. Once again, *histoire* gives way to histrionics as Lecoq presents a highly dramatized performance of his "roman" to Plantat and Gendron:

> Il ne racontait pas seulement le drame, il le mimait, il le jouait, ajoutant l'ascendant du geste à l'empire de la parole, et chacune de ses phrases reconstituant une scène, expliquait un fait et dissipait un doute. Comme tous les artistes de génie, qui s'incarnent vraiment dans le personnage qu'ils représentent, l'agent de la sûreté ressentait réellement quelque chose des sensations qu'il traduisait, et son masque mobile avait alors une effrayante expression.
> — Voilà donc, reprit-il, la première partie du drame. (144)

> [He not only narrated the drama, he mimed it, acted it out, adding the power of gesture to the authority of the word, and as each of his sentences reconstructed a scene, a fact was explained, a doubt eliminated. Like all gifted artists who fully identify with the characters they represent, the detective genuinely experienced something of the feelings he was con-

veying, and his ever-changing, masklike face took on a frightening expression.

"So there, he went on, "you have the first part of the drama."]

One story engendering another, Plantat is maneuvered into producing a manuscript in his possession, the (multiple) authorship of which is left ambiguous at this stage in the narrative. This is the missing text whose existence had been posited by Lecoq as the motive for the murder of the countess and whose story-content helps to complete gaps in Lecoq's own reconstruction of the crime. Written partly by the countess's first husband as a journal recording the progress of his gradual poisoning by his adulterous wife and her lover (the present missing count), and completed by the countess after his death, it occupies a hefty ten out of the twenty-eight chapters comprising the novel. And yet, despite its quasi-autonomous status as the story of the origins of the present crime, its subordination to the story of the investigation is maintained. Indeed, the manuscript proves to be a "murderous" text, the posthumous instrument of the dying husband's revenge. By binding the two adulterers forever together in unholy matrimony (Plantat is to make public its contents if their marriage fails to proceed), the existence of the manuscript is responsible for the death of both the countess and, ultimately, the count himself. For it is in a frenzied attempt to gain possession of this incriminating document that the count is driven to murder the woman he now abhors, but to whom he is "textually" bound. Given its presentation to the reader in the form of yet another dramatized reading, this time by Plantat, our attention is drawn once again to performance and reception issues, the mode of telling revealing almost as much as the chilling facts of the tale itself. Indeed, it is the passionate nature of Plantat's delivery that serves to confirm Lecoq's suspicions that Plantat has still more to reveal.

Despite the length of the interpolated story, the novel does not end here. The investigation continues, the final resolution of the mystery being deferred for another seven chapters. For critics like Jean-Claude Vareille, these long analects, common in Gaboriau's novels (and in those of his successors such as Conan Doyle), illustrate the essentially hybrid nature of the early detective stories, which he views as transitional forms, unable fully to shake off the shackles of the popular novel from which they derive.[18] Vareille concludes that the presence of these mini popular novels in the *roman policier archaïque* is proof of his contention that "le roman policier est la mise en scène de la genèse d'un roman populaire" [the detective novel stages the

genesis of the popular novel].[19] But this is not a persuasive view of a
genre that seems anxious to establish its novelty—to signal its textual
ancestry while at the same time staging its own genesis as a dis-
tinctively new kind of text.[20] Such a conclusion would also ignore the
particular intratextual framing of the embedded narrative in *Le Crime
d'Orcival*, for an ironic recapitulation of the plot occurs soon afterwards.[21] Forced to disclose his personal interest in the outcome of
the case, Plantat confesses his love for Laurence, the young daughter
of the mayor of Orcival who, it seems, has eloped with her lover, the
count, after faking a suicide note to her parents. In an impassioned
plea to the detective, he begs Lecoq to find a way to spare the innocent Laurence the shame of a public trial, alluding to the sensational-
ism of the events of the earlier crime in these terms: "Est-ce qu'il ne
réunit pas, ce procès, toutes les conditions qui assurent le succès des
drames judiciaires? *Oh! rien n'y manque, ni l'adultère, ni le poison, ni la
vengeance, ni le meurtre. Laurence y représentera l'élément romanesque et
sentimental.* Elle deviendra, elle, ma fille, une héroïne de Cours d'Assises. . . . Les journaux la rendront plus publique que la fille des rues,
chaque lecteur aura quelque chose d'elle" (353–54, italics added)
[Didn't the trial bring together all those conditions necessary to the
success of judicial dramas? *Oh! there was nothing missing, neither adultery, poison, vengeance nor murder. Laurence will provide the romantic, sentimental element.* Laurence, my daughter, will become a heroine of the
Assises. The newspapers will expose her more publicly than a woman
of the streets, every reader will have access to a part of her]. By
drawing attention to the sheer melodramatic *excess* of the story we
have just been reading, the text can exploit the more extravagant
aspects of the plot for its popular appeal, while at the same time
ironically distancing itself from what it has clearly designated as a
highly successful formula.

At the level of story, Plantat's involvement with one of the more
peripheral players in the *théâtre du crime* allows Gaboriau to produce a
final narrative arabesque that deflects the plot away from the trajectory suggested earlier by Lecoq in the scene with which this analysis
began. In this way the focus is kept squarely on the detective, both as
investigator and dispenser of justice. In compliance with Plantat's
desires, the novel ends not with due process of law, but with a man-
hunt organized by Lecoq culminating in the staging of a "scene of
justice" outside the limits of the investigating magistrate's control.
Although at this stage of the investigation the detective shifts from
the more passive role of master interpreter to that of active redresser
of wrongs (recalling the *justicier* figure prominent in popular serials
of the period),[22] Lecoq refrains from direct intervention in the

climactic scene of confrontation with the murderer that follows. True to his role of *metteur-en-scène*, the detective occupies a position off-stage, in the wings. As the narrator informs us: "M. Lecoq est un de ces hommes qui ne laissent rien au hasard de l'inspiration, qui pré-voient tout, qui règlent les actions de la vie comme les scènes de théâtre" (389) [M. Lecoq is one of those men who leave nothing to the inspiration of the moment, who anticipate everything, who plan everything that happens in life like scenes in a play]. Since, as we have been reminded, Lecoq is one of those people who leave nothing to chance, it must be assumed that he knowingly engineers the mur-derer's death through the agency of the young and "innocent" Lau-rence. (The latter shoots the count with one of his own pistols when he balks at the idea of suicide as a means of preserving his honor.) A murderer by proxy, the detective concludes: "Voilà . . . un misérable *que j'ai tué* au lieu de l'arrêter et de le livrer à la justice. En avais-je le droit? Non, mais ma conscience ne me reproche rien, c'est donc que j'ai bien agi" (396, italics added) [So *I have killed* a scoundrel instead of arresting and handing him over to the courts. Did I have the right to do so? No, but my conscience is clear, since I acted appropriately]].

Having defeated his rival player in the "théâtre du crime," Lecoq's final act is to hand over the pregnant Laurence to le père Plantat, who willingly accepts the role of surrogate father to the unborn child. The novel thus ends with the transformation of the detective into virtual assassin, completing a circular structure that repeats the crime with which it began and blurs the boundaries between criminal and detective, self and other, author and reader in the text. At the same time, as a denouement to a novel obsessed with the theatrical, the double murder structure[23] hints at a genealogy that extends beyond its immediate popular contemporaries to a more distant ancestor, the Greek tragedy that introduced the first literary detective-cum-murderer, Oedipus himself.[24]

NOTES

1. Emile Gaboriau, *Le Crime d'Orcival* (Paris: Encre, 1985), 130. Subsequent page references will be incorporated into the text. All translations are my own. *Le Crime d'Orcival* was first published in daily installments between October 1866 and Febru-ary 1867 in both *Le Soleil* and *Le Petit Journal*. The work was commissioned by Moïse Millaud (financier and owner of several newspapers) following the success of Gaboriau's first *roman judiciaire*, *L'Affaire Lerouge*, published in serial form in 1865.

2. The veiled allusion to Balzac's *La Comédie humaine* as narrative intertext (La société, voilà mon théâtre" ["Society is the theater of my fiction"]) is a further allusion

to the world of fiction as the reference point for questions of *vraisemblance* in this novel.

3. Marie Maclean, *Narrative as Performance: The Baudelairean Experiment* (London and New York: Routledge, 1988), 76.

4. Lecoq is a master of disguise, his study resembling an actor's dressing room with its array of wigs and costumes, makeup and other accessories. Throughout the investigation he appears in different physical guises to the astonishment of his "audience." There is even some doubt expressed that an essential Lecoq exists behind the protean forms he assumes: "Il est vrai que M. Lecoq a l'air qu'il lui plaît d'avoir. Ses amis assurent bien qu'il a une physionomie à lui, qui est la sienne, qu'il reprend quand il rentre chez lui . . . mais le fait n'est pas bien prouvé" (60) [It is true that M. Lecoq changes his appearance at whim. His friends are quite certain that he has a countenance of his own that he assumes when he goes home . . . but that has not been proved beyond a doubt]. As critics like Jean-Claude Vareille (*L'Homme masqué, le justicier et le détective* [Lyon: Presses Universitaires de Lyon, 1989]) point out, references to masks and disguise and the foregrounding of the gap between seeming and being are common in popular novels of this period, establishing connections with the carnivalesque as opposed to the realist tradition.

5. Following Marie Maclean's argument that "major novels of all periods have used embedded dramatic models over the centuries from *The Golden Ass* to *David Copperfield* . . ." (*Narrative as Performance*, 13), my contention is that self-conscious allusions to the theater have a specific generic function in detective fiction.

6. Geoffrey Hartman, in *The Fate of Reading* (Chicago: The University of Chicago Press, 1975), 206, draws a distinction between the "whodunit" and what he calls the "whodonut," a collective label for postmodern versions of detective stories that refuse the reader the satisfactions of a strongly localized and visualized "scene of pathos." It could be argued, however, that every detective story is "a story with a hole in it" since, although Robbe-Grillet and others referred to by Hartman frustrate our desire to know definitively what happened in the past, every story of an absent crime is a fiction produced by the detective that more or less fits the evidence. The failure of a detective figure to produce such a coherent account simply offers greater opportunities for the reader to step into his shoes.

7. The term used by Gaboriau, "roman judiciaire," in some ways more accurately reflects the concerns of these novels, given their preoccupation with issues of justice. But the designation "roman policier" draws attention to their distinctive focus on the investigative part of the judicial process and the preeminent role of the detective figure.

8. See especially Dennis Porter, *The Pursuit of Crime: Art and Ideology in Detective Fiction* (New Haven and London: Yale University Press, 1981), 24 ff; Vareille, *L'Homme masqué*, 45; Lits, *Le Roman policier: Introduction à la théorie et à l'histoire d'un genre littéraire* (Liège: Éditions du C.E.F.A.L., 1993), 75 ff.

9. Maclean, *Narrative as Performance*, xi.

10. In fact the theatrical potential of *Le Crime d'Orcival* was soon recognized and exploited with its production as a play, a drama in five acts, by Edgard Poucelle, a friend of the novelist, and Henri Mendel. The first performance was in 1878, five years after Gaboriau's death.

11. Like the ill-fitting glove in the O. J. Simpson real-life courtroom drama that triggered the defense's mantra "if it doesn't fit, you must acquit," the prosecution's case stands or falls on questions of narrative plausibility.

12. Once the *roman policier* is established as a genre, the reference point is not only the theatre, but also commonly the genre itself, textual performance being mea-

sured implicitly against the preestablished rules of the game. As early as 1887 in *A Study in Scarlet,* Sherlock Holmes measures his performance as a detective against that of his two most illustrious predecessors, Dupin and Lecoq:

> "You remind me of Edgar Allan Poe's Dupin. I had no idea that such individuals did exist outside stories."
>
> Sherlock Holmes rose and lit his pipe. 'No doubt you think that you are complimenting me in comparing me to Dupin," he observed. "Now, in my opinion, Dupin was a very inferior fellow . . ."
>
> "Have you read Gaboriau's works?" I asked. "Does Lecoq come up to your idea of a detective?"
>
> Sherlock Holmes sniffed sardonically. "Lecoq was a miserable blunderer," he said in an angry voice.

13. As quoted by Lits, *Le Roman policier,* 26.

14. Ibid.

15. "J'ai fait comprendre à tous ces gens l'indécence de leur curiosité" (59) [I made all these people realize how indecent their curiosity is], says M. Courtois, the mayor of Orcival, in a reference right at the beginning to the curiosity of the "crowd" that the text disingenuously decries.

16. As readers we are repeatedly positioned as a privileged audience having access to disclosures never revealed to the wider public. Plantat stresses, for example, that the real circumstances of the countess's remarriage remained unknown to the outside world:

> — Et le public n'a jamais rien su de l'horrible guerre intérieure.
> — Le public n'a jamais rien soupçonné. (291)
>
> ["And the public never knew anything about the horrible war being waged between them."
> "The public never suspected a thing."]

17. When Lecoq first appears at the scene of the crime, the narrator sketches the following unflattering portrait of the typical policeman: "Il est entendu, en France, que chaque état a son extérieur particulier et comme des insignes qui le dénoncent au premier coup d'œil. . . . En vertu de cette loi, l'employé de la rue de Jérusalem doit avoir l'œil plein de traîtrise, quelque chose de louche dans toute sa personne, l'air crasseux et des bijoux en faux" (61) [It is an accepted fact in France that each person, depending on his station in life, has distinctive external features, like insignias that reveal all at one glance. . . . In accordance with this law, the employee from the rue de Jérusalem should be shifty-eyed, have a sinister air, a grimy appearance and wear fake jewellery]. A few pages further on, Lecoq himself admits: "La police— c'est bête comme tout—est mal vue" (63) [The police—it's crazy—are held in low esteem], and, later still, he ruefully comments to Plantat: "En France, monsieur, la police a contre elle non seulement les coquins, mais encore les honnêtes gens" (341) [In France, Monsieur, the police have not only the criminals against them, but also law-abiding, decent folk].

18. Vareille, *L'Homme masqué,* 66–67.

19. Ibid., 65.

20. This is in fact how Vareille views the later detective novel: "Cette mise en scène d'une recherche, cette chronologie de l'enquête et cette chronologie du drame . . . qu'est-ce d'autre sinon l'imbrication d'une création et d'une histoire créée, d'une écriture et d'une fiction, d'une énonciation et d'un énoncé . . . ? Le roman policier

qui construit/reconstruit par bribes une aventure qui finit par être cohérente apparaît ainsi comme le récit de la genèse d'un texte . . ." (*L'Homme masqué*, 172) [This staging of a quest, this double chronology—of the quest and of the drama—what else is it if not the interweaving of an act of creation and a created story, of a writing and of a fictional text, of an enunciation and an utterance . . . ? The detective story, which in piecemeal fashion constructs/reconstructs a story that finally hangs together coherently, thus seems to represent the story of the genesis of a text . . .].

21. On intratextual framing generally, see Gale MacLachlan and Ian Reid, *Framing and Interpretation* (Melbourne: Melbourne University Press, 1994).

22. For a detailed analysis of the relationship between the detective and the *justicier* figure, see Vareille, *L'Homme masqué*.

23. As one of the characters in Michel Butor's *L'Emploi du temps* remarks: "Tout roman policier est bâti sur deux meurtres dont le premier, commis par l'assassin, n'est que l'occasion du second dans lequel il est victime du meurtrier pur et impunissable, du détective qui le met à mort . . . par l'explosion de la vérité" (Paris: U.G.E., «coll. 10/18», 1972), 214 [Every detective novel is constructed around two murders, of which the first, committed by the murderer, provides the opportunity for the second, in which he is the victim of that pure and unpunishable murderer, the detective, who engineers his death . . . through the explosion of the truth].

24. Butor's character George Burton again makes this link: "Le détective est le fils du meurtrier, Oedipe, non seulement parce qu'il résout une énigme, mais aussi parce qu'il tue celui à qui il doit son titre, celui sans lequel il n'existerait pas comme tel . . ." (215–16) [The detective is the offspring of the murderer Oedipus, not only because he solves a puzzle, but also because he kills the person to whom he owes his name and his very existence . . .].

The Daughter's Triangle: *Fatal Attraction* and *The Piano*

NAOMI SEGAL

TRIANGLES ARE EVERYWHERE IN RECENT THEORY. IN THIS ESSAY I want to suggest how the structure can be understood in a number of different ways, culminating in a contrast between two recent films about adultery. To begin with, a quick tour of geometrical space.

First, we have from narratology the triangular nature of the reading process, understood as a series of negotiations made between two imaginary figures, the implied author and the implied reader, across the "third person" of the text. None of these figures is stable or single. The reader is plural in both space and time, the author an amalgam of a body in history and an impossible ambition, and both are multiplied by the fantasies generated by the image of the other in each's variable head; the text too is both a concrete object and a gap peopled virtually by the characters, geography, and teleology of a fiction. Reading is thus both a contract and a tightrope act.

A second triangular structure superimposes two ways of thinking about the relation between generations—genealogy, reproduction. In 1878, Samuel Butler wrote: "It has, I believe, been often remarked that a hen is only an egg's way of making another egg."[1] This is most startling, perhaps, because of the way it exposes our uncertain idea of priority, always fraught with difficulty when it comes to chickens and eggs. In nature—and most overtly in what natural scientists like to call the "lower" species—a male is only a female's way of making another female; praying mantises and even sea horses bear witness to this. In human culture, however, patriarchy has turned the natural structure on its head. Social arrangements between the sexes have always ensured that a woman is merely a man's way of making another man. Thus women are passed from fathers to husbands and transmit the latter's family names to sons, who keep those names, and to daughters, who most often lose them. The genealogical model is essential if we are to understand how the apparently closed binary of the couple becomes social, narrative, etc., because it is itself the middle term of a triadic communicative structure that absorbs it. Our other triangles, from oedipal or adulterous back to the textual contracts we make and break in reading, will be haunted by this restless genealogy, always on the move and juggernaut-like in its unconcern for the claims of the dyad.

Psychoanalysis is obviously the most established of the modern triangular theories. In Freud's classical oedipus complex, the nuclear family consists of father, mother, and male child. Less obviously—but in this it is typical of narratives generated since romanticism—it is a triangle viewed from the position of the son, grown-up now perhaps, but still unconsciously thinking as a child. He desires his mother, perceives a threat of castration from the father, and concedes defeat, abjuring sexuality and entering a social contract that will fit him finally to make and terrorize other little boys. Reading Freud through feminism, we become aware that the move by which the boy accepts that he must join his father rather than beat him derives less from fear of castration than from the dismissal of the mother/sister whom he believes to be "already castrated." Such valueless women are not worth serious desire, which is transferred to those things properly valued by a men's world, and sexuality is put aside, to be brought out again later in a way that will never accord it conscious priority in the things that matter to men.

Freud himself offers another model that supports this reading of the oedipal drama, in his discussion of the generation of the "smutty joke." A man desires a woman; she refuses his advances, ideally (in Freud's view) because of the presence of a rival male that "would make seduction out of the question."[2] When, in pique at the woman's refusal, the first man tells a smutty joke about her, it is to the second man that he tells it. The final move is a conciliatory one, bringing both men's sexual tension to an end: "through the first person's smutty speech, the woman is exposed before the third [the rival], who, as listener, has been bribed by the effortless satisfaction of his own libido."[3] Somehow, in all this, the hostility both toward the rival and toward the rejecting woman has disappeared—to the former because he is now treated with friendship, to the latter because she has been made to disappear, or rather, has been transformed into a narrative. Implicitly undercut in the "lower levels of society" where, Freud suggests, women even sometimes tell the jokes themselves, this structure holds good at the higher levels and supremely, I would like to suggest, in the high cultural level we call literature. In fiction, the oedipal dismissal of the woman turns her into that virtual object, a text.

We are moving toward the most familiar triangle of all, the one that forms the common plot of the "great" bourgeois nineteenth-century novels.[4] For this, the key theorist is surely René Girard, who sees in the workings of desire a universal structure of distancing. In *Mensonge romantique et vérité romanesque* (translated as *Deceit, Desire, and the Novel*),[5] he argues that desire is always conditioned by a model or mediator in whom the desirer may have a greater libidinal investment than in the overt object of the passion. Thus, both in fiction and experience the intense relation of jealousy may be not just the catalyst but the generator of a sexual obsession. This would be to see adulterous or transgressive desire as always oedipal, and indeed the fictional examples seem designed to support that view. Not only are they almost always presented as the desire of a young man for an older, married woman, but they seem to rely more than anything on the frustration born of the impossible wish. In a sparkling development of Girard's theory, Eve Kosofsky Sedgwick has mapped out the typical gender-structure of this triangularity. She argues that the topos of rivalry in which two men do battle over the (alive or eventually dead) body of a woman is best understood if we regard the engagement of the two men with each other as the primary dyad, and the desire for the woman as the mere pretext for their more crucial encounter.[6] In what she calls "homosocial desire," the triangle shortens into a hidden or repressed relation between men.

Persuasive as Sedgwick's reading of the rivalry plot might be, it does not adequately explain those two archetypal subgroups of male-authored nineteenth-century fiction, the *récit* and the novel of adultery. In both we repeatedly find the hero's most powerful passion directed toward the maternal figure. It is, after all, she who dies. The supposed oedipal parricide is replaced by a matricide that more exactly reflects the ousting of the woman in the plot of the smutty joke. In the *récit* the father- or rival-figure is carefully placated, regretted or displaced; it is the maternal figure who is disempowered or murdered. Similarly, in the novel of adultery, the husband functions as a cuckold: foolish, amiable even, blustering perhaps but not really a hate-figure. Think of the saintly Alexei Karenin, guilty of nothing worse than sticking-out ears; or the unimaginative Prussian von Innstetten or the silly husbands in the fictions of Stendhal, Maupassant or Flaubert.

If the husband is not really the rival in the plot of the novel of adultery, who is? Well, let us not forget that, true to her oedipal origins, the beloved in these texts, unlike her lover, has children. In a late *récit*, *Dominique*, we find the protagonist frankly reacting to his beloved's grief at her sterile marriage by being "impitoyablement jaloux" [pitilessly jealous]—of a child whom the author cannot even allow to exist![7] If, as I want to suggest, it is the child rather than the husband who is the real object of jealousy in these triangular texts, then we must look out for two quite distinctly gendered versions—depending on whether her child is a son or a daughter.

My analysis of a group of canonical novels of adultery shows that, when the desired woman is the mother of a son, her son tends to fall ill just at the moment when the love affair is beginning. He rarely dies, but his illness may be the cause of her abandoning the hero (in Flaubert) or undergoing the torments of guilt (in Stendhal). In either case, we see the stranglehold of patriarchal convention wherein the husband owns the right to pass his name legitimately through his wife to his son replaced by the more phantasmic menace of the author-God holding the rights of life or death over her maternal passion for her child. By contrast to this blighted but familiar icon, mothers of daughters are a rare thing in male-authored fiction; when they do occur, they are always transgressors—prostitutes, murderesses or adulteresses. It is as if the self-reproduction of a mother having a daughter were, to the author, already a kind of punishment, scarcely better than sterility. At the same time, the mother/daughter couple is spotlighted by a kind of fascination, as the place where the masculine authorial imagination stops and wonders. The mother/daughter pair appears in these adulterous texts framed and occulted in some enclosed space—a garden, a room, a cell. Hester Prynne stands forth in the opening scene of *The Scarlet Letter*, displayed on the prison steps, a grey-clad sinner with, on her breast, the bright embroidered A whose meaning is never spelled out and the pretty baby dressed likewise in ornately decorative scarlet: the two are equally badges of her crime, and we do not need to be told that her child must be the anti-icon, a daughter. Daughters in the novel of adultery do not fall ill; instead they simply fall (like their mothers) and often cut themselves, visibly presenting the excess of female blood to be read as more scarlet letters. And what happens when their mothers die? Both Hester and Anna's bastard daughters, like the neglected legitimate offspring of Emma Bovary and Effi Briest, end up fostered by their mother's husbands. In this way, the genealogical chains close up again on the transgressive outsiders.

Turning now to our own life and times, I will compare two fictions produced in the last ten years. Both were immensely popular films, breaking box-office records in the USA and elsewhere, and provoking critical and general interest beyond anything their directors had received before. Prior to *Fatal Attraction* (1987), Adrian Lyne was known for *Flashdance* and *9½ Weeks*, both reckoned to be glossy and essentially superficial exercises. Jane Campion's *Sweetie* and *An Angel at My Table* had won critical acclaim and awards, but were unpopular or unknown by the general public. *Fatal Attraction* and *The Piano* caught the attention of the moment and speak, it seems, very powerfully to the preoccupations of the last two decades of this century.

What I shall examine in this essay is how the principle of triangularity works differently, both in structure and in a more general psychological functioning, in these two films. At the risk of starting over-simply, I want to work inward from a symmetrical assumption: that *Fatal Attraction* is a powerful negative myth of contemporary masculinity and *The Piano* is an equally powerful positive myth of contemporary femininity. Both their residual enigma and their production of overdetermined explanations (the British Film Institute offers an at-a-glance list of around seventy longer articles and reviews on each) attest to their resonance. What exactly is it they do?

Again, to start simply: what are the common elements between them? Both films have a plot that turns upon the question of adultery and each uses a triangle as its basic form. In both, the trio of adults is supplemented by the addition—which, however, I would suggest, makes for a more complex triangularity rather than some other figure—of a female child and, parallel or supplementary to her, other objects or creatures intermediate between the "fully human" and the land- or cityscape.[8]

In 1980s and 1990s mainstream cinema, particularly USA films, sons appear as the third person in unhappy families where the wife is to be ejected from a domesticity that runs better without her.[9] *Kramer v. Kramer* is only the most popular of these myths.[10] They roll comfortably on from an oedipal origin and what Leslie Fiedler identified as long ago as 1960 as a peculiarly American alienation from adult sexuality and nostalgia for the ostensibly unsexed bonds of boyhood.[11] More recently, we find the male body feminized in increasingly comical (read: safe) ways to take over further areas of women's space. Robin Williams and Arnold Schwarzenegger, with a little technology, will make better mothers than their wives ever could, and the latter is undoubtedly a more reliable kindergarten teacher than the Nicole Kidman character in *Malice*.[12]

Given this vocabulary of the sympathy-for-father genre, it is perhaps surprising to find that Dan Gallagher (from whose viewpoint the film is wholly presented) has a daughter—more still, we might think, that his perfect wife has one. Good mothers in male-authored fictions generally have sons and lose them only when they cease to deserve them. That Beth Gallagher has a daughter, however short-haired, suggests something of the prehensile ambiguities of her role in the triangular plot in which she will be in turn the reject, the haven and the killer.

Much more ink has been spilled over Dan and Alex, and I will return to them. But let's begin with the surprisingly matrilinear wife. Most reviewers, whether grudgingly or with relief, recognize that Beth is no dishrag. We must believe that Dan has little reason to cheat on her, and that he can enjoy a pleasant future with her, even if they avoid baths for a few months. She must be not so much less as differently sexy from the excessive Alex, who thrills for only a very short time, after which she begins to spill. Beth differs not by being unattractive but by offering, feature for feature, hair, eyes, and mouth that invite rather than threaten—her gaze is dewy, her smile humble, her hair flowing, whereas Alex's are respectively demanding, knowing, and controlled. Yet the wife is, paradoxically, less sexually available than her rival. He can have her but he can't have her (a planned nude scene between them was never shot) because first the (male) dog and then the child are placed in between them. This same dog is mutely included in the adulterous weekend: in a day, he witnesses outdoor frolics and indoor grapples, two plays at death and their outcomes, and he eats the evidence in a plate of cold spaghetti sauce; later, the daughter and her (female) rabbit will be brought similarly into the drama of Alex's invasions after first having taken the place of sexual intimacy between the husband and the wife.

Crucially, triangularity is presented in *Fatal Attraction* as invasive. True to the tradition of adulterous plots, it is the story of an outsider breaking in and breaking up. Like the scapegoat in tragedy or detective fiction, that outsider is finally dispatched in order to save (or perhaps simply patch) the original unit, whose inner faults s/he has less exposed than disguised. Alex Forrest, as her name suggests, is the wild by which the safe is demarcated. Whether in the cluttered New York apartment or the well-acred suburban homestead, she presents the black hole that forces itself into completion. What she invades is warm, cozy, threatened, and imperfect. Implosion is also explosion. To return to Beth, we need to look again at how her desirability is represented. Not available but enclosed.

We frequently see Beth half-undressed, making up or getting ready for her bath. But she always seems complete because she is in her right place, in front of a mirror. Applying lipstick, she reproaches her daughter for parodying women's titivations. Before the glass, she checks the colors on her skin: rouge, bruises. At one point, the most erotic moment they share, Dan comes up behind her and gazes (he at her, she at herself, and both at the couple they make) upon the mirrored image of their marriage. In parallel, much later, while he is downstairs making a conciliatory cup of tea,[13] she examines her reflection again, twice in his shaving mirror, then in her larger one; and in the latter frame, as she wipes away the steam, Alex's face appears behind her. Of course, this types the outsider as both intervening on and belonging inside the scheme she ruptures. Beth is potentially the same sort of woman as Alex: less libidinous perhaps but more sadistic, for we only witness Alex's attacks on herself, whereas it is the two goodies, male and female, who threaten murder,[14] and while he rehearses it with detailed ferocity, she carries it out.

If triangularity is conceived as invasion in this myth, we have seen that it is not just Alex who threatens the closure of the framed space. We have seen that it is already disrupted internally by the stops that its internal "extras" present to desire. Dan, as the truism goes, seeks something outside the marriage that he doesn't find inside it. That it is something he only fleetingly or superficially wants is unimportant; he is not happy in the frame as Beth, we are constantly assured, is happy. Beth moves from one enclosure to another. She is a *femme d'intérieur* in every sense (except in the extraneous pun of her offering an inside to others: no one enters her).[15] When she is outside her gilded cage and set in motion, she very quickly shatters.

While Beth is engaged in the panicky drive that will break her into the pieces that only her own violence can mend, the narrative intercuts to Alex whizzing up and down the big dipper with Beth's daughter. Side by side and perfectly safe, they are on the rails while the mother is driving off them. The increased pace of Alex's wickedness has been marked in a number of inroads. First she had borrowed the husband without the wife's knowledge, harassed him and entered their space by means chiefly of the telephone, whose fetishistic audibility gets louder as it creeps nearer and nearer to the no longer properly monogamous bed. Soon she herself arrives at their home posing as a buyer, and takes away the new phone number. In her next attack, the acid burns but does not penetrate the car: only the skin of the Volvo is marked, but her abusive cassette is taken first into his car, then his "den"—where it is Beth who scares the life out of him by her gentle arrival. Then the boiled rabbit, tragicomically taken from hutch to pot, and the moment of confession that has Dan ejected from the family space, Ellen lifted, and Beth hospitalized.

Alex's wish to be included begins to become pathological only from the point at which she lays claim to a good reason for it. She tells Dan she is pregnant. Despite the views of some critics, we never know for sure if this is true—her vomiting in the garden after watching the schmaltzy scene of family and pet is surely justified psychologically as much as physically, and could *you* imagine voluntarily riding the big dipper in the first trimester? But it does not really matter. She claims it and Dan and Beth believe it. This child is both rival and sibling to Ellen; it could explain such uncertainties as why Alex does no harm to her baby's older sister and why Dan tries repeatedly to kill them both but only his unrelated wife can take over that killing. More importantly, it makes her a doubled threat to the family. Her child offers the negative image of their legitimacy. Her attack is no longer that of the simple outsider but of the inversion of relatedness that upturns theirs.

Who has penetrated whom? For all Alex's come-on, Dan enters her body (this is a movie about unsafe sex) and cannot ever wholly come out again. Whether literally in the fetal residue—"How do you know it's mine?" he predictably stutters—or in the need that she retains, he is in Alex as much as she is in him. He repeatedly breaks into her apartment, though it is not locked. If she always rises up again when injured like a cyborg or a vampire, so does he, after teasing her with a faked heart attack in the park. Alex's pregnancy is, as Karen Durbin points out, just as much Dan's.[16] But it is she, not Beth, who has a mother's rights over him. It is she who practises the kind of sex that impregnates, ignoring the props and fetishes that, by contrast, Beth arrays between herself and Dan. Alex's child makes her more immediate, Beth's makes her less.

Her child makes her uncanny because Alex is the enclosure of the pre-oedipal, pre-sexed, the more-herself-half-his. Beth's role is to be contained, not to contain. She alone of all the four protagonists is secure in the joint affection of living parents. Her child is no longer in her and, androgynously shorthaired, ungainly in girly costume, aged somewhere between five and six (her parents do not agree on this), hangs ready like a fruit to drop into the oedipal moment where her father waits hungrily. She practices the proposal scene from a play, watches junk TV and learns card tricks from her grandfather; she can already answer the phone and pass messages to Mommy. She is on the way to being a mediator and seems to hold the marriage together, but actually, like the other "third persons," she holds it apart.

Too much has been written about the ending of *Fatal Attraction* for me to want to add much here. Mandy Merck unusually shows its consistency with the rest of the film, all of which can be read as a representation of the child's-eye view of the primal scene. At earlier moments, she argues, both Alex and Ellen have been lookers-in on the couple; now in the final frames, the daughter is safely offstage. As first Father, then Mother, attempts to kill the woman who has come between them, the child who has come between them—a child who was previously aroused from bed by raised voices—fails to appear at the primal scene. As the camera surveys the film's bloody climax, the reverse look we expect to be given, Ellen's look, is withheld. Instead, I would argue, we are invited to take up her vantage point, to watch another white-clad lover struggle and die in the intimate surroundings of the family bathroom, and to be as shocked as a child. The exaggerated and implausible horror of Alex's death (a Grand Guignol finale which displeased realist critics) is rendered psychologically appropriate by our own infantilized viewpoint, which replaces that of the little girl, seen only in the film's final, notorious close-up of the Gallagher family photograph.[17]

This is surely a correct reading of the psychological buzz that the climax gave viewers, not least the good wives of bad men, and that Sherry Lansing and Adrian Lyne justify in clearly orgasmic terms.[18] But there is another, if only momentary and only implicit, viewpoint within the final scene—that of Alex through whose (dead or undead?) eyes we witness her drowning. We shall see another resurrection from drowning in our other film, also viewed from the lower depths upwards and also marking the limits of the disposal of female desire. Alex is being finished by the nuclear family, Ada is about to start one. How differently does triangularity function in this declaratively "women's film"?

To recapitulate: *Fatal Attraction* is provocative because it both uses and inverts the familiar version of the adulterous triangle. An outsider threatens an established dyad; but because that outsider is a woman she threatens it differently. In this traditionally penetrative fantasy of sexual irruption, the subject of forced entry is female and familial: she enters more insistently because she is an already containing space, herself both penetrated by and penetrative of the man's psychological space.

I use the term "penetration" reluctantly because I want to enter the continuing "sex wars" debate without getting caught in its most common traps. I do not want to identify the two modes of desire represented by these two films with male and female practice—that would be patently simplistic. I am not sure that the consequences of gendering them masculine and feminine are altogether useful, leaving unbroached as it does the question of same-sex desire and its place in any gender binary. But it is true that *The Piano*, understood for various reasons as being a "women's film," moves more women more powerfully than it seems to move men, and that this effect (which I share) requires explanation.[19] Clearly, the music, visual sweep, and erotic buildup is part of it. But I think there must be something more to explain why this film appears to transcend the bounds of the masculine images of desire with which our culture so massively familiarizes us, women and men, gay and straight.

So let me try to distinguish the two modes in other ways. In *Fatal Attraction* the sex represented is avid, noisy and violent. Quite deliberately, we know, the three most violent scenes, all taking place in kitchens and bathrooms, the most "bodily" parts of a house, set up an analogy between the choreography of sex and murder. The only moments of missionary-position *corps-à-corps* are Dan's two attempts to kill Alex, in which shot-reverse-shot shows the equally contorted faces of murderer and murderee such that we can neither distinguish homicidal from sexual violence nor the status of aggressor and victim. Let us call this mode of desire "invasive," noting that it is the mode most commonly presented to us in cultural products hitherto. The triangle of invasion, desire as breaking and entering, the colonization of resistant space by an outsider who might be ejected. Love and death in the western world.

In *The Piano*, it is also a question of the entry into a person's protected space and of colonization. Desire is triangulated and co-optative but differently so. The key differences are temporal and spatial, using the inevitability, the step-by-step of desire in a way that replaces sadism with curiosity, and showing how bodies can reach each other in a mode that somehow resembles the playing of a piano.

The adulterous triangle in this film consists of a woman and two men, the most common pattern in traditional representations of adultery that, with their oedipal freight, tend to show an already assigned woman desired by a younger man. But here the married woman stands at the apex of the triangle, insistently focalized, alongside neither of the men. And, somewhat like Alex and very much like Hester Prynne, she starts out doubled by an illegitimate daughter whose existence declares her sexuality and represents one mode of access between her and the world.

Ada's muteness is not explained and is presented in the first frames as a state that she has both chosen and is powerless to reverse.[20] "Not a handicap but a strategy," a multiplication and dissemination of the possible resources of communication,[21] her silence marks out very clearly the way in which an originating choice (or "will," as the characters describe it) both frees up and restricts the actions that follow. This film, like the other, multiplies and fetishizes the channels between subject and object; but it reverses the triangulation that sees the "third" element as invasive, and presents it instead as a putting out, a means towards the other. Where Beth's daughter was a possession that could be stolen from her, Ada's daughter is an extension of herself that is broken from her. It is not surprising that when Beth is hurt it is by a shattering of the whole body, and when Ada is hurt it is by the cutting off of one of her fingers, the spoiling of a complete set, what her mutilator calls "clipping her wings."

There are many other objects and modes of mediation—indeed, what some viewers dislike about the film is the relentless (oddly, simultaneously over-obvious and over-arty) stylization of these devices. Bonnets resemble scallop shells "designed to concentrate acoustic information,"[22] crinolines are houses, skirts leading reins, shirts dusters, the wooden slats of a packing case or a rough-hewn cottage let sound out or voyeurism in, and the visual sweep of the camera combined with the concentration of close-up brings together natural lighting, predominance of forest-greens and subaqueous blues to alternate the fantasies of being-lost-in and emerging-out.

The piano is, of course, the main fetish-object: both desired thing and part of self, it is bulky, inert, biddable and sensual; its cumbersomeness and beauty make it the possession no one can hold with certainty, like their own body.[23] It ends the film imagined undead beneath the sea and still, even after Ada's graphic birth out of the amniotic bubble, keeping one version of her body suspended umbilically above it. In the opening moments of the film, in a shaft of red only rarely seen,[24] and through which (like the light seen through fingers, behind which a child might hide its face, thinking that makes it invisible) a piping voice identifies itself as Ada's "mind's voice," she announces that she stopped speaking when she was six. This, we discover, was just after or just before she began to play the piano. Thus the instrument allows the child's preservation as voice inside her body and its voluntary-involuntary expression, a model of psychoanalytical *Aufhebung*.

We are tempted perhaps to think it is Flora's voice. Unlike the Maoris, whose difference is marked fairly carefully in superiority and mimicry,[25] her doubling of her mother is both functional and reciprocal. It is a double Venus that is brought forth and landed on the beach, and the use of the child as substitute for voice is shown when she pronounces Ada's aggressive message to the sailor and only escapes his fist by hiding in her mother's skirts. She has the rights of monogamous enjoyment of her mother: like Ellen, she is there in the bed when the husband visits at the end of the day and it is her he offers to kiss rather than the woman.

The child and the piano are alternative communicators of the woman's physical desire. For Stewart, both Ada and her piano are his to buy and sell; Baines at once recognises its mediatory function. He first takes her to it, standing as audience to the complete unit of mother/child/instrument on the beach; then he uses it to bring her to him, listening silently as she reappropriates it by playing. From this point, the child as mediator becomes redundant to the newly formed unit of woman, piano, and man. It is, of course, essential that Baines cannot read, so that the instrument is at first the only means of communication between them. Gradually, through the simultane-ously comic, threatening, and reassuring eroticism of Baines's clumsy "bargain," the woman's body reenters the communicative circuit, replacing both piano and child.

We will return to the development of dyadic communication in a moment. First, there is more to say about the human mediators. Flora, cast off as she becomes the object rather than the interpreter of her mother's will and co-opted by the patriarchal-symbolic society of the Scottish colonizers, makes an expected move from the mother/daughter cell into the fostering oedipal. Continuing to wear her angel costume—the Hebrew for "angel" means "messenger"—she will act as transmitter of judgment and carrier of keys. But before the story is over, she will undergo a second transfer, from Ada's bed to Baines's, and she will end up turning healthy cartwheels in another triangular family, the least traditional of all.

Stewart plays his assigned role as disruptor of adulterous love; but he, too, is used as something peculiarly connective. In the interlude of her imprisonment, Ada plays only in her sleep, and when she makes an unexpected move toward her husband, seems to "play" on his body in a similarly somnambulist way. What makes this moment so affecting is that it remains in excess of what it proposes. Ada's erotic approach is not simply the redirection of a sexual appetite that Baines has aroused and Flora cannot satisfy. There are two scenes of her night visits: in the first, the screenplay describes her motive as "a separate curiosity of her own"; in the second, she is "moved by his helplessness, but distanced, as if it has nothing to do with her."[26] With a detachment hanging somewhere between compassion and cruelty, Ada touches but will not let herself be touched. But what unmans and maddens the husband most is how she touches him: with the back of her hand upon the back of his body. This special mode of caress is reserved elsewhere only for the sea, the child, and the piano.

In most European languages, the word used for the keys of a piano is associated with the faculty of touch (French *touches,* Italian *tasti,*

German *Tasten*) and connected with a verb used of blind or quasi-blind feeling, groping (*toucher/tâtonner, tastare, tasten*). In stressing her silence as strategy rather than disability, Campion is both right and wrong: Ada has extended the reach of her senses, transferring voice into an extra modality of touch. Stewart is unmanned by this, Baines understands and reciprocates. It is this that makes the sexuality of this film unusual.

George Baines's mediation between cultures is etched on his brow, and it is not simply what makes him a cross between Tarzan and Mellors, it is also the sign of his bilingualism, the ability, like Ada's, to transfer himself and his desire from one mode to another. She cannot speak, he cannot read; she plays, he listens; she touches, he touches. Like Stewart, Baines talks stiltedly—here, Harvey Keitel's struggle with the accent came in useful—and, like him also, he struggles to hear Ada speaking, but whereas the former intuits her wishes "in his head," Baines helps her to move her voice out onto the surface of her skin.

Colonization comes from and operates by the structures of capitalism: grading, marking, and counting out. Analogous to piano keys and fingers, numbered territorial stakes measure out the landscape and buttons are supposed to pay for it. These are Stewart's coinage. Baines and Ada begin with black and white keys, black overclothes and white underclothes; but at a certain moment, the bargaining stops and with it the grading of access that is undoubtedly one mode of the erotic, creating an appetite in both the heroine and the audience. Baines is, after all, like the husband, a colonial exploiter, but less absolutely, not so much an owner as a mediator and interpreter. Implicated nonetheless, he buys the piano and expects to buy Ada; but let us not forget that Ada is as hard a bargainer as he is and it is he who stops the negotiations first.

Erotic violence is not always chaotically invasive: Sade, quite the contrary, creates an atmosphere of *graded* cruelty by his obsession with enumeration, space within space, sectioning off of days, cells, or tortures. It is no chance that Stewart cuts off just one finger: he can then grade the threat on into the future, "another and another and another." Thus the gentle striptease of the unerect Baines is also potentially coercive, but he stops when he has reached her skin. What follows is the transformation of the temporal erotic onto a multiplied surface that is the whole extent of the person (inside and out, we are to understand) now accessible without destruction.

In *The Piano,* then, adulterous triangularity is reinterpreted: it is no longer the structure of the other who invades or irrupts into an enclosed thing that can be punctured or shattered. It becomes instead the condition of the complex movements of desire through its own involuntarinesses into diverse forms that meet other forms at the tips of the fingers. Both these fictions are post-AIDS: *Fatal Attraction* is indeed about the perils of penetration, of man by woman and woman by man, of hallowed spaces by their own fracturability and violence, and of frames by the seduction of a false imaginary. *The Piano* is about the extensability of desire upon a surface that is its own mediation.

NOTES

A shorter version of this article appears in Nicholas White and Naomi Segal, eds., *Scarlet Letters: Fictions of Adultery from Antiquity to the 1990s* (London: Macmillan, 1997), 109–22.

1. Samuel Butler, *Life and Habit* (London: Trübner, 1878), 134.

2. Sigmund Freud, *Jokes and Their Relation to the Unconscious*, trans. James Strachey, ed. Angela Richards, vol. 6 of *The Penguin Freud Library* (Harmondsworth, U.K.: Penguin, 1976), 142.

3. Ibid., 143–44.

4. See my *The Adulteress's Child* (Cambridge, U.K.: Polity Press, 1992) as well as Judith Armstrong, *The Novel of Adultery* (London: Macmillan, 1976) and Tony Tanner, *Adultery in the Novel* (Baltimore and London: Johns Hopkins University Press, 1979). Tanner's analysis highlights "the connections or relationships between a specific kind of sexual act, a specific kind of society and a specific kind of narrative" (12). The adultery plot goes back, of course, to medieval literature; see Denis de Rougement's vast survey, *L'Amour et l'occident* (Paris: Plon, 1939).

5. René Girard, *Mensonge romantique et vérité romanesque* (Paris: Grasset, 1961), translated by Yvonne Freccero as *Deceit, Desire, and the Novel* (Baltimore: Johns Hopkins University Press, 1965).

6. Eve Kosofsky Sedgwick, *Between Men: English Literature and Male Homosocial Desire* (New York: Columbia University Press, 1985).

7. Eugène Fromentin, *Dominique*, ed. Barbara Wright (Paris: Garnier, [1863] 1966), 274.

8. Both films, interestingly, attach a male dog to the female child, and use the dog for humorous or even louche moments based on the animal's propensity to lick.

9. See Tania Modleski, *Feminism without Women* (New York and London: Routledge, 1991), especially chap. 5.

10. In "The Mirror Cracked: The Career Woman in a Trio of Lansing Films," *Film Criticism* 12, no. 2 (winter 1987–88): 28–36, Roslyn Mass observes the representations of strong women who always meet a bad end in films produced by Sherry Lansing; among these are *Kramer v. Kramer* and *Fatal Attraction*. Betty Caplan points out that, for a single working woman, Alex is seen very little at work: "In Work but Out of Sense," *Guardian*, 12 May 1988, 25.

11. Leslie Fiedler, *Love and Death in the American Novel* (London: Jonathan Cape, 1967).

12. See Colleen Keane, "Recent Thrillers: Postmortem Play and Anti-Feminism," *Metro Magazine* 97 (autumn 1994): 20–22.

13. In a generally excellent article, Jean Désobrie points out the recurrence of steaming liquids in the invasion of Alex into the Gallagher family, *Cinémascopie: propos sur le cinéma contemporain* (s.l.: Roger, 1989), 139–40.

14. This is pointed out by Shaun Usher in "The Great Attraction," *Daily Mail*, 15 January 1988, 26. A similarly cynical view of the yuppie couple and their like is given by Michael VerMeulen in "Manhattan Transfer," *Sunday Telegraph*, 7 February 1988, 21.

15. The term *femme d'intérieur* is difficult to translate by a single phrase: roughly, "homemaker," literally, "woman of indoors/inside."

16. Karen Durbin, "The Cat's Meow," *Village Voice*, 15 December 1987, 90: "What Douglas experiences as a result of his fling with Glenn Close reminded me of nothing so much as that classic female nightmare (and luckless female reality), the unwanted pregnancy: a huge, distressing, apparently endless consequence he cannot rid himself of. And all because the poor guy had a little fun. Hey, is life unfair or what? He even tries to get an abortion but Alex is having none of it. Sorry, fella, she says, *you can't get an abortion*. 0 role reversal! 0 bitter joy!"

17. Mandy Merck, "The Fatal Attraction of *Intercourse*," *Perversions: Deviant Readings* (London: Virago, 1993), 210–11.

18. See Adrian Lyne, in an interview with Brian Case, "Out of Lyne," *Time Out*, 13–20 January 1988, 31: "You see, if you build up a lot of empathy for the married man and his family—and I based a lot of it on mine—and then say, sorry fellas, he's going to jail, you're left alone, that's it—I don't think that's fair. I mean, you're giving the audience the foreplay and then . . ." Or Sherry Lansing, less graphically, in Mass, "The Mirror Cracked," 33: "I love the ending we have. It is eminently satisfying."

19. See Lizzie Francke, [no title], *Sight & Sound* (November 1993): 224: "For a while I could not think, let alone write, about *The Piano* without shaking. Precipitating a flood of feelings, *The Piano* demands as much a physical and emotional response as an intellectual one. . . . Not since the early days of cinema, when audiences trampled over each other towards the exit to avoid the train emerging from the screen, could I imagine the medium of film to be so powerful."

20. Kate Pullinger, who wrote the book of the film (abandoned by Jane Campion after a couple of chapters), explains that "Ada is mute because at six, when she contradicted the adults, she was ordered not to speak again that day and she decided to stay silent for ever," Marianne Brace [no title], *Guardian*, 18 April 1994, 11. Whatever the originating event—and why should it not be the smallest of traumas?—the result is necessarily something other than its occasion.

21. See Campion's interview with Ian Pryor, [no title], *Onfilm* 10, no. 9 (October 1993): 25; also Valerie Hazel, "Disjointed Articulations: The Politics of Voice and Jane Campion's *The Piano*" (paper delivered to the Centre for Women's Studies, Monash University, Melbourne, March 1994).

22. Adam Mars-Jones, "Poetry in Motion," *Independent*, 29 October 1993, 26.

23. Campion, who cites one of her motives as the wish "to explore the relationship between fetishism and love" (Katherine Dieckmann, "Jane Campion," *Interview* 27, no. 1 [January 1992]: 82), stresses the characteristics of the piano as inert object and a number of critics note the analogy with the ship of *Fitzcarraldo*. But it is interesting to remember that her original title referred not to the object but to *The Piano Lesson*, which has been followed exactly in the French version, while the Italian pluralizes it into *Lezioni di Piano*.

24. For example, in the patterned curtain behind which Baines waits naked, in Flora's Red Riding Hood cloak, and in the blood that splashes on her white apron.

25. Campion has claimed that the original interest in making a film set early in New Zealand colonial history arose from her fascination with the "European cross-dressing" of Maoris in the mid nineteenth century (see Geoff Andrew, "Grand En-

trance," *Time Out*, 20–27 October 1993, 24). More generally, she contrasts her "strange heritage . . . as a *pakeha* New Zealander" with the Maori sense of history, in the screenplay of *The Piano* (London: Bloomsbury, 1993), 135. She has since been accused of orientalism and her portrayal of the Maoris in the film as too simplistically based on a noble savage/repressed Britishers contrast. See for example the debate between Richard Cummings and Stella Bruzzi in the letter pages of *Sight & Sound* (February 1994): 72 and (March 1994): 64.

26. For these two quotations see the screenplay of *The Piano*, 90, 93.

A Father and His Fate:
Intertextuality and Gender

CHRIS WORTH

> Ah, this is a great day to me . . . The day when my daughter returns to the house where she will rule when I have left it. Pleasure is deepest when it depends on our dear ones rather than ourselves. I look to the end of my life with a settled mind. I shall live on in my grandchildren, here where I was born, bred, look to die—. (199)

So declares Miles Mowbray, the monstrous, world-creating head of the household in Ivy Compton-Burnett's *A Father and His Fate*. The passage comes from near the end of the novel, as one of his three legitimate daughters returns from her honeymoon—she has married her cousin, Malcolm Mowbray, who is also Miles's heir. "You are quoting a poem," notes the newly married Ursula, only to meet with a flat denial that might be considered a paradigmatic example of commonsense resistance to post-structuralist ideas about the authenticity of speech acts: "No, I am not. The words came into my head of their own accord. And I never quote other people. I use my own words or none. I should have thought you would know that." It is not surprising that someone who so completely embodies, indeed parodies through excess, the rule of the father as Miles does should insist that his speech originates in himself alone, free from any ambiguous context, parasitic quotation, or dangerous supplement. But there is more to Miles's insistence than merely a stubborn and naive trust in the originary logos—his troubles with language are only part of his struggle to assert what he believes to be his natural role as father of his household, and his failure to arrest the flight of signifiers is metonymic of the fate that awaits him in his attempt to continue to play the patriarch.

A Father and His Fate was published in 1957 but is set, like most of Ivy Compton-Burnett's work, in a vaguely pre-First World War environment whose details, such as they are, have more to do with textual restriction than social realism. In it Miles Mowbray has taken his role of head of the family to extraordinary lengths. His attempt to

71

"live on" has driven him to increasingly aberrant practices. He has tyrannized over his own family, taken Malcolm out of his dead brother's family to play the role of his heir, been complicit in the bizarre disappearance and reappearance of his wife, proposed in her absence to marry the young woman with whom Malcolm was in love, and used lies and distortions in an attempt to retain the moral high ground despite the discovery of evidence of his egocentric behavior. He has assimilated himself to a myth of paternalistic hegemony, but in circumstances that have led to that hegemony being constantly mocked and subverted, not only by the voices and actions of the women and boys who surround him, but also by the ironies of life and language themselves. The passage quoted above evokes Miles's monstrous egotism concisely. The usually exogamic proceedings of marriage in this case return Ursula, the bride, to her *father* and *his* house. "Pleasure" is arrogated to himself by Miles even as he denies that he can take pleasure. He constructs his death primarily as the beginning of a genealogy originating in him. Even the fact that he will have to vacate his house at death is subject to reterritorialization: only because he leaves the house *to* someone does leaving have meaning. Endings themselves are imaginable because *he* looks to them, imagines them. In his gaze death takes its form.

At the same time the paragraph shows how duplicitous the tools are with which he attempts to reign. Already he has smuggled into the patrilineal genealogy he is constructing a necessary deviation. Conception is a matter of chance. Since his own children are all female the entailed inheritor of his estate is not his son but his nephew. His own genetic line will have to be secured by an appeal to the female, by Malcolm accepting Ursula. Hence the emphasis on the daughter's rule, which is clearly presented in this paragraph (the first of the chapter) as extending beyond the domain of the tea table over which Miles's own wife presides. To accept Ursula's potential for rule would be already something of a retreat from his earlier effort to ensure that he will "live on" not only in his direct descendants but also in the inheritor of his estate, whether Malcolm, whom he attempts to shape, or another child. For it is possible that it is not Ursula he has in mind as the future ruler of the house, but the unnamed daughter of Malcolm by an earlier marriage—as Malcolm's daughter she is not of his own line, but suppose she were his own illegitimate daughter, would this then legitimate her as his heir? That Compton-Burnett is interested in the paradoxes of this example of what Deleuze and Guattari call "movements of deterritorialization and processes of reterritorialization"[1] is suggested by the plots of others of her books, for example *Mother and Son,* in which Julius adopts the three children of his brother, knowing that they are his own illegitimate family, only to find that his own son and heir, Rosebery, is in fact the child of another man.

Language itself proves equally duplicitous ground for Miles. At the point in the novel from which this quotation comes, Miles is endeavoring, after a series of reversals, once again to place himself as the benevolent and legitimate male center of his household. Stretching out his hand to catch a phrase from the vortex of language to define his new role as aging patriarch, he gestures around at his house "Where I was born, bred, look to die." But his catch is a slippery one, for it is indeed a quotation, just as Ursula warns him, a woman's phrase, a line from Christina Rossetti's poem "Italia, io ti saluto."[2] Intertextuality subverts the romance of authentic meaning. The phrase by which he tries to reinforce his identity merely exposes his dependence on the shifty grounds of language. The fate of Miles in *A Father and His Fate* is to find that all his attempts to ensure, or to *will*, the continuation of a monologistic patriarchy are similarly undermined.

In this essay I should like to show how Ivy Compton-Burnett explores in a fictional mode a range of tropes of deterritorialization, heteroglossia, and subversion. I deliberately use a bricolage of terminology, for I am not interested in "proving" some theory using Compton-Burnett's text. Rather, I am interested in how such an idiosyncratic writer exploits genre and language to expose the mythic and comic nature of the patriarchal imagination. There has been considerable debate about the extent to which Compton-Burnett can be read as a feminist author.[3] Many have doubted whether a writer so little interested in female role models or in the evocation of social realities has a place in the pantheon. Her cool and apparently superficial style is divisive too, as repellent to some as it is attractive to others (Virginia Woolf found it hard to stomach, for example). But although the women and boys who surround Miles fail to challenge directly his relentless will to power and are frequently in antagonistic relations with one another, in their words, in their silences, and in their actions they form communities of dissent that model some of the many strategies of resistance that can be mounted against the naturalization of a male myth of power. Mary McCarthy called Ivy Compton-Burnett's fictions "subversive packets"[4] and *A Father and His Fate* is a characteristic example of these packets. Part of my argument is, then, that the novel is concerned with a female "language," not in the essentialist sense that Miles, for example, understands such a concept, but rather in the shape of practices that survive male myths of power and meaning, that do not accept the notion of the

originary word, that deny that meaning is created only through male
uses of language. To say this is not to imagine an identifiable "female
voice," but rather to contribute to the project that Marie Maclean
described in *The Name of the Mother* and "Narrative Involution" as a key
function of gendered criticism, "to identify the interplay of discourse
within the text,"[5] to give a central place to the concept of
heteroglossia.

It would be impossible to talk at length about the passage I have
quoted without contextualizing it in the whole novel. The cast of
characters in *A Father and His Fate* is dominated by the family group
outlined in the figure below, whose intricacies need to be grasped for
the plot to make sense. Miles Mowbray inhabits the role of pater-
familias. At the point at which the novel opens Malcolm has been
installed as his uncle's heir—the estate is entailed, so it is not Miles's
whim alone that has decided this. Audrey, the youngest of Miles's
daughters, is now grown up, but Rudolf and Nigel, whose ages are
difficult to determine, appear to be boys still. In addition to the
Mowbray family group there are some outsiders: one is a mordant
butler, Everard, who plays a regrettably small role; another is Miss
Gibbon, the superannuated governess of Miles's children, who is
both a commentator and a carefully manipulated *ficelle*; Miss Man-
ders is Miss Gibbon's double in Eliza's household; and the fourth
outsider is an interloper, Verena Gray, a very attractive young woman
who comes to live with Eliza's family. The dispatcher of the action is
Miles's decision to take himself and his wife off to inspect some
distant overseas property, in a manner so carelessly contrived as to
belong to the dream world it in part signifies. Their departure, remi-
niscent of the Bertrams' in *Mansfield Park,* precipitates change. Verena Gray is wooed by Malcolm in the absence of the (castrating)

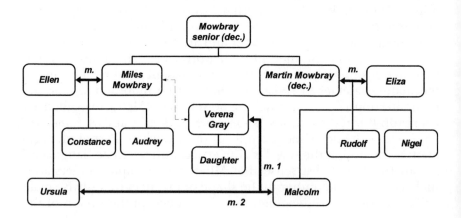

father figure of Miles; she agrees to marry him. But then Miles returns, having been involved in a shipwreck. Announcing that his wife
is dead, he quickly exercises a kind of droit de seigneur and proposes
to marry Verena himself. She is more than happy to transfer her
affections from the substitute heir to the head of the household (and
to the more virile of the two characters). At this moment, however,
and it seems with a degree of reluctance, Ellen Mowbray reappears
and is reinstated beside her husband. She has, it is gradually revealed, been living in the locality supported by an unknown benefactor through the intermediation of Miss Gibbons (later it is revealed
that Miles himself has been the benefactor, so he actually knew his
wife was alive during his engagement with Verena). Verena reasserts
her claim over Malcolm and promptly marries him, giving birth to a
daughter somewhat earlier than might have been expected. She
quickly tires of him, however, and deserts him and the child. It is after
this traumatic history and his divorce that Malcolm is able to marry
Ursula and so bring the two sides of the house together in that
manner so satisfactory to Miles.

These complications in the plot need to be spelled out since much
of the conversation that comprises the bulk of the text refers to them
only indirectly. (But since the novel is also about the framing of
knowledge, the dramatic ironies of displaced knowledge, and the use
of knowledge, no plot summary like this quite catches the essential
Compton-Burnett quality of subtle and complex interactions between speaker and situation.) As in so many other texts about fathers,
issues of legitimacy and authority abound. From the beginning everyone is aware that inheritance, important in itself, stands always in a
metaphorical relation to genetic survival. Malcolm, who comments
on himself that "I have been received into my uncle's house to imper-
sonate the son they should have had. My character is that of substitute and second-best," is as conscious as anyone that he is an instrument to another's survival. Mary McCarthy puts it elegantly: "All
testatory wills in Compton-Burnett are in fact puns on the enslaving
human will, which is plotting to survive death."[6] Paradoxically the
entail does not appear to "bind" Miles; he positively enjoys the notion
of having to hand on the estate to Malcolm, rather than allowing it to
descend to his daughters, because he imagines himself part of a
patrilineal genealogy that will extend into the infinite future as into
the past.

It is often noted how the dominance of Ivy Compton-Burnett's
father seems to be enacted in such fictional characters: the entail-
ment of an estate on the male line of a family, no matter how distant
the degree of relationship involved, was associated with the kind of

renaming that produced "Compton-Burnett." This name is not to be
decoded as a combination of partners, but as the survival of a patrilineal family name through purchase, through the willing of property, or through marriage—that is, as a sign of accession to an inheritance that is also a subordination. As Hilary Spurling shows,[7] not only
did Compton-Burnett's family name arise in such circumstances,
those circumstances and the role of the sons in the Compton-Burnett
household were constitutive fields of Ivy's own existence. In her work
names are rarely trivial. And as the child of a second wife she was also
made very aware of the tension between stepsisters, between those
who thought of themselves as authentic and legitimate and those
who were interlopers. All her novels demonstrate a fascination with
the dynamics of bizarre family life[8]—it is quite typical that at the end
of *A Father and His Fate* Verena's child has a (step)grandfather who is
her (actual) father and (genetically speaking) her great-uncle, or
that Ursula is triply related or subjected to male power, as daughter
of the head of the household, as wife of the heir, and as stepmother
of the future heir.

Practically, financially, almost every character is dependent on
Miles. Compton-Burnett is always brutally frank about the realities of
power and money in the kinds of families she uses in her fiction,
although she unashamedly deploys them as artifices. Meaning too is
legitimized by being authorized; truth is the origin of meaning, but
only the father can settle what is true. When Malcolm claims the right
to reorder things in the way he wants, to substitute his authorizing for
that of the absent Miles, he is quickly disabused by Constance (the
most conservative of the daughters, as perhaps her own name figures). Here is their deconstructive exchange concerning the house
where Malcolm and Verena will live when they get married, which
Malcolm decides will not be Miles's residence:

> "That is for Father to say."
> "It is for me, and I have said."
> "You know you cannot say it on your own authority."
> "I have done so," said her cousin.
> "But you know the words mean nothing."
> "They mean what they say."
> "No words have meaning, unless they are related to truth."
> "These are more than related. They are true."
> "Father will settle that question and many others." (63)

Needless to say, it is to Miles's house that the couple eventually
returns.

But the characters who look to Miles for meaning and for money also see through him. They know about his pretensions, they expose the gaps between his language and his actions, and they exploit the possibilities of language itself to subvert his rule. In Compton-Burnett's writing, the "complex geography of social ruses," in Michel de Certeau's phrase, is mapped with acute consciousness of ironies and paradoxes. Talking of folktales, de Certeau notes how "They are deployed like games, in a space outside of and isolated from daily competition, that of the past, the marvellous, the original. In that space can thus be revealed, dressed as gods or heroes, the models of good or bad ruses that can be used everyday. Moves, not truths, are recounted."[9] So, too, in the artificial world of these novels a similar "art of practice" is deployed, creating a tactical manual or cookbook whose "moves" are drawn up like those of a chess game—the linguistic play and family dynamics are complex, rule-bound, and yet strangely familiar. Compton-Burnett has her characters resort to a number of resistance practices to combat their exclusion from financial independence. Verena's embrace of the center of power, for example, is an example of a traditional female oppositional practice.[10] The lady-companions discover things, revealing or withholding information. Malcolm fails in his attempts at direct confrontation, which reveal him to be not the usurping bastard but the substitute suffering son. The boys Rudolf and Nigel are excluded so totally from any source of authority or power they can take on the prized role of the fool, the commentator whose excesses are licensed—one of the pleasures of the book is their satiric commentary on the adult world. Even Ellen's mysterious acquiescence in her withdrawal from the household is clearly a resistance practice (as is her disconcerting return from the dead). And then there are the subtextual "involutions or incorporations"[11] of nonverbal responses, silences, looks, shared recognitions, and glances in the text, not narrated directly, but allowed to emerge from the complex dialogisms of the reported speech that constitutes the majority of the novel. These ruses are played out primarily in language.

The novel is like a self-extracting program (to use a contemporary metaphor), expanding into a suite of applications. In order to understand what is going on readers have to decode the functions of the actants and the hierarchy of events from sparse clues in the mass of dialogue and reframe them outwith the experimental conditions of the novel. Within the text human monsters and unlikely heroes struggle in the constrained exchanges of a late nineteenth- or early twentieth-century middle-class milieu, their weapons those of modern literate engagements: analysis and rhetoric, wit and sarcasm.

Readers are drawn into the struggle by the enigmatic nature of the prose. To follow the almost entirely dramatized speech, we have to imagine the speakers and their audiences and be conscious of the constant double-voicing of speech, for in this respect Compton-Burnett is supremely a Bakhtinian. Almost every utterance in the book is not only heard by a recipient, but also overheard by other recipients, or heard ironically or in multiple senses by listeners. And as readers delight in what is going on, so too they are torn between recognition (and self-recognition) and repudiation. In this environment knowledge is potential power and language is a constant source of contention, as the direct speeches of characters to each other are supplemented by the crisscrossing unspoken significations, muttered and murmured exchanges that are half-heard, misunderstood, repeated, re-sited. The echoes of people's words reverberate through the whole text, dogging their utterers with the past and structuring the future or fate of all of them.

In the case of the Rossetti quotation Miles is acutely conscious that not only his language, but his authority is being called into question; he responds accordingly with another attempt to restore certainty to language. His position, however, has been grossly compromised by the revelations that have been accumulating about his own misuses of language. He has prevaricated, equivocated, lied outright. He has written letters that have miscarried and shown his duplicity (there are many such uses of written material in these novels). His behavior has shown the weakness of his claim to any kind of moral authority. Yet he retains a belief in his own power to determine meaning. The following exchange illustrates the complex interweaving of voices involved:

"Well, I suppose the poet and I said the same thing. We might easily do that. I mean we might by chance. I don't suppose there is so much difference between poets and ordinary—and other people. Well, we see there is not."

"It is woman in this case," said Constance.

"A poetess?" said Miles, as though hardly accepting this as an authentic term. "Well, of course I was not quoting her. I am sure I was not."

When Miss Gibbon interrupts to ask him if he has any objections to citing a female, Miles responds even more firmly:

"I should not quote anyone. And naturally I should not quote a woman. What man would?"

"A man did," said Audrey.

"Would a woman quote a man, Mr. Mowbray?"

"Well, I suppose so, if she quoted anyone. She would not quote another woman. We can be sure of that."

"So women have not much success in the matter of quotation."

"Well, they have other kinds of success."

"And in this case this one, Mr. Mowbray."

"Yes, the poet was Christina Rossetti, Father," said Constance.

"Rossetti was a man," said Miles, in a manner of meeting success himself.

"Christina was his sister."

"Oh, he had a sister? Well, that was different. I suppose it ran in the family. That proves what I said." (199–200)

The intertext that Ursula identifies introduces the notion that language, rather than allowing self-definition, may instead defer it, attaching the speaker not to a divine presence but to an infinitely extended chain of signifying texts. Monstrous Miles may be, but his fate is to find his every move subverted. In this instance he tries flat denial as well as the argument for chance repetition. Even more disturbing than the notion of the intertextual circulation is the suggestion that he could use the language of a woman. Miles uses "poetess" exactly as feminist theory insists discriminatory gender terms are used, to denigrate. The inauthenticity of the term stands in Miles's mind for the inauthenticity of the thing itself. To him female speech is utterly distinct from male speech because it is essentially derivative, while male speech is originative. Poetry, romantically seen as the closest that language comes to the divine, must be especially free from the contamination of secondary speech. In another of Compton-Burnett's novels, *Men and Women,* Jermyn refuses to marry Millicent because she turns out to be a better poet than he is, and he does not want such an "unnatural" distribution of talents in his family. If anything, Miles's response to being confronted with the derivativeness of his own language is even more intense: "naturally I should not quote a woman. What man would?" Miles's position rather nicely exemplifies Bakhtin's notion of monologism, in which "All ideological creative acts are conceived and perceived as possible expressions of a single collective consciousness, a single spirit";[12] Miles's ideology would indeed transform "the represented world into a *voiceless object*"[13] if it were unchallenged. But of course it is challenged, because he cannot make use of language without also using the already-spoken, the dense network of speech genres, or, in this case, the words of others, the word of the Other, of a woman. "The unique speech experience of each individual is shaped and developed in continuous and constant interaction with others' individual utterances. This experience can be characterized to some degree as the process of *assimilation*—more or less creative—of others' words (and not the words of a language). Our speech, that is, all our utterances (including creative works), is filled with others' words, varying degrees of otherness or varying degrees of 'our-own-ness.'[14] It is not hard to imagine what Miles's response would be to this view of language. By being revealed as a man quoting Christina Rossetti he is confronted with a monstrosity (in his terms), an alterity within, the copresence of male and female within language. Since his place in the world is already under threat of delegitimation and defiliation, he appeals desperately to nature, to the agreement of his listeners, to the order of society, in order to repudiate the idea.

Bakhtin's insistence on heteroglossia, on the othering of language, which is such anathema to Miles, theorizes what is an essential practice in the exchanges that take place in a Compton-Burnett novel. The use of clichés, the restricted range of diction, the fascination with quotations, significant names, and dim allusions often noted by critics[15] are all part of her exploration of the circulation of language: "These words of others carry with them their own expression, their own evaluative tone, which we assimilate, rework and re-accentuate," continues Bakhtin, as if describing the constant play with framing, overhearing, irony, mistaking, punning, and accentuation that characterizes the extended language games she deploys.

In *A Father and His Fate,* language and genealogy are seldom separated from each other. So central is the question of genetic inheritance for Miles that even a genius for poetry becomes explicable, even in a woman, when shown to be a familial trait, one that can be passed down a (male) line. Indeed it might be that his relief is to find a "natural" parallel for the complex means by which he is passing on his own seed. For while Constance is denying the (il)logic of Miles's attempt to prove that his quotation is free from alterity, the immediate consequences of her change of subject are the beginning of a demonstration that he is aware that in life too legitimacy is a fiction (Gentile quotes Cixous: "Paternity, which is a fiction, is fiction passing itself off as truth"):[16]

> "But why not keep to your own interests? [says Constance] As Malcolm's child is a girl you may have a grandson to succeed you. And I have an impression that you feel a bond between yourself and his daughter. She may need your protection the more, that she is not your grandchild. She will have no mother in the house."
>
> "She will always be my charge," said Miles, in a grave tone. "She is in an uncertain place. . . . Her claim is the stronger that it is not a recognized one, that by some it would not be accepted. Ah, the little one is safe under my roof." (197–98)

The exchange is given point by the imminent revelation that the baby, who is supposedly Malcolm's and his first wife's, Verena's, child, is in fact Miles's illegitimate daughter, and hence indeed exists in "an uncertain place" (the uncertainty reinforced by Compton-Burnett's ruthless refusal to attach a name to the child). She is both Miles's own youngest daughter and oldest grandchild. Illegitimate at conception, legitimated left-handedly by the marriage of Verena to Malcolm after Ellen's return, then delegitimated by her mother's divorce of Malcolm, she is about to be relegitimated in being nominated as the rightful heir to the Mowbray fortune or fate, although her sex and history still ensure that Miles's hopes are being realized only through deviation, sinisterly. How is the revelation going to come about? Because Miles will offer to take down some high clothes drawers (he is both ingratiating himself with the family and competing with the boys, who are now taller than him). "Yes, we will let Father show his prowess," says Constance (201). Unfortunately, discarded (unfolded) in these drawers, where they had no right to be, are undergarments belonging to Verena. Everyone can read the signs. Yet again Miles finds himself betrayed by a language whose meaning he cannot determine.

Miles's monstrousness lies as much in his attempt to control meaning and deny a voice to the women and men he is surrounded by as in his control of the real inheritance. At the beginning of the novel it seems as if legitimacy and authority cohere in him. Both are progressively unraveled in the course of the book, shown to be fictions by which his real power (financial and possibly legal) is naturalized. Because his power is mediated, primarily through language, he can never free it of parasitic voices, re-voicings, intertextuality. He can never escape the heteroglossia of language any more than he can be a tyrant with no subjects (Caliban's great insight). The passages I have been looking at are only cases of Miles's many battles with monsters, with the teratology of language. He always loses, and yet is never defeated. As in all of Compton-Burnett's writing, the authoritarian figure is not discarded: he is revealed as being maintained by the multiple interacting and resistant figures who sustain but also scorn him. Under the myth of benevolent patriarchy he would have them accept, they exchange their other stories, their other modes of life, their other practices. At the end of the novel Compton-Burnett pictures him as struggling in his role, supported or buoyed up by others who have accepted, for their own ends, the symbolic world that he appears to represent. His survival at the end is no accident, because his fate is to suffer, not to escape.

Marie Maclean's work consistently explored the ways in which theories of language, literature, and culture could expose the symbolic means by which human beings attempt to maintain their authority over others. And she equally consistently perceived the multitudinous ways in which groups and individuals subvert and mock the monologies of rule. Her own rich and complex engagement with the name of the mother was one expressive kind of reply to the myth of male-centered thought that Miles articulates. But the dense and challenging fictions of Compton-Burnett constitute a reminder that it is not solely within the academy that these issues can be explored. As Marie would herself have been the first to acknowledge, writers of fiction have been leaders in confronting the myth of the rule of the father or reenvisaging the role of the father in language.

Notes

1. Gilles Deleuze and Félix Guattari, *A Thousand Plateaus: Capitalism and Schizophrenia,* trans. Brian Massumi (Minneapolis: University of Minnesota Press, 1987), 10.

2. The poem, from Rossetti's *A Pageant and Other Poems* (London: Macmillan, 1881), reads:

> To come back from the sweet South, to the North
>   Where I was born, bred, look to die;
> Come back to do my day's work in its day,
>   Play out my play—
> Amen, amen say I.
> To see no more the country half my own,
>   Nor hear the half familiar speech,
> Amen, I say; I turn back to that bleak North
>   Whence I came forth—
> The South lies out of reach.
>
> But when our swallows fly back to the South,
> To the sweet South, to the sweet South,
> The tears may come again into my eyes
>   On the old wise,
> And the sweet name to my mouth.

(R. V. Crump, *The Complete Poems of Christina Rossetti: A Variorum Edition,* 3 vols [Baton Rouge: Louisiana State University Press, 1979–90], 2: 74–75.)

3. See Kathy J. Gentile, *Ivy Compton-Burnett* (Basingstoke, U.K.: Macmillan Educational, 1991), chap. 1.

4. Mary McCarthy, "The Inventions of I. Compton-Burnett," in *The Writing on the Wall and Other Literary Essays* (London: Weidenfeld and Nicolson, 1970), 143.

5. Marie Maclean, *The Name of the Mother: Writing Illegitimacy* (London and New York: Routledge, 1994) and "Narrative Involution: The Gendered Voices of the Text," *Rivista di letterature moderne e comparate* 48, no. 2 (1995): 113–25 (p. 113).

6. McCarthy, "Inventions of I. Compton-Burnett," 116–17.

7. Hilary Spurling, *Ivy When Young: The Early Life of I. Compton-Burnett, 1884–1919* (London: Victor Gollancz, 1974) and *Secrets of a Woman's Heart: The Later Life of Ivy Compton-Burnett, 1920–1969* (London: Hodder and Stoughton, 1984).

8. See Susan Crecy, "Ivy Compton-Burnett: Family as Nightmare," in *Lesbian and Gay Writing: An Anthology of Critical Essays,* ed. Mark Lilly (Basingstoke, UK: Macmillan, 1990).

9. Michel de Certeau, *The Practice of Everyday Life,* trans. Steven Rendall (Berkeley: University of California Press, 1984), 22–23.

10. See Maclean, *Name of the Mother,* 90–92.

11. See Maclean, "Narrative Involution."

12. Mikhail M. Bakhtin, *Problems of Dostoevsky's Poetics,* ed. and trans. Caryl Emerson (Minneapolis: University of Minnesota Press, 1984), 82.

13. Ibid.

14. Ibid., *Speech Genres and Other Late Essays,* trans. Vern McGee, ed. Caryl Emerson and Michael Holquist (Austin: University of Texas Press, 1986), 89.

15. For example, McCarthy, "Inventions of I. Compton-Burnett" and Charles Burkhart, ed., *The Art of I. Compton-Burnett: A Collection of Critical Essays* (London: Victor Gollancz, 1972).

16. Gentile, *Ivy Compton-Burnett,* 66.

Places in the Library: Language and Authority in Annie Ernaux's *La Place*

PHILIP ANDERSON

THE OPENING PASSAGE OF ANNIE ERNAUX'S *La Place* is the site of a negotiation of authority on two levels. On one level, the authority of the author-narrator is at stake. The negotiation of the narrative contract between teller and audience opens here with the telling. Indeed, insofar as author is narrator, that negotiation has already begun with the paratext.[1] On another level, that of the tale, the author-narrator as protagonist negotiates another contract of authority. What is recounted in the opening passage is her taking the "épreuves pratiques du Capes"(11)[2] [the practical test for the Capes[3]] that were to give her authority to teach and, more generally, authority over language and knowledge, the figure of which is the Library. I want to argue here that *La Place*, in its ongoing negotiation of the narrative contract, in its exchange between teller and audience, mediated by language, is a renegotiation of that authority in and over the Library, a reworking of the law governing that authority, so that readership of the text becomes assent to a new canon, such that the Library includes within it (and so becomes) another place, that of *La Place*, in which writing is righting the wrong of exclusion of the author-narrator-protagonist's father, de-authorizing of the protagonist that the author-narrator was, and authorizing the other father's daughter she desires thereby to become. I want to argue that the text engages with rewriting and rereading the Name of the Father. The argument will bear on two passages that frame the text and, deploying the figure of the library as Library and the Library as canonical discourse and knowledge, as Language and Knowledge, constitute a *mise-en-abyme* of the textual stake, the ultimate point of *La Place*.

Where the reader crosses the threshold of the text in the company of an author-narrator who is (as paratext and her discourse show) a middle-class intellectual, the protagonist, the author-narrator's sometime self, has crossed a threshold too. She has crossed a series of increasingly powerfully filtering boundaries—material boundaries

of and within a school[4] that can be seen as metaphoric representations of less material *épreuves*—to be admitted to a library, "une bibliothèque au sol en moquette sable" (11) [a library with sand-colored
carpet]. There remains one more *épreuve*, one more boundary or
threshold to be crossed, before she is no longer just a visitor to the
place metonymically represented by this (or any other) library, before she is permanently admitted with full rights to the Library and
her present passivity becomes the initiative of the insider.[5]

Before the protagonist's eyes is, indeed, the figure of what she
wishes to attain through full and permanent right of entry to this
place, through achieving her place in the Library: "Une femme cor-
rigeait des copies avec hauteur, sans hésiter. Il suffisait de franchir
correctement l'heure suivante pour être autorisée à faire comme elle
toute ma vie" (11) [A woman was correcting papers haughtily, un-
hesitatingly. All that was required was to get through the next hour
properly to be entitled to do what she was doing for the rest of my
life]. The woman teacher is the figure of unquestionable and unquestioning exercise of legitimate power through and over language
and the knowledge it informs. But the figure and the concept it
represents can be convincing or absurd. At this point one is reminded that the author-narrator-protagonist is not necessarily monolithic, but can be discontinuous. If the *je* of the *énonciation* is the *je* of
the *énoncé*, they are nevertheless separated by history, by time and
change. It is clear, for example, that the narrator views herself as
protagonist from the other side of the *épreuves,* which, in the *énoncé*
and for the protagonist, are yet to begin and which legitimate
writing—or rather, as the figure of the woman teacher shows, legitimate a certain writing while marking other writing as *inadmissible.*
Two views of the figure of the teacher can be read through the
narrator's words on her as a model for a life's work. As free indirect
discourse, the words mark the protagonist's view of the teacher as an
object of admiration and envy, as a model whose power the protagonist would exercise with equal conviction, good conscience, and satisfaction, as the figure of her own legitimate empowerment. As the
expression of the narrator's cynicism, however, the words construct
the teacher as arrogant, excessively sure of her knowledge, her "right-
ness," and her righteousness, too secure in her power too un-
thinkingly assumed, a representative of a fate narrowly and luckily
missed. They ironize the protagonist's view of the teacher, constructing it as at best naive and at worst testimony to alienation and bad
faith. Both views see the teacher's place in this library as figuring
authority in the Library, power over and through Language and
Knowledge (each of these capitalized nouns becoming something

unique, designating something absolute); they diverge in their espousal or refusal of that authority and of the absolute nature of the language and knowledge that underpins it and is underpinned by it.

The actual lesson the protagonist-candidate gave, canonical in subject matter ("vingt-cinq lignes . . . du *Père Goriot* de Balzac" (11) [twenty-five lines from Balzac's *Old Goriot*]) and presentation (the lines of the text are numbered for the classical explication de texte), is passed over quickly by the narrator. It is presented only through the inspector's rather unfavorable view of it in a rapid transition to what is called "cette cérémonie" (11) [that ceremony], the evaluation meeting with the examiners, which will come to overshadow the lesson as the real "objet de l'épreuve" (11) [object of the test]. The candidate follows the ceremony with some difficulty, in contrast to the inspector's active command of it and the other examiners' total familiarity with its code, demonstrated by the perfect timing and unison of their participation in it. She is totally unfamiliar with the code governing proceedings, unable therefore to participate in the ceremony or predict its outcome, and caught unawares by its closure when she learns she is "reçue" (11) [passed]: "D'un seul coup, d'un même élan, ils se sont levés tous trois, l'air grave. Je me suis levée aussi, précipitamment. L'inspecteur m'a tendu la main. Puis, en me regardant bien en face: 'Madame, je vous félicite.' Les autres ont répété 'je vous félicite' et m'ont serré la main, mais la femme avec un sourire" (11) [As one, as if moved by a single impetus, they all three got up, looking solemn. I got up too, hurriedly. The inspector held out his hand to me. Then, looking me straight in the face: "I congratulate you." The others repeated "I congratulate you" and shook my hand, but the woman did so with a smile]. The now successful candidate's reaction to this performance of what might be seen as a predictable rite of passage is all the more surprising for being unsignaled and unexplained in this opening passage that, as narrative rite of passage, becomes less than predictable, less than predictive, less than reassuring as exposition or establishing scene on the level of the *énoncé*, and more interesting as problematization of the narrative voice on the level of the *énonciation*.

The sentence that presents that reaction develops through three powerful movements. First the ceremony, now closed, is presented as totally preoccupying, absorbing, engrossing, even obsessive: "Je n'ai pas cessé de penser à cette cérémonie . . ." [I couldn't stop thinking about that ceremony . . .]; then the incessant nature of that preoccupation is undercut by the adverbial phrase ". . . jusqu'à l'arrêt du bus . . ." [right up to the bus stop]: the obsession is suddenly cut short at the apparently most trivial of boundaries; finally the emotional thrust of this paradoxically "temporarily ceaseless" thinking over the ceremony is made clear: ". . . avec colère et une espèce de honte" [with anger and a kind of shame].

Nothing in the account of the ceremony prepares the reader for this anger and shame. Moreover, these emotions are immediately eclipsed, not just at the bus stop, but in the letter the protagonist writes to her parents announcing her success but silencing her anger and shame, and by the further ellipsis of time and emotion that takes the reader to the mother's response. Its curiously formulaic reticence also marks something unspoken, something else (like the father's voice subsumed in the mother's miming of appropriate phrases, the parents' happiness invested in the daughter's assumed pleasure) for which these words stand: "Le soir même, j'ai écrit à mes parents que j'étais professeur 'titulaire.' Ma mère m'a répondu qu'ils étaient très contents pour moi" (12) [That very evening I wrote to my parents telling them I was a "qualified" teacher. My mother answered that they were very happy for me]. Why the anger and shame? At whom are they directed? Why do they stop at the bus stop? Does the protagonist's apparent acceptance of her status as "professeur 'titulaire'" ["qualified" teacher] through her affirmation of it signify their total eclipse? Is the protagonist's affirmation of her new status unequivocal? Does the narrator's recounting of that self-affirmation ironize it? Multiple answers suggest themselves.

The protagonist could have been disappointed in her own professional performance, at the idea, supported by her inability to predict the outcome of the ceremony, that her performance was borderline, only just worthy of a pass, giving her minimal authority. She could have been angry at the ceremony itself, seen as summary justice without right of response or evaluation of circumstance; or at the inspector who asserts his hierarchical dominance over everyone and, in particular, holds her in suspense about her result; or again, at the curiously incongruous woman *assesseur* in pink shoes who offers the complicity of a smile and the symbolic infringement of the dress code, but no real support against what might be read as patriarchal high-handedness. The protagonist's "espèce de honte" [kind of shame] could be felt for the examiners, for the woman *assesseur* in particular, rather than or in addition to being felt for herself as victim. But it could also be shame at her own belief in empowerment when the ceremony shows her to be powerless before her "superiors." Or again, she could have been angry and ashamed at her own silence through a ceremony read as humiliation, especially if her silence had been exchanged for power to use the discourse that angers and shames, "avec hauteur et sans hésiter" [haughtily and un-hesitatingly], against the weaker still, the pupils excluded from the library she was in and who cannot question the teacher's question or respond to the teacher's summary judgment of their response.

However one reads the anger and shame, they are cut short, unceasing as far as the bus stop, gone in the letter home. Perhaps the bus stop represents the threshold of the real world outside the closed world of the school; perhaps it is the threshold of the world of material demands, practicalities, and concrete decisions. Perhaps, then, the ceremony is dismissed in the face of real life and its demands, its threats, and the advantages it offers. Perhaps the place in the Library is accepted as a necessary evil or simply as a relatively good thing. Certainly in some sense we witness an act of repression here and the turning to the world of a public figure whereby the "professeur 'titulaire'" stands in the stead of an angry, shameful self.

This opening passage, through which so many possible voices speak against one another and set so many faces against one another undecidably, receives no further clear contextualization. It is set in temporal relation to the death of the author-narrator-protagonist's father on the levels of the real and the imaginary, inviting a shift from contiguity to a relationship of some form of identity, of being of the same order, but no other direct contextualization. It sits, then, at the head of the text, throughout the reading of the text, as unmet demand in terms of contextualization and resolution, so that the author-ization of one or other, some or all, of the voices in the *concours de voix* vying to speak the text and give it a face becomes the stake of *La Place*. Who speaks in Annie Ernaux's name when the text says "je"? Who speaks on whose silence? Those are the questions the opening passage puts. The answer is fought out through the *concours de voix* that the whole text works through. The whole text responds— though not necessarily in the end in a totally unequivocal manner— to its opening uncertainty of authority. In a very real sense the authority of the text is founded at the level of the *énonciation* rather than the *énoncé*, through the discursive struggle of which it is the site.

Another fragment of the text, a fragment that follows the text's major "cycle," moving from the father's death and its provocation of the desire to write the life—"écrire au sujet de mon père" (23) [write about my father]—through to the death rewritten,[6] does, however, respond more directly to the opening passage. It contextualizes both the opening scene of the taking of a place in the Library and the whole writing and reading of *La Place* as a discursive struggle, as the taking of another, different place in the Library, and as the making of this place/*Place* in the Library (and therefore the Library itself) other.

In this passage near the end of *La Place*, the author-narrator as clever schoolgirl protagonist and her father, both for the first time, go to the municipal library of their town. The status of the library as sacred site of language and knowledge, and of language and knowledge as one and universal, is marked by the metaphor of library as church. Both *culte* and *culture* share monumental architecture: the library is entered—significantly, in this case, "un dimanche après la messe" (111) [one Sunday after mass]—via "le grand escalier de la mairie" (111) [the main staircase at the Town Hall]. They are both celebrated in a space set apart, in which the manners of the outside world are no longer operative, which is entered with hushed reverence and, for those who do not know the liturgy, with trepidation: "On n'entendait aucun bruit derrière la porte. Mon père l'a poussée, toutefois. C'était silencieux, plus encore qu'à l'église, le parquet craquait et surtout cette odeur étrange, vieille" (111) [Not a sound could be heard on the other side of the door. My father tried it, however, and it opened. All was quiet, even more so than at church, the floor creaked and , more striking still, that strange smell of oldness]. Both focus on a sanctuary. In the municipal library, the librarian-priests keep vigil at a raised counter-altar rail that separates the profane from the holy: "Deux hommes nous regardaient venir depuis un comptoir très haut barrant l'accès aux rayons" (111) [Two men watched us approach from a very high counter that barred access to the stacks]. Characteristically, the father can only bring his child to the Library. He cannot induct her into its rites. He does not know its language and liturgy. He cannot speak for his daughter here: "Mon père m'a laissé demander: 'On voudrait emprunter des livres'" (112) My father let me ask: "We'd like to borrow some books"]. The child's words are far more than the expression of cultural innocence because they are spoken not for herself alone but for both daughter and father. "On" means "nous" here, as the librarian's rejoinder makes clear: "L'un des hommes aussitôt: 'Qu'est-ce que vous voulez comme livres?'" (112) [One of the men, straight back: 'What sort of books do you want?"]. This *vouvoiement* addressed to a twelve-year-old designates her as spokesperson for her father, and books are provided for both of them. The expression of cultural innocence becomes expression of cultural ignorance, designated as such by the infantilizing choice of books, when the child's words or her silence are not hers alone, but proferred for the father and, indeed, are his words or silence in her mouth, the evidence of her cultural heritage, her absence of cultural capital, of "savoir d'avance" (112)[7] [knowledge in advance].

The child's inability to answer the librarian's question is read as cultural ignorance, as the choice of books made for daughter and father shows: firstly, because it is made for them, in their place, telling them (and readers of the text) that they have no place in the Library other than the one that is given to them; secondly, because the nature of the choice (Merrimé and Maupassant, shorter and lesser elements of the canon, at least at that time considered to be texts for the younger or less sophisticated reader) shows that the only place they can be given is on the margin, on the threshold. They are subject to the law of the Library (subjected to canonical choice) rather than subjects of it (they have no authority, no jurisdiction here).

Father and daughter implicitly refuse their subjection to the law of the Library because they exercise their only power in relation to it: the power of self-exclusion. They refuse to return to the library and infringe the only rule by which it governs them directly—the return date: "Nous ne sommes pas retournés à la bibliothèque. C'est ma mère qui a dû rendre les livres, peut-être, avec du retard" (112) [We didn't go back to the library. My mother must have taken the books back, maybe, late]. Self-exclusion from the library, which is exclusion of self in the bourgeois world of which libraries are the temples, is total on the father's part. One day he says to his daughter, now embarked on simultaneous transitions to womanhood and middle-class ideology: "Les livres, la musique, c'est bon pour toi. Moi je n'en ai pas besoin pour *vivre*" (83—author's emphasis) [Books, music, they're okay for you. *I* don't need them to *live*]. But the daughter, on the other hand, does return to the Library, she does turn to bourgeois selfhood. It is precisely there, as visitor and aspirant to it, on its threshold, that we find her in the book's opening passage. She aspires to be a subject of that jurisdiction that the Library represents, subject to it but also initiator of the juris-diction, pronouncing the law. She aspires to unquestioning and unquestioned exercise of legitimate power through and over language and the knowledge it informs.

Now the key to absolute power and absolute knowledge is absolute language. In a sense, the protagonist had always known that. It is the sense of her not just correcting her father's bad French, but declaring any variation, alteration, or infringement of standard French to be non-existent: "Puisque la maîtresse me 'reprenait,' plus tard j'ai voulu reprendre mon père, lui annoncer que 'se parterrer' ou 'quart moins d'onze heures' *n'existaient pas* (64) [Since my school teacher corrected me, later on I wanted to correct my father, tell him that "se parterrer" or "quart moins d'onze heures"[8] *did not exist*]. The

Library—the bourgeois library governed by its strict canon—is a function of a single, uniform, monolithic, homogeneous mother tongue, identical for all who exist in it and through it, radically exclusive of difference but also, therefore, radically egalitarian—logically—within itself. But what the protagonist discovered in the "cérémonie" that does not follow her "épreuve," in fact, but becomes the "épreuve" itself, the rite that gives right of passage, can be summarized in the words of Deleuze and Guattari: "Il n'y a pas de langue mère, mais prise de pouvoir par une langue dominante dans une multiplicité politique"[9] [There is no mother tongue, but a power takeover by a dominant language in a political multiplicity]. For what the examiners substitute for the supposedly homogeneous, equal space of the Library, when they admit the protagonist-candidate to it, is firstly the headmaster's office—"le bureau du proviseur" (12)—where, one assumes, the desk reconfigures the space of the municipal library of the candidate's childhood, and, secondly, an unexpected and incomprehensible discourse that they master—actively (in the case of the inspector) or passively (in the case of the *assesseurs*), in its verbal aspect—equally, perfectly, apparently spontaneously, and in unison, and whose point seems to be to show the candidate that she cannot. Because it reveals the Library to be an ideological illusion, the authorizing ceremony the examiners preside over is quite precisely de-authorizing, constituting the "successful" candidate as *répétiteur* of an illusory mother tongue and de facto subject of a discourse of power and subjection. She is "titulaire" [qualified] in a double sense: she is given a form of authority, but that authority involves no real power, an agency that involves no real production and is restricted to being an agent of social reproduction and control. She is empowered to disempower herself by accepting her title, substituted for her father's name, conferred in the Name of the Father.[10]

What is at stake when we enter *La Place*, what has been at stake, we see clearly as we leave it, is the configuration of a place in the Library—acceptance by the protagonist of the place already awaiting her there (but which has as its contiguous event and its logical corollary the death—real and symbolic—of the father: he who is refused and refuses bourgeois selfhood and minimally—in silence—affirms a selfhood that is outside bourgeois ideology), or her rewriting and reconfiguring—as author-narrator and therefore protagonist of a remembering (*remémoration-remembrement*)—of the space of the Library. The author-narrator does not accept the myth of the Library but engages with its reality of discursive conflict to construct not just her own place in it, but the place too, the living place, of the dead father, the metonymic place of a social class and its discourse. That is not just self-authorization; it also involves the authorization of the reader.

NOTES

1. Biographical and cover notes to the edition of the text in Gallimard's "Collection *Folio*" identify author with narrator. Moreover, the epigraph can be read as identifying the text as literary, as "writerly" in its deliberate manipulation of language, and confessional.

2. Unless otherwise indicated, all quotations refer to Annie Ernaux *La Place* (Paris: Gallimard [Collection *Folio*], 1984.) All translations are my own.

3. The *Capes* (*Certificat d'aptitude professionnelle à l'enseignement secondaire*) is a teaching qualification.

4. A school, especially a modern French school, is itself an area that one cannot enter at will. The protagonist has been admitted to "la partie réservée à l'administration et au corps enseignant" [the area reserved for administrative and teaching staff] (11).

5. The protagonist's present passivity is both semantically and syntactically marked: she can only "actively" wait, subject to the call of others, object of their summoning. This contrasts with the apparent activity of the teacher, who makes autonomous and summary judgments on work she has set.

6. In a sense the "cycle" moves from the mother's words announcing the father's death—"Elle a dit d'une voix neutre: 'C'est fini'" [She said in a flat voice: "It's over"] (13)—to the repetition of those words—"Juste au tournant de l'escalier, elle a dit doucement: 'C'est fini'" [Just at the bend in the stairs, she said softly: "It's over"] (110). Those words repeated mark the end of (hi)story that begins after the account of the discovery of the desire to write and the difficulty of writing: "L'histoire commence quelques mois avant le vingtième siècle, dans un village du Caux, à vingt-cinq kilomètres de la mer" [The story starts a few months before the 20th century, in a village of the Caux, twenty-five kilometers from the sea (24). They mark the end of that text, but not its metatext, the context that concerns us here.

7. My nominalization of the infinitive in the text: "A la maison, on n'avait pas pensé qu'il fallait savoir d'avance ce qu'on voulait, être capable de citer des titres aussi facilement que des marques de biscuits" [At home, we hadn't thought you had to know in advance what you wanted, be able to quote titles as easily as biscuit brands] (112). In this sentence, too, we deal with a problem of *énonciation*, of attribution of words to voice. One can read it as the words of the twelve-year-old grocer's daughter, the protagonist, so that the metaphoric association of book to biscuit becomes an expression of cultural innocence. But one can also read it as the words of the middle-class intellectual author-narrator, and suspect in the metaphor the condescending view of father and daughter that also comes from the librarians, a view reflected rather than a view espoused, undoubtedly, but at least a view recognized.

8. These are regional expressions.

9. Gilles Deleuze and Félix *Mille plateaux* (Paris: Minuit, 1980), 14.

10. The protagonist's title ("professeur 'titulaire'"), which Guattari uses to tell her parents of her new identity, is conferred by the delegated authorities (and notably the Inspector as Patriarch) over the Library. Her acceptance of it involves renouncing her father's identity founded in self-exclusion from the library. It should

be noted here that the protagonist's accession to the "bourgeoisie à diplômes" [educated middle class] (96) also takes place by marriage, by that taking on of another('s) name, that of the husband with whom, symbolically, she will sleep on the eve of her father's funeral in her father's deathbed, in more than one sense "le seul lit à deux places" [the only double bed] (19).

and
The Telling of Performance

Producing the Voice in Erotic Narrative

PETER CRYLE

I SHALL ATTEMPT IN THIS ESSAY TO RAISE A SET OF QUESTIONS ABOUT the representation of desire, pleasure, and femininity in narrative. My concern will not be to develop any sort of argument from first principles, but to consider these questions insofar as they are already "answered"—often brashly or glibly—in a certain kind of story. Brashness of a sort will in fact surround, and indeed define, the very object of my study. One might speak here of the crassly "feminine." It will quickly become apparent, moreover, that I have drawn little or nothing from the well of psychoanalytical theory, preferring to focus on a quite particular fictive discourse, while gesturing toward its broader significance. I shall take as my corpus that rather un-distinguished body of texts we are wont to call erotic literature, and as my emblem that sometimes noble, but more often vulgar form of punctuation, the exclamation mark. I hope to show how exclamation comes to signify, in writing, the ritual circularity of enunciative intensity and libidinal truth.

In *La Volonté de savoir*, Foucault describes the historical formation of what he calls *le dispositif de sexualité*. While his analysis is largely devoted to the questioning practices informing the Catholic rite of confession, he is able to define his topic most evocatively by referring to Diderot's erotic novel, *Les Bijoux indiscrets* (1748): "Ce dont il s'agit dans cette série d'études? Transcrire en histoire la fable des *Bijoux indiscrets*. Au nombre de ses emblèmes, notre société porte celui du sexe qui parle. Du sexe qu'on surprend, qu'on interroge et qui, contraint et volubile à la fois, répond intarissablement"[1] [What is the object of this series of studies? To transcribe into a history[/story] the fable of *Les Bijoux indiscrets*. Among its emblems, our society wears that of the sex that speaks. The sex that is caught in the act, and questioned. Both constrained and voluble, it replies with inexhaust-ible chatter]. Foucault's interest is in the utterance of sexuality, as it is called forth and called for by the confessor's questioning. He merely takes Diderot's fable as an emblem, having nothing in particular to say about the fictional representation of such utterances. I shall attempt here to show that so-called erotic fiction tends to develop both a poetics and a thematics of utterance, finding ways of performing erotic talk, and concomitant ways of referring to it. Following Foucault's lead while taking a parallel path, I shall focus on the representation of confession in these texts, on the notion of truth as a product of ritual intimacy, and on the modes of expression that are proper to it. My concern will not be just to "find" the truth of sexuality. That has been done repeatedly, and can only take us through an unduly brief circuit of self-confirmation. Rather, I wish to dwell on the thematic opportunities that such a discourse makes available to narrative, on the local inflections of meaning that it requires. In other words, beginning with *Les Bijoux indiscrets,* I shall examine what kinds of *histoire* have been made in literature out of Foucault and Diderot's *fable.*

Foucault notes that the power to evince confession is represented thematically in Diderot's novel: it is concentrated with comical simplicity in a magic ring given to the sultan Mangogul by a genie. When Mangogul points the ring at a woman and twists it, her vagina (*bijou*) begins immediately to recount its past experiences. The magic, Foucault suggests, lies in the direct articulation of sex with speech, whereby the truth comes flowing out as a genital avowal that reveals any words uttered by mouth to have been primly duplicitous. Somewhat beyond the scope of Foucault's study, however, is the actual quality of spontaneous story-telling that is produced by forced "indiscretion." Mangogul's pro-voking, his calling forth of the truth, compels his victims to give voice to their sexual experiences in language over which they have no control. What kind of writing, what kind of narrative serve to signify spontaneous veracity? What are the characteristics of genital speech? It must be said that Diderot's novel is more interesting for the fact that it allows these questions to be asked than for any richly complex answers that it may give, although the narrative is briefly troubled by the issue from time to time. When, for example, Mangogul points his ring toward the sleeping Thélis, we read the following account of events: "Je m'en souviens encore, comme si j'y étais, dit incontinent le bijou de Thélis: neuf preuves d'amour en quatre heures. Ah! quels moments! que Zermounzaïd est un homme divin!"[2] ["I remember it as if I were still there," said Thélis's jewel, going on without stopping. "Nine demonstrations of love in four hours. Ah! What moments! What a divine man Zermounzaïd is!"]. This could be heard as quite revealing talk, complete with the lover's proper name, but it is not received as such in the novel. The *bijou* is described as speaking "incontinently," in a way that is too immediate or too elliptical for Mangogul's narrative purposes.

To his ears this kind of talk is a failure of eloquence, so that even as it pours forth it serves to hide (*dérober*) something from him. He twiddles his magic ring so as to produce a more finely tuned, more detailed narrative: "Mangogul, qui désirait s'instruire des particularités du commerce de Thélis avec Zermounzaïd, que le bijou lui dérobait, en ne s'attachant qu'à ce qui frappe le plus un bijou, frotta quelque temps le chaton de sa bague contre sa veste, et l'appliqua sur Thélis, tout étincelant de lumière. L'effet en parvint bientôt jusqu'à son bijou, qui mieux instruit de ce qu'on lui demandait, reprit d'un ton plus historique" (126) [Mangogul wanted to know the details of the intercourse between Thélis and Zermounzaïd, which the jewel was keeping from his grasp, for it was only going on about the things that most interest a jewel. He rubbed the setting of his ring against his coat, and applied it to Thélis all sparkling with light. The effect was soon felt on Thélis's jewel. Now with a better a idea of what was required of it, it went on in a more historical tone].

Mangogul's requirement that spontaneous talk have a properly recognizable form serves to remind us, as Foucault would have wished, of the exigent nature of confession as a discipline. But the particular narrative discipline chosen is also the mark of Mangogul's classicism. The disjointed language he first hears appears to him only a *dérobade,* a refusal to respond properly. He has to insist, via a metaphor of light and clarity, in order to be told the truth in its proper historico-narrative form.

It is appropriate here to speak of Mangogul's "classicism" because we see him requiring that supposedly nonnarrative language be transformed into its worthy opposite. The fact is, of course, that unruly talk is not banished from the domain of literature, and is actually present in the text. What is more, Thélis's vaginal utterance signifies its (quite relative) incoherence in particular, recognizable ways: it contains only short phrases, with strong punctuation, and includes a number of exclamations. These are presumably the signs of what "strikes" a *bijou* most, but they are present here without being valued by the most authoritative character in the novel. They are practiced episodically, but not owned by any official poetics. The same kind of discrepancy, the same disturbance of the classical, occurs in Crébillon's *La Nuit et le moment* (1755). When invited to tell a story by his companion Cidalise, Clitandre declares that the situation in which they find themselves, in a boudoir, is generically inappropriate for proper storytelling: "Si vous saviez à quel point je raconte mal dans un lit, vous ne voudriez sûrement pas m'y transformer en historien"[3] [If you knew how poorly I tell stories in bed, you surely would not want to turn me into a historian in this place]. But the neat

opposition between "historical" narration and pillow talk is not maintained throughout Clitandre's verbal performance. He does tell
something of a story as part of his seductive conversation, and Crébillon's text follows that seduction to the point where Clitandre finally achieves his goal. Politely but eloquently, he gives voice to the
impossibility of eloquence at that moment: "'Ah! Madame! . . . ma
joie me suffoque; je ne puis parler.' [Il tombe, en soupirant, sur la
gorge de Cidalise, et y reste comme anéanti]" (IX:64) ["Ah!
Madame! . . . My joy takes my breath away. I cannot speak." He falls
with a sigh on Cidalise's breast, and lies there as if exhausted]. This
we must take to be just the kind of talk that can and ought to go on in
a boudoir, since it is an avowal of pleasure, but we are required, if we
respect the explicit rules of the text, to oppose it to proper storytelling. In that sense, La Nuit et le moment, like Les Bijoux indiscrets, brings
together erotic avowal and a form of poetic disavowal. In the fifty
years that follow, erotic fiction will in fact be less and less disturbed by
the supposed discrepancy between civilized talk and sexual babble. It
will learn to (re)produce the babble, to organize its representation,
and to assert its truth at key moments in narrative.

It could be argued that there is no historical shift of note here,
merely the continuance of a tradition going back to Aretino in which
exclamatory talk serves as a privileged semiotic vehicle for desire.
This is just how Gustave Colline sees it. In fact, he goes so far as to say
that erotic literature in general is characterized by "la langue assez
décousue, ponctuée d'exclamations et de monosyllabes" [rather disjointed language, punctuated by exclamations and monosyllables].
This was the case in the Ragionamenti, according to Colline, and the
pattern has hardly varied since.[4] That is too hearty a generalization, if
only because it excludes or at best marginalizes a whole class of
refined libertine texts, including Diderot's and Crébillon's. Yet there
is something in the claim that deserves attention, and that can lead us
back to Foucault. At the very least, it can be noted that there is a
subgenre of erotic fiction, in fact a quite dominant one in French
texts of the seventeenth century, that answers to this broad description. It represents, as in Aretino, intimate conversations between
women during which expressions of emotion and sudden changes of
direction—interjections, or yielding to other forms of discursive
temptation—are said to occur, and occur in the saying. This is the
case, notably, in L'Académie des dames (1655), L'Escole des filles (1660),
and Vénus dans le cloître (1682). These texts are in fact confessional in
an informal sense, confessional partly because of their informality.
Their show of unpredictability and their regular indiscipline are the
marks of true feminine talk—true, of course, by circular definition.

The three French texts can even be said to coincide historically with the emergence of the religious confession studied by Foucault.

At this point, "disjointedness" has its full value as a (conventional) mark of spontaneity. When the language of sex is allowed (and required) to come spilling out, it is likely to be marked by sighs, cries, and exclamations. Producing these vocalizations, drawing them out from women characters in particular, becomes the business of a confessional erotic discipline that is both enacted and recounted in fiction. This talk is undoubtedly a grammatically plain and lexically spare branch of the *dispositif de sexualité*, and as such is neglected by Foucault. Yet it goes on no less volubly than the elaborate discourses of pastoral confession and psychoanalysis. As Foucault's theory, if not his actual analysis, helps us to see, disjointed language may be no less a discursive formation for its relative inarticulacy. Indeed, there is a linguistic practice of "inarticulacy," in which talk keeps on coming, in discourse that is breathless and continually interrupted. This discourse is recognizable precisely as one that signifies, by its shape, the loss of shape and the loss of all reticence.

It does not follow from this, however, that the signification of disjointedness is stable throughout four centuries of erotic narrative. To suppose that would be to ignore everything Foucault has to say about the history of sexual discourses. The question is a more subtle, but also a more helpfully immediate one. How, if at all, does exclamatory talk come to be articulated with a thematics of confession, supposing that the two do in fact converge at certain historical points? When, and where, does exclamatory talk count as the utterance of sexual truth? Not in the *Ragionamenti*, at any rate. In Aretino's text, exclamations are of interest for their acoustic qualities, undeniably, but the primary focus of description is on their extraordinary variety. Here is a passage, in translation, representing the festive profusion of an orgy as an orchestration of cries: "tous s'accordèrent pour le faire en mesure, comme s'accordent les Musiciens ou les Forgerons en levant le marteau, et, chacun attentif au final, on n'entendait que des: Aie! aie! — Embrasse-moi! — Tourne-toi bien. — Prête-moi ta petite langue! — Donne-la-moi! — Prends-la! — Pousse plus fort! — Attends que j'y sois! — Va donc! — Serre-moi bien! — A l'aide! L'un parlait en murmurant, l'autre criait en miaulant, on aurait dit une bande de sol, fa, mi, ré, ut, et c'étaient les yeux renversés, des soupirs, des secousses, des convulsions"[5] [all agreed to do it together as choristers sing in unison, or more to the point, as blacksmiths hammer in time, and so, each attentive to his task, all that one heard was: "Oh my God, oh my Christ!" "Hug me!" "Ream me!" "Push out that sweet tongue!" "Give it to me!" "Take it!" "Push harder!" "Wait, I'm coming!" "Oh Christ, drive it into me!" "Holy God!" "Hold me!" and "Help!" Some were whispering, others were moaning loudly—and listening to them one would have thought they were running the scales, *sol, fa, me, re, do]*.

This is both a kind of vulgar symphony and a flamboyant list, in which all the exclamations serve to display the range of sounds produced in pleasure. Yet the range itself, even when exhibited in near-perfect simultaneity, hardly constitutes a moment of confession. This is order made out of disorder, but it is fun rather than truth. "Expression" takes place joyously, in the uttering of instructions, animal noises, and sighs, without any revelation of erotic interiority. Even when, at another point in Aretino's text, the orchestration is more polished, it does not give rise to climactic avowal. There is a collective performance of pleasure in which the eight participants sigh in unison. Their sighs do not signify the triumph of narrative circumstance as the compulsion to speak what lies deep within: they simply come together like a well-disciplined wind ensemble, producing a blast of such force that it could have blown out eight torches (I:59).

There is a great difference between this and the blurting out of desire, presented as a revelation, and therefore as a narrative event in its own right. We come closer to a Foucaldian narrative moment in *Vénus dans le cloître*, where a priest is drawn despite himself into disturbing the sacramental roles of confession. While listening to a young penitent's account of libertine behavior, he is tempted by the man's beauty into an exclamation of enthusiasm: "Ah, qual gusto! signor."[6] This breaking out of desire, in a foreign tongue indeed, reverses the roles and makes the confessor into the confessee. But for the event to count in full as a moment of truth, it would need to generate further narrative, and that does not happen. The revealing exclamation is only an amusing twist at the end of an anecdote. A later novel, *Les Amours du chevalier de Faublas* (1793), shows how exclamation comes to be put in a strong narrative place, as something decisive, yet relatively banal. The young Faublas is indulging in a romp with one of his mistresses, but makes the mistake, so often repeated since in popular comedy, of blurting out the wrong name, that of his first, virtuous love: "Mais par une singularité que je n'entreprendrai pas d'expliquer, l'image des vertus les plus pures vint, au sein du libertinage, se présenter à mon esprit troublé; et, ce qui n'est pas moins digne de remarque, je m'avisai de vouloir parler dans un de ces moments, où l'homme plus étourdi, exempt de toutes distractions, ne laisse échapper que de courts monosyllabes ou de longs soupirs étouffés. Ah! Sophie! m'écriai-je! j'aurais dû dire: Ah! Coralie!"[7] [But for some strange reason that I will not attempt to explain, the image of the purest virtues appeared in my troubled mind, right in the midst of a libertine frolic. Furthermore, and this is equally noteworthy, I found myself speaking in one of those moments where the dizziest man, free from all distractions, lets out only short mono-syllables or long muffled sighs. "Ah! Sophie!" I exclaimed. I should have said, "Ah! Coralie!"]. The dramatic point is, of course, that the superficially wrong name, surrounded by sighs and monosyllables, is the profoundly right one. When "undistracted" by social awareness, Faublas utters the name that is closest to his heart, slipping unguar-dedly into the exclamation of truth. On such a moment of revelation, the story turns.

Sometimes in the eighteenth century, especially in more pastel-hued texts, the sigh itself takes on thematic status as a timely erotic effusion. This allows the narration to remain quite decorous, partly because the sigh itself is the most nobly insubstantial of bodily ema-nations, and partly because the language of description need not be interrupted by exclamatory talk. In *Acajou et Zirphile* (1744), for exam-ple, a young man and a young woman who have been enclosed in adjoining gardens are drawn into a love story through a dialogue of sighs:

> Un jour que le prince était plongé dans ses réflexions auprès de cette palissade, il laissa échapper un soupir: la jeune princesse, qui était de l'autre côté dans le même état, l'entendit; elle en fut émue; elle recueille toute son attention, elle écoute. Acajou soupire encore. Zirphile, qui n'avait jamais rien compris à ce qu'on lui avait dit, entendit ce soupir avec une pénétration admirable; elle répondit aussitôt par un pareil soupir.
>
> Ces deux amants, car ils le furent dans ce moment, s'entendirent réciproquement.[8]

> [One day when the prince was deep in thought near this fence, he let out a sigh. The young princess, who was on the other side and in the same state of mind, heard it. She was moved. She gathered all her powers of attention and listened. Acajou sighed again. Zirphile, who had never understood anything that had been said to her, understood that sigh with admirable intelligence. She replied with a similar sigh of her own.
>
> These two lovers, for they became so in that instant, heard and under-stood each other].

Entendirent, in this context, is a pun, and a happy one, signifying both "heard" and "understood." When the two have found a way to com-municate face to face, the same kind of language persists between them: "Ils se touchent; ils gardent le silence; ils laissent cependant échapper quelques mots mal articulés" (43) [They touched each other. They remained silent. And yet they let out a few poorly articulated words]. They have no need to adjust their language in order to adopt a "more historical tone," as in Diderot. Poor articulation, here, is more richly communicative than any other, and its utterance has been a crucial event in the story. At the same time, however, the narration that refers to inarticulacy remains itself quite "historical," and retains its polish.

In *Kanor* (1750), sighs have similar dramatic effects. Babillon, the young heroine, appears for a moment to have been killed in a fall. This provokes from her would-be lover, the young Zaaf, a tragic cry that is modulated into a deep sigh: "Il s'aperçut qu'elle ne respirait plus; il fit un cri terrible et douloureux et, en s'approchant encore davantage, il ne put retenir un soupir profond"[9] [He noticed that she was no longer breathing. He let out a terrible cry of pain, and drawing closer, could not hold back a deep sigh]. That he should go from a cry to a sigh may well be the mark of parody, since it allows the story to move between two registers of effusive language, but it demonstrates nonetheless the power of inarticulate sounds to effect narrative transformation, for the sigh, which is said to come from deep within the prince—"[il] partait du saisissement et de la tendresse de son cœur" (127) [it came from the shock and affection of his heart]—reaches the princess and revives her, bringing about the happiest of erotic confluences: "ce souffle brûlant parut ranimer son amante et lui rendre la vie; ses yeux s'entrouvrirent et, à son tour, elle soupira si juste, que le petit souffle qui partait de son cœur vint se mêler et se confondre avec un second soupir, tout de feu, que le charme de la retrouver vivante tira de l'âme du Prince" (127) [this burning breath seemed to revive his lover and bring her back to life. Her eyelids fluttered, and she in turn sighed so appropriately that the little breath that came from her heart joined and mixed with a second, fiery sigh that the delight of finding her alive drew from the soul of the prince]. The careful numbering and the playfully detailed physics, when applied to zephyr-like sighs, account for the production of what we can identify as full-blown effects of love: "Ces souffles si disproportionnés s'unirent, à peu près comme une vapeur légère, comme le plus doux zéphyr s'unirait à un tourbillon impétueux. C'était précisément cette union et ce mélange, qui étaient le talisman décisif" (127) [These disproportionate breaths were united, almost as a light vapor, the slightest of zephyrs, would be united with an impetuous whirlwind. This union and this mixture were exactly what was required as the decisive talisman].

In *Les Nonnes galantes*, which also dates from the mid-eighteenth century, we find the sigh once again revealing the heroine's "trouble secret," and her lack of self-control. The man who is with her has no trouble interpreting this as a symptom: "Cette tendre émotion de sa jeune maîtresse ne valait-elle pas bien pour lui la plus flatteuse déclaration?"[10] [Was not this tender emotion in his young mistress tantamount for him to the most flattering declaration?]. Indeed, in this novel such behavior is given a certain status, and a conventional place, by the existence within the convent of a "cabinet des soupirs" [room of sighs]: "Et le lecteur remarquera que jamais endroit ne fut mieux nommé: ce cabinet, en effet, qui était au milieu du jardin, ne paraissait destiné qu'à être le secret confident des secrètes peines des jeunes nonnes amoureuses. C'était là où elles allaient se rappeler le souvenir de bien des moments heureux trop rapidement écoulés, ou se plaindre des obstacles que le sort opposait à leurs tendres désirs" (120) [The reader will observe that no place was ever better named. This small room in the middle of the garden seemed destined only to be the secret confidant of the secret sufferings of young nuns in love. It was here that they came to recall the memories of happy moments that had been all too fleeting, or to complain of the obstacles that fate put in the way of their tender desires]. There is thematic room here for that other, parallel form of confession, the erotic sigh, gathered and concentrated in its own topical place.

Théophile Gautier's *La Morte amoureuse* (1836), for all its haunting mystery, performs a remarkably straightforward thematic reprise of the sigh as declaration. The narrator-hero, a priest, is summoned to the bedside of a dying, indeed apparently dead woman whose identity is unknown to him. To his surprise and deep regret, this woman proves to be Clorimonde, the one he had loved and lost at the moment of his entry into the priesthood. Struck by the "singulier hasard" [strange event of chance] that has led him to find her once again just as he appears to lose her forever, he expresses his regret in the most natural (or most culturally apposite) bodily manner: "un soupir de regret s'échappa de ma poitrine" [a sigh of regret came from my breast]. This subdued expression of desire, by a further, perhaps more productive, coincidence, is answered by another sigh. Is it, he wonders, just his own sigh echoing around the bedroom, or is this a second sigh, emanating from the "dead" woman in response to his own? The echo itself is again the decisive phenomenon, and the indication that their love has been literally revived.[11]

Erotic fiction that is both more vulgar and more challenging, as it develops at the end of the eighteenth century, includes such narrative effects as those produced by the revealing sigh, while extending the range of bodily expressions and, in particular, representing the impact of such expressions on the writing itself. Gentle sighs may stand euphemistically, in polished fiction, for more forceful utter-

ances and more substantive bodily emissions, but the point to be
noted for a thematics and poetics of climax is that they stand in the
same narrative place. In more vulgar stories, the sigh is not necessarily exhaled through the noble orifice, as we find in the following
episode from Andréa de Nerciat's *Les Aphrodites* (1793): "Déjà le
comte, dans un moment de délire assaisonné des exclamations les
plus passionnées, est allé jusqu'à déposer un baiser fixe et mouillant
sur cette bouche impure [the anus] de laquelle, en pareil cas, il serait
disgracieux d'obtenir un soupir . . ."[12] [Already the count, in a moment of folly seasoned with the most passionate exclamations, had
gone so far as to place a lingering wet kiss on that other, impure
mouth from which, in such circumstances, it would have been un-
couth to call forth a sigh]. Yet this jocose symmetry, parallel to that of
Les Bijoux indiscrets, reveals in its own way that the narrative force of
bodily emissions in late eighteenth-century erotic stories of a more
vulgar sort builds on an established thematic. Nerciat maintains the
value of exclamatory expression as one of the marks of *délire,* and of
passion. A sigh, whatever might later have been said to the contrary in
"Casablanca," is still a sigh. However delicate and playful, however
uncontrolled or even obscene, the sigh is equivalent, for its decisive-
ness, to other forms of ejaculation. When, in *La Nouvelle Académie des
dames* (1774?), two lovers are locked together in the most passionate
embrace, desire and pleasure pass between them in a mingling of
sighs and a liquefaction of breath that give full erotic substance to
respiration: "une bouche étroitement collée sur la sienne lui com-
muniquait tous mes soupirs; sa langue était un trait qui faisait passer
chez moi tout le feu qui le consumait"[13] [a mouth that was tightly
glued to his communicated all my sighs directly to him. His tongue
was a dart that passed into me all the fire that burned within him].
Sighs and exclamations may be no less profuse here than in the
Ragionamenti, but they are now no longer countable, since they form
an erotic flux. The tongue, in this context, is a sexual organ, whose
dominant role reflects the directly communicative value that has
come to be invested in inarticulate utterance.

   The language of sighs and cries is able to function discursively and
thematically for the precise reason that it is a language, no matter
how spontaneous or unprecedented its manifestations may seem.
Indeed, by a paradox I have already alluded to, the written sigh, the
written exclamation signify in this way because they codify breathing
and breathlessness. This point seems to have escaped Michel Camus,
even as he was accurately identifying the linguistic patterns. In a
preface to *Le Triomphe des religieuses, ou Les Nones babillardes* (1748),
Camus distinguishes the habitually seductive discourse of polite ex-

change, carried on even in bed, from that which marks "l'acmé ou le *raptus* érotique" [the erotic acme or *raptus*]. The latter is characterized by "des petits points spasmodiques" that disturb the flow of civilized conversation. The cause of this disruption, says Camus, is something profoundly unspeakable: "La langue est impuissante à rendre compte de ce qui, par nature, dans l'intensité même de l'acte d'amour, échappe à toute formulation ou à toute expression adéquate. C'est le feu même de la vie qui est passé sous silence. . . . Le langage de l'esprit doit s'articuler sur le langage du corps pour en arriver à satisfaire la faim sexuelle"[14] [Language is powerless to render that which, by nature, in the very intensity of the act of love, is beyond formulation or expression. The very fire of life is then left unspoken. The language of the mind must be articulated with the language of the body in order to satisfy its sexual hunger]. This analysis seems to me not so much wrong as unsubtle, in that it fails to mark a historical distinction between libertine discourse of the eighteenth century and a full-fledged romantic understanding of Desire. To speak, as Camus does, of the interruption of language under the compulsion of inner fire and sexual hunger is to fail to notice that there is also a language of interruption helping the reader to evoke these secret forces of compulsion. More to the point, it is also almost certainly an overinterpretation of the way ejaculatory language works in *Le Triomphe des religieuses,* or for that matter *La Nuit et le moment,* assimilating them to a later thematics that features (and articulates) unspeakable moments of overwhelming truth. More helpful to a history that wishes to avoid anachronism are the remarks of Jean Marie Goulemot in a preface to *La Messaline française* (1789). Goulemot notes that what he calls "cette difficulté presque ontologique à exprimer la jouissance" [the almost ontological difficulty of expressing pleasure] is partly overcome by the use of an established set of adjectives and nouns that are "strictly coded," and by "les points de suspension . . . comme si la jouissance ne parvenait à s'exprimer que par l'abolition de ce qui avait projet de l'exprimer, le récit lui-même. Les points de suspension, les blancs typographiques sont autant de signes pour désigner ce que les mots sont impuissants à dire"[15] [suspension marks, as if pleasure only managed to express itself through the abolition of that which had aimed to express it, the narrative itself. Suspension marks and typographical blanks are so many signs for designating what words are powerless to say]. This is not a definitive failure of language, as Goulemot rightly observes. It is the "constat d'un échec . . . qui finit, par une dialectique propre à l'effet d'écriture, par se donner à lire comme une expression réussie" (291) [recognition of a failure that eventually, by a dialectic proper to the writing effect, offers itself for reading as a successful expression]. The difficulty of expression, while regularly encountered, is domesticated by a kind of semiotic etiquette.

A stronger challenge to erotic representation, one that will not be satisfied with classical libertine convention, is pronounced by the narrator of Nerciat's *Le Diable au corps* (1803). What must be written out are not so much the words passing between lovers, but all the subverbal things that characterize amorous exchange at its most passionately vigorous: "Où trouver un historien qui, vraiment digne d'écrire les fastes du *monde foutant,* serait capable de saisir les mots, les demi-mots, les accents, les soupirs, les sanglots mille fois plus éloquents que les plus belles paroles"[16] [Where can we find a historian who is truly worthy of these festivities of the *fucking society,* and able to capture the words, the half words, the tones of voice, the sighs and the sobs that are a thousand times more eloquent than fine words?]. A historian worthy of the task would achieve a "historical tone" by conveying the flow of half-words: unlike Diderot's Sultan, he would render the intermittent flow directly, in all its communicative power. Nerciat's reflexivity here is, of course, to be read as a playful rhetorical gesture setting before his reader and himself the image of eloquent babble as the true language of fucking. There is still something classical in this concern with eloquence and in the debate about poetics that is allowed to go on in the novel. Yet at the same time he begins to glorify the subverbal in ways that would have been unthinkable fifty years earlier, inviting us to focus on the aesthetic qualities (now) inherent in the semi-articulate. Two lovers are described in another of his novels as communicating in a language that is more eloquent than that of the most polished rhetorician: "Ils ne peuvent plus proférer que des accents confus, mille fois plus éloquents que les plus beaux tours de force de l'esprit académique" (*Les Aphrodites,* II:185) [They can only speak in confused tones, which are a thousand times more eloquent than the figures of academic wit]. Not words, but "accents"—meaningful sounds or qualities of voice—are the matter, the communicative substance that passes between truly eloquent lovers.

Whether or not there is a drama of profundity at work here, whether we ought to feel anguish at the supposed ontological difficulty of expression is a moot point. Most of the eighteenth century seems generally to regard breathless language in much the same way as it does crumpled skirts or half-laced bodies, fluttering eyelashes or rosy cheeks: all are revealing in the same pleasurable way. They are to be enjoyed as marks of an erotically coded *désordre.* Yet the insistence on eloquence that we find in Nerciat and in some of his early nineteenth-century contemporaries is a step toward a rather different understanding: the notion of a superior erotic language, made of something other than, better than, words. Pigault-Lebrun's narrator, in *La Folie espagnole* (1801), invites us to imagine a language that is rhetorically beyond all others because it is morphologically and phonetically on the near side of words: "soupirs brûlants sont le seul langage qu'ils emploient: quel autre vaudrait celui-là?"[17] [burning sighs are the only language they use. What other language would be equal to that?] What other language, indeed? Presumably not that which we read in *La Folie espagnole*. The nineteenth century will soon be troubled, in its very concern with the literary, by the thrust of this question: how is it to harness for erotic narrative the power of the semi-articulate? It hardly suffices to talk about such language, although it does happen quite often that texts are content to refer to the eloquence of inarticulacy, without seeking to perform it in any way. This happens typically in novels of the late nineteenth century that gesture toward such language without "evoking" it, in any literal sense. Is that because to write out breathlessness would detract from the generic dignity sought by many fin de siècle erotic novels? Instead of an attempt to render an unarticulated bodily truth, they tend to offer lyrical idealizations of the subverbal. *Demi-volupté* (1900), by Ernest La Jeunesse, glories in the fact that the lovers' cries are freed from signification: "Ils ne parlèrent pas: de petits cris pas humains leur montaient aux lèvres, en la saveur des baisers: de petits cris l'un pour l'autre, se répondant en même temps comme des oiseaux et comme des frissons de la foudre"[18] [They did not speak. Little non-human cries came from their lips, among the flavor of kisses: little cries meant for one another, answering each other at the same time like birds or flashes of lightning]. In René Saint-Médard's *L'Orgie moderne* (1905), the absence of any comprehensible code allows such (half-)talk to be qualified as celestial: "Leurs bouches étaient unies, nouées dans un baiser sans fin, et ne se séparaient que pour proférer des onomatopées sans signification dans notre langue, mais qui doivent être l'idiome du ciel"[19] [Their mouths were united, bound in an endless kiss, and they separated only to speak onomatopoeias that have no meaning in our language, but must be the language of heaven]. Novelistic writing of this kind seems to have given up all hope of espousing or reflecting erotic language, being content to indulge in a kind of metalinguistic nostalgia.

Talking about the inarticulate is not the most demanding task, nor even the most characteristic of erotic narrative. Beyond the blandly thematic, beneath and around it, a veritable poetics of disjointedness is often at work. We have already seen that the practice of exclama-

tory writing, established to some degree since Aretino, was not authorized, not fully owned by narratorial discourse in such texts as *Les
Bijoux indiscrets* and *La Nuit et le moment*. The fact is nonetheless that it
persisted, and became more elaborate. It has to be said that the
formal features of such writing remain uncomplicated, nay, rudimentary: lines of text are punctuated by exclamation and suspension
marks, the alternation of which seems to constitute a rhythm of
emphatic disjointedness. Eighteenth- and nineteenth-century writing often displays these features, not to signify undisciplined conversation or festive noise, as in Aretino and his immediate successors,
but to echo the *accents* or the voice of pleasure. These formal traits
appear well established by about 1740, and are maintained into the
nineteenth century. Most of them are present in the stylized representations of spontaneity that occur in Crébillon's novels. Montade, a
character in *Tableaux des mœurs du temps dans les différents âges de la vie*
(1750), utters and owns his pleasure in repetitive first-person verbs:
"J'achève . . . j'achève . . . je n'en puis plus" [I am finishing . . . I am
finishing . . . I cannot last any longer]. To which his lover is said to
reply, for even extreme pleasure is conversational in Crébillon: "Je
meurs de plaisir! . . ."[20] [I am dying of pleasure! . . .]. It is as if the
sentences were always dying and finishing, compelled to do so by the
circumstances of their enunciation—as if the force of the exclamation itself caused the suspension. More complicated and sustained
instances can be recounted, and even greater disorder presented,
but it will be rhetorically more of the same.

A degree or two beyond Crébillon's text in this regard is *Le Triomphe des religieuses* (1748), which is dotted with exclamations, and
which actually breaks up the longer words used to speak pleasure:
'Eh! . . . Eh! . . . Eh! . . . tu me tues . . . ar . . . rête, je me . . .
meurs"[21] [Hey! . . . Hey! . . . Hey! . . . You are kil . . . ling me . . .
Stop . . . it, I am dy . . . ing]. Disintegration into monosyllabic elements is quite widespread in pornographic writing of the later eighteenth century, and is still to be found in modern texts of the same
type. In his pornographic writing, Restif de la Bretonne seems to
favor full-voiced, open vowels, adding to the usual punctuation a few
circumflex accents for wider stretching of the mouth, and greater
sonority: "Je pa . . . ars! . . . Je décha . . . arge! . . . Hââh! . . ."
(*L'Anti-Justine*, 1798)[22] [I am goo . . . one! . . . I am discha . . . rging!
. . . Hââh! . . .]. Here, even the monosyllabic *pars* cannot resist the
word-rending force of the heart. And in *Lettres galantes et philosophiques de deux nones* (1797), we find a striking utterance about—and
performance of—breathing: "Mon cœur . . . Hélas! . . . mon cœur
pal . . . pite, et mon . . . ha . . . leine ex . . . pire"[23] [My heart . . .

Alas! . . . My heart is pal . . . pitating, and my brea . . . th ex . . . piring]. Such breathlessness may have something broadly in common with the racy dialogues of Aretino's Nanna and Pippa, as Gustave Colline pointed out, but it is importantly different from them in at least one respect. The language of desire and pleasure claims to be expiring at its high point, uttering as if with its last breath the death of language—except that this death is repeated endlessly, and repeated in language. When the drama recurs from page to page, and from line to line, what is spoken is no more than a *petite mort* of the most routine kind.

The second half of the eighteenth century understands exclamations and interruptions as signs of an erotic state that it often refers to as *vivacité*. A veritable set of symptoms now makes if possible to identify desire as a (temporary) condition of the whole body: suddenness of movement, quickening of the blood, breathlessness of speech. Indeed, a sudden change of state is itself to be read as a symptom: "Les passages imperceptibles de la tranquillité aux mouvements les plus vifs, de l'indifférence au désir, n'étaient plus des énigmes pour moi" (*Histoire de dom Bougre,* 1741)[24] [The imperceptible shifts from stillness to the most lively movement, and from indifference to desire, were no longer riddles to me]. Sometimes, the eyes reveal all: "ses yeux m'avaient déjà prévenue, ils m'avaient peint la vivacité de ses désirs" (*La Nouvelle Académie des dames,* 76–77) [her eyes had already enlightened me; they portrayed the liveliness of her desires]. At other times the inner circulation of fire shows itself on the outside in a whole range of ways: "son teint était animé, ses yeux me lançaient des regards perçants, qui m'obligeaient de perdre contenance chaque fois que ma vue se portait sur la sienne; et la rapidité de ses gestes, de ses mouvements, ne laissait que trop apercevoir le feu dont il était dévoré" (*Amélie, ou Les Écarts de ma jeunesse*)[25] [his complexion was bright; his eyes cast piercing looks at me, making me lose my self-control each time I saw him looking at me; and the rapidity of his gestures and movements made it only too clear that a fire was consuming him from within]. When this state is evoked in first-person narration, the description itself tends to be symptomatically disjointed: "mes genoux fléchirent, ma voix s'éteignit, j'étais absorbée; cependant je brûlais de mille feux" (*Vénus en rut,* c. 1785).[26] [my knees buckled, and my voice failed me. I was absorbed. At the same time, I was alight with a thousand fires].

With the full development of a romantic discourse of desire as rapidity of circulation and intense fullness of the body, the *cri* will come to be powerfully expressed in metaphors of substance. Whereas eighteenth century texts often played with the equivalence of sighs and other kinds of emission, allowing for their succession and alternation, romantic narrative makes all expressions coincide in time as symptoms of the body in climax. The materialization is spoken as a claim and claimed to be spoken in Nogaret's *L'Arétin français* (1787):

> Ah! la liqueur divine
> Circule à grands flots, s'achemine . . .
> Es-tu prêt? . . . Je décharge . . . Ah! mon
> Dieu! que c'est bon![27]

> [Ah! the divine liquor
> Is circulating in great waves, and making its way . . .
> Are you ready? . . . I am unloading . . . Ah! My
> God! How sweet it is!]

When circulation reaches its point of greatest activity, erotic physiology is said to compel the utterance, "I discharge." The economy that builds up sperm within the body is connected in narrative with the very capacity to speak, allowing (and requiring) oral outpouring to coincide with genital emission. This is never more clear or more strongly overdetermined than in the favorite exclamation of Revolutionary eroticism, "foutre!" Through the word's double sense, as an obscene verb meaning to copulate and a vulgar name for sperm, "foutre!" celebrates the fulfilment of desire while naming the substance that is its most direct physiological expression. The term is not a new exclamation, and is in fact mentioned, although not properly uttered, in *Tableaux des mœurs du temps dans les différents âges de la vie* (1750) as a mark of masculine conversation,[28] but it is only at the end of the century that it commands a place in narrative as a sign of discharge.

Whereas writers such as Crébillon talked about such forceful enunciation and even alluded to obscenity without actually performing it, writing at the turn of the century goes a step further. Nerciat manages to produce the obscenity of *foutre!* as the most telling verbal symptom, all the while surrounding it with protocols of tact. On one occasion, he seems to respect the old libertine etiquette, referring to the double meaning without actually writing out the exclamation, although the reference and its narrative significance are unmistakable: "[Hilarion] tombe sans connaissance après avoir mâlement articulé (soit plaisir, soit douleur) le *mot* grenadier de ce dont il vient de si bien réaliser la chose" (*Le Diable au corps*, IV:138; original emphasis) [Hilarion fell unconscious, after pronouncing the grenadiers' word that corresponds to the thing he had just carried out with such success]. Whether he feels pleasure or pain matters infinitely less for narrative than the intensity of his experience. And in expressing what he feels, he utters "the word" that all true males come to utter in that extreme circumstance, whether they be soldiers or, like Hilarion himself, men of the cloth. Indeed, such is the natural compulsion at work here that the same manly expression is heard to come spilling out of the mouths of Nerciat's most vigorous female characters. The marquise, in *Les Aphrodites,* is about to engage with a young nobleman who has made his way into her apartment disguised as a servant. Here is the imperative of desire with which she summons him to action: "Foutre! s'écrie-t-elle, mets-le donc" ["Fuck!" she exclaimed. "Just put it in"]. After this has been blurted out, Nerciat's narratorial tact comes belatedly into play, so that the unbridled directness of the marquise's talk is followed by a lengthily apologetic "editorial" note, in which the narrator invites his readers to a kind of brainstorming session, pretending to hope that they will contribute more seemly expressions that might satisfy the double exigencies of truthful vigor and sociable refinement: "Je déteste (comme sans doute tous les lecteurs délicats) ces malheureux moments où des femmes dont on a la meilleure opinion, et qui ont été bien élevées, s'abaissent aux indécences, à la brutalité du plus ignoble vulgaire . . . Je prie les gens d'esprit et ceux qui auront l'expérience de ces sortes de conjonctures de m'adresser quelques tournures de bon ton, quelques jolies phrases qui, sans affaiblir les situations, puissent suppléer à des obscénités, véritables taches dans cet historique et très moral ouvrage. Nous avons essayé de *triomphez donc . . . d'achevez ma défaite . . . de faites-moi mourir . . .* , etc. Tout cela ne nous a pas paru valoir cette énergique *foutre! mets-le donc! . . .* Quel dommage qu'on ne puisse accommoder la bienséance qu'aux dépens de l'expression ou de la vérité! . . ." (I:150; original emphasis) [I hate (like all delicate readers, no doubt) these unfortunate moments where women of whom one has the highest opinion, and who are well mannered, stoop to indecency, to vulgar brutishness at its most ignoble. . . . I beg people of intelligence and those who have experienced this kind of circumstance to send me some distinguished expressions, some pretty phrases that will not weaken these situations, but will take the place of obscenities, for they are very much a stain on this historical and highly moral work. We tried "Wreak your will . . . ," "Complete your triumph . . . ," "Bring me to my end . . . ," etc. None of them seemed to be equal in value to that energetic "Fuck! Just put it in! . . ." What a pity that propriety can only be satisfied at the expense of expressiveness or truth! . . .].

We can note in passing that the direct expression of climactic pleasure is deemed to be grossly unfeminine, thereby indicating the extent to which the value of exclamation has narrowed and intensified since Aretino. The main point to note, however, is that the long-windedness of Nerciat's editorial comment does no more than demonstrate, and apologize for, the superiority of short-winded language in the representation of desire. He feigns unease at the stain made on "historical" narrative by this exclamation, but that is merely a polite way of negotiating change, and insisting that ejaculation have its place in the heart of the story. It is no surprise to find the same woman and others exhaling their *foutre!* at other times in these novels. The Comtesse is heard to say "quite loudly": "Ah foutre! . . . fou . . . ou . . . tre! voilà du plaisir . . ." *Le Diable au corps*, V:112)[29] [Ah Fuck! . . . Fu . . . u . . . uck! There's pleasure for you . . .]. Such phrases are climactically overdetermined. They are cries of pleasure in every sense: both immediate symptoms of what is occurring within, and instantaneously reflexive celebrations of its occurrence.

In keeping with this materialization of voice, utterances can assume all the qualities of bodily fluids. Sade's libertines, who are eager consumers of the substances emanating from their victims, can be seen to drink in sighs just as they might absorb base forms of excreta.[30] Here is an example from *La Nouvelle Justine* (1797) involving the monk Clément: "osant mêler l'amour à ces moments d'effroi, sa bouche se colle sur celle de Justine et veut respirer les soupirs qu'arrache la douleur"[31] [he dares to mix love with moments of fright, and his mouth adheres to Justine's as he seeks to breathe in the sighs provoked from her by pain]. Another scene from the same novel actually dramatizes the equivalence of tears and sperm, showing the two to be produced at the same time, and in response to the same stimulus. Justine and Juliette have just learned the tragic news of their father's death, to which Justine responds, as is her wont, by bursting into tears. Juliette shows what she is made of, quite literally, by bursting into another substance. She brings herself to a climax of pleasure in front of her weeping sister, sighing as she "ejaculates": "Poursuivant ensuite son opération, la putain soupira; et son jeune foutre, éjaculé sous les yeux baissés de la vertu, tarit la source des larmes que, sans cette opération, elle eût peut-être versées comme sa sœur" (*La Nouvelle Justine*, VI:34)[32] [Going on with her exercise, the whore sighed, and her young fuck, ejaculated before the downcast eyes of virtue, dried up the source of the tears that she might otherwise have shed like her sister]. Juliette has found something stronger to do than to weep: she mingles sighs with "sperm," and gives vent to both grief and pleasure in the same action. The "mixing" of love and terror that occurs in Clément's encounter with Justine and the coincidence of tears and sperm in the contrastive sisterhood of Justine and Juliette can both be read as examples of a practice of narrative intensity that develops at the very end of the eighteenth century. We see the coming together of narrative interest and physiological substance in ejaculatory moments. This is what one might call the qualitative dimension of intensity: the fact that sexual discharge is loaded with other kinds of significance than the merely physiological.

A further contribution to intensity, dialectically related to this one, is the production of "spontaneous" blasphemy at moments of extreme pleasure. In this domain, Sade's libertine heroes are unrivaled virtuosi, although the range of variations is rather limited. Dolmancé uses the classically impious "sacredieu!" (*La Philosophie dans le boudoir*, III:437), but adds to it more richly offensive couplings of the sexual and the divine, such as the following: "Sacré-foutu dieu, comme j'ai du plaisir! . . ." (III:439) [Holy fucking God, what pleasure this is! . . .]. His densest and most concentrated ejaculation is the quintessentially obscene "foutredieu!" (III:437), which constitutes a metaphysical counteraffirmation at, and as, the point of greatest intensity. Blasphemy, in this instance, is both a source and a symptom of pleasure.

One of the functions of exclamation in Sade is to produce intensity as climactic coincidence by calling for it imperiously. Not for his master libertines the insidious subtlety of the confessor's art, nor the whimsical short-circuit of Mangogul's borrowed magic. What they require and achieve is a proper timing of discharge somewhat akin to the sighing in unison described by Aretino's Nanna. But whereas in the *Ragionamenti* this event was a happy coincidence, preceded and followed by less successful ones, in *La Philosophie dans le boudoir* it reliably occurs on time, in response to orders that are themselves powerful ejaculations. Dolmancé exhorts his colleagues to unload all at the same moment: "Chevalier, tu t'emportes, je le sens . . . Attends-moi! . . . attends-nous! . . . O mes amis, ne déchargeons qu'ensemble: c'est le seul bonheur de la vie! . . ." (III:468) [Chevalier, you are getting carried away, I can feel it . . . Wait for me! . . . Wait for us! . . . Oh my friends, let's make sure we unload together: it's life's only happiness! . . .]. And when such a moment is about to arrive, the desire for unison spills forth, this time from the Chevalier, as an urgent command: "Déchargez! . . . déchargez toutes deux, mon foutre va s'y joindre! . . . Il coule! . . . Ah! sacredieu! . . ." (III:458) [Unload! . . . Unload both of you. My fuck will soon join yours! . . . It's flowing! . . . Ah! Sacredieu! . . ."]. As the first person singular, "je décharge!" appropriates the second person and expands compellingly into the plural—"déchargez! déchargeons!"—the utterance of pleasure comes out as the call for a particular form of narrative. In much the same way, the heroine of Gamiani longs for, indeed cries out for, the pleasure of crying out: "se toucher, se mêler, s'exhaler corps et âme dans un soupir, un seul cri, un cri d'amour! Fanny! Fanny! c'est le ciel!"[33] [to touch each other, to mingle, to feel body and soul expiring in a sigh, a single cry, a cry of love! Fanny! Fanny! It's heaven!]. What is expressed thus is not just the climax of desire, but the desire for climax.

As part of the developing thematics of intensity, in which Sade's work plays a key role, the sheer quantity of ejaculation is deemed to be an object of interest. Loud exclamations are no more absent from earlier erotic narrative than gentle sighs, but loudness appears now to take on new value. In *Thérèse philosophe* (1748), which remains in touch with a classical narrative tradition, a former prostitute who is recounting various incidents and eccentricities from her career tells a story about a particularly vociferous bishop with whom she had had dealings: "Imagine-toi que, soit par un goût de prédilection, soit par un défaut d'organisation, dès que sa Grandeur sentait les approches du plaisir, elle mugissait, et criait à haute voix *haï! haï! haï!* en forçant le ton à proportion de la vivacité du plaisir dont il était affecté, de sorte qu'on aurait pu calculer les gradations du chatouillement que ressentait le gros et ample prélat, par les degrés de force qu'il employait à mugir *haï! haï! haï!* Tapage qui, lors de la décharge de Monseigneur, aurait pu être entendu à mille pas à la ronde, sans la précaution que son valet de chambre prenait de matelasser les portes et les fenêtres de l'appartement épiscopal."[34] [Well, either because it was his preferred taste or because of something in his make-up, as soon as His Grace felt the onset of pleasure, he bellowed, and cried out at the top of his voice, "Aye! Aye! Aye!" increasing the volume in proportion to the strength of pleasure he was feeling, in such a way that one could have calculated the gradation of stimulation experienced by the stout prelate, according to the degree of loudness with which he bellowed, "Aye! Aye! Aye!" This noise would have been heard a mile away during Monsignor's discharge, were it not for the fact that his valet took the precaution of padding the doors and windows of the episcopal apartment]. All this is a *goût*, a *manie*, a diverting eccentricity told as one of a series, and providing the possibility of playful mensuration. It makes of the bishop a potentially laughable object of scandal, rather than a champion of desire.

It is amusing and instructive to observe that several sentences from *Thérèse philosophe* are reproduced almost verbatim in *Gamiani*, eighty-five years later. To talk of plagiarism here is hardly relevant, since the thematic significance of the description has changed in a quite fundamental way. This has now become a description of Gamiani's outstanding erotic performance—in this particular scene, with animals—in which the voice of desire takes on superlative qualities, reaching new heights of frenzied utterance: "La comtesse criait à haute voix: Hai! hai! hai! forçant toujours le ton à proportion de la vivacité du plaisir. On aurait pu calculer les gradations du chatouillement que ressentait cette effrénée Calymanthe" (123) [The countess cried out at the top of her voice, "Aye! Aye! Aye!" increasing the volume in proportion to the strength of pleasure she was feeling. You could have calculated the gradations of stimulation felt by this frenzied Calymantha]. Of another young woman in the same novel, it is said: "Sa joie, ses transports éclatent en une gamme de oh! et de ah! mais sur un ton si élevé que la mère entend" (123) [Her joy and delight burst out in a scale of "oh"s and "ah"s so loud that her mother heard them]. The true voice of pleasure in this context is loud, high-pitched, and spectacularly "indiscreet," and the range of exclamations is the thrilling scale of an individual vocal performance, rather than the din of carnival.

Between the time of *Thérèse philosophe* and that of *Gamiani,* Sade's fiction had helped add thematic value to the sheer quantity of ejaculation. His heroes distinguish themselves by their stentorian utterances of pleasure. Here is Juliette's description of the unparalleled "crises" of Durand: "Rien n'égalait les crises voluptueuses de la Durand. De mes jours je n'avais vu de femme décharger ainsi: non seulement elle élançait son foutre comme un homme, mais elle accompagnait cette éjaculation de cris si furieux, de blasphèmes tellement énergiques, et de spasmes si violents, qu'on eût cru qu'elle tombait en épilepsie" (*Histoire de Juliette,* IX:428) [Nothing could compare with the voluptuous crises of Durand. In all my life I had never seen a woman discharge like that. Not only did she shoot out fuck like a man, but she accompanied her ejaculation with such furious cries, such energetic blasphemy, and such violent spasms, that one would have thought she was having an epileptic fit]. It is not true, of course, that nothing equals the force of Durand's discharge: it is matched quite regularly by almost every other Sadian master libertine. Certainly, Gernande's dramatic performances, in the different versions of Justine's story, are described in lavish detail, but most of the others are also accorded the honor of quantitative hyperbole. In *Les Cent vingt journées de Sodome,* the Duc de Blangis comes down to breakfast expressing astonishment at the sound emitted by his partner in crime Curval: "Peut-on brailler, peut-on hurler comme tu le fais en déchargeant! dit le duc à Curval, en le revoyant le vingt-

trois au matin.'" . . . "'—Ah! parbleu, dit Curval, c'est bien à toi
qu'on entend d'une lieue à m'adresser un pareil reproche!'" (I:292)
["How can anyone bray and shout the way you do when unloading?!"
said the duke, when he saw him again on the morning of the twenty-
third. "By damn!" said Curval, "it is hardly up to you who can be heard
from a league away to reproach me with such a thing!"].

This last example displays yet another way in which the confluence
of exclamations contributes to the thematics of intensity. Blangis and
Curval practice what might be called second-order ejaculation, mar-
veling at each other's utterances. They comment on, draw attention
to, and echo, quite literally, the vocal power of each other's climax.
Exclamations of this sort, in the form of narratorial cries of wonder,
occur from time to time in earlier literature, and *Kanor* (1750) provides a nicely lyrical example: "Quel aimable désordre dans les
discours! Quel trouble enchanteur dans les sens!" (138) [What
charming disorder in their talk! What enchanting disturbance in
their senses!]. But this is a gently reflexive account of disorder,
passed on in the narration itself. It is quite another matter when
novelistic characters utter cries of admiration that surround and en-
hance great moments of intensity. In that sense, Mme de Saint-Ange
plays to perfection the role of the subordinate libertine when she says
to Dolmancé, just after he has uttered a string of libidinal exclamations: "Comme tu blasphèmes, mon ami!" (*La Philosophie dans le
boudoir,* III:437) [How you blaspheme, my friend!]. She is provoked
by the force of his utterance into her own, tributary exclamation, just
as the hypothetical admiring reader is doubtless supposed to be.
"How he exclaims!" we should all exclaim, as we follow this model,
echoing in chorus with the intensity of climactic pleasure.[35]

Such intensity leaves an opportunity for irony, and that opportunity is nicely exploited, in a way that defines and mocks the theme,
in Gautier's *Mademoiselle de Maupin* (1835). The climax of this story is
in fact just the kind of powerful convergence of narrative and erotic
interest that we have been considering. The hero, d'Albert, discovers
finally that the beautiful young man to whom he has been distur-
bingly attracted for some time is in fact a young woman in disguise.
He finds out the truth about Mademoiselle de Maupin, and fulfills
his desire for her, when she obligingly comes to visit him in his room,
dressed in all her feminine splendor. Now, this event provokes absolutely no cries of wonder on the part of the narrator. Indeed, the
reader is reminded that such a reaction would be quite out of place,
since the truth has long since been made apparent in the telling. The
practice of secondary ejaculation is inverted, in a display of nar-

ratorial composure: "qui fut étonné?—ce n'est ni moi ni vous, car vous et moi nous étions préparés de longue main à cette visite; ce fut d'Albert qui ne s'y attendait pas le moins du monde"[36] [Who was surprised? Not me or you, for we have been prepared for this visit. It was d'Albert, who was not expecting it in the least]. "Our" comfortable distance from the hero makes it possible to attend closely to his utterance of surprise—and presumably desire and pleasure—"Il fit un petit cri de surprise tenant le milieu entre oh! et ah! Cependant j'ai les meilleures raisons de croire qu'il tenait plus de ah! que de oh!" (408) ["He uttered a little cry of surprise situated about halfway between "Oh!" and "Ah!" Nonetheless, I have every reason to believe that it was more like an "Ah!" than an "Oh!"]. Not only is this *petit cri* at the opposite end of the scale from the shrieks of Gamiani or the bellowing of Gernande: the very fussiness with which it is described signifies irony, by leaving room for thoughtful attention to the exact phonetic qualities of the utterance. Such fine discrimination is foreign to, and subversive of, the discourse of spontaneous intensity.

Fin de siècle erotic narratives do not develop the poetics of inarticulacy to any degree, but they do heighten the thematic seriousness of exclamation by surrounding it with knowing medical discourse. Beyond Sade, beyond *Gamiani,* and sadly beyond irony, they tend to spell out the significance of erotic utterance as the revelation of sexual truth. *Le Roman de Violette* (1883) allows us to measure this thematic development with some precision, because it has so many other features in common with the most classical erotic fiction, as I showed in *Geometry in the Boudoir.*[37] There is a drawn out process of initiation in which the hero, a professor of medicine, supervises the sexual awakening of a beautiful child-woman who has come into his care by chance. He takes advantage of her infatuation with him in order to play the role of teacher and, eventually, of lover. For all its self-conscious gentleness, this process leads to an intense climax for Violette, and the climax is heard by a practiced, analytical ear. When the young woman cries out in pleasure, he hears the voice of the soul, hears the immanence of the soul in a bodily convulsion, and hears the true meaning of inarticulacy: "A partir de ce moment, ce ne fut plus de sa part que des cris inarticulés qui se terminèrent par un de [c]es longs spasmes où passe l'âme entière"[38] [From that moment onward, she produced only inarticulate cries that ended in one of those long spasms in which the soul is fully expressed]. The profound truth comes spilling out in an avowal of illness, fire, and death: "C'est de la rage! c'est du feu! . . . Oh! . . . Oh! . . . je meurs . . . prends mon âme . . . tiens . . ." (534) [It is rabies! It is fire! . . .

Oh! . . . Oh! . . . I'm dying . . . Take my soul . . . Here it is . . .]. The narrator-hero has waited patiently for this moment. He has prepared the climax by ensuring that his pupil is sufficiently mature to experience the fullness of pleasure, and to confess its fullness in the audible language of the psyche. Later in the novel, the hero displays the same alliance of voyeurism and medical know-how when he overhears two women at the height of their pleasure. Their words are said to be "unintelligible," but he listens carefully to the "muffled sighs" and the "râle d'amour" [rattle of love]. It is even possible for him to make out (*distinguer*) the name of a lover (578), for he hears all the key elements in what is uttered so breathlessly. The pleasure of women coincides perfectly with the intellectual satisfaction of the doctor hero as the revealing sounds come gushing out. Their well prepared and well-observed utterance makes pleasure and truth happen together.

Erotic narratives of the climactic kind do not just dramatize the utterance of pleasure: they confirm and indulge a particular form of knowledge that permits the confident recognition of symptoms. The symptoms in question are not to be thought of as transhistorical, for they vary considerably even across the eighteenth and nineteenth centuries. In the mid eighteenth century, there is pleasure to be had in reading the signs of desire-and-pleasure in others, whether as *vivacité, langueur,* or the movement between them. But when, from about the time of the Revolution, desire is understood and represented as accumulated energy, demanding to be released through discharge, the old codified marks no longer suffice. Recognizing desire and its promise of pleasure in mid eighteenth century fiction was a subtle art, if a somewhat stylized one, involving the reading of half elegant disorder. In contrast, many texts of revolutionary times affirm the task of recognition to be quite straightforward, although this apparent ease masks a fundamental difficulty—a difficulty aggravated, if not produced, by a newly constituted narrative order. Since the moment of pleasure is now taken to be the point about which meaning is organized, that moment must be quite distinctive. There must be no doubt that pleasure is occurring right at this time, as the decisive event. But then, the question can be asked, how is the climactic pleasure of women to be discerned with the requisite clarity and certainty?

Brantôme, in *Les Dames galantes* (1666), did not make a problem out of this. He simply marveled at the extraordinary things that women had been said to do at times of great pleasure, providing a remarkably varied list of eccentricities, rather than a coherent description of symptoms:

J'ai ouy dire et conter à plusieurs amans advanturiers et bien fortunés qu'ils ont veu plusieurs dames demeurer ainsy esvanouyes et pasmées estans en ces doux alteres de plaisir; mais assez aysement pourtant retournoient à soy-mesme; que plusieurs, quand elles sont là, elles s'escrient: "Hélas! je me meurs!" Je croy que ceste mort leur est tres-douce. Il y en a d'autres qui contournent les yeux en la teste pour telle delectation, comme si elles devoient mourir de la grande mort, et se laissans aller comme du tout immobiles et insensibles. D'autres ay-je ouy-dire qui roidissent et tendent si violemment leurs nerfs, arteres et membres, qu'ils en engendrent la goute-crampe; comme d'une que j'ay ouy dire, qu'y estoit si subjecte qu'elle n'y pouvoit remedier. D'autres font péter leurs os, comme si on leur rehabilloit de quelque rompure.[39]

[I have heard tell by some adventurous and successful lovers that they saw ladies faint and swoon in the sweet transformations of pleasure. But they came to quite easily after. Some, when they are in that state, exclaim, "Alas! I'm dying!" I believe that death to be a most pleasant one. Others roll their eyes and their heads about during pleasure, as if they were going to die a real death; they become quite still and unfeeling. I have heard of others who go rigid. Their nerves, arteries, and limbs are so taut that they cramp up completely. I have heard of one who was so given to this that she could do nothing to avoid it. Others have bones that crack, as if they were recovering from a fracture.]

Rather than telling a story, Brantôme is producing here a paradigmatic inventory whose very range is the main source of interest, and of descriptive pleasure, as in the earlier quote from Aretino. He is not seeking to identify the distinctive pleasure whose appearance will mark a narrative climax. Whatever he has to say about women's pleasure is marked by its extraordinary, perhaps even ludicrous, variety, but this old theme—*la donna è mobile*, even in this respect—will not serve the purpose of a strictly narrative eroticism of the kind that developed toward the end of the eighteenth century. These manifestations are too diverse, and too scattered. What is needed, so that climax can be seen to occur, is a well defined set of symptoms. Needing either to solve or deny this problem, texts of the late eighteenth century often do both of those things at once, by committing to a thematics that is radically opposed to the wondrous diversity evoked by Brantôme and Aretino. They regularly describe women's pleasure as if it were recognizably singular, corresponding in every particular to that of men.

Male desire is never more conveniently visible, nor more truly physiological, than when it manifests itself organically, as visible erection. Not for true republicans the mincing subtleties of libertine discernment: revolutionary eroticism responds best to the undenia-

ble evidence of an erect organ. Here is an example in which rustic
simplicity is itself endowed with erotic value, precisely for its directness: "Ce rustre frais et gaillard ne voyait point passer Claudinette
dans le village qu'aussitôt son vit se redressât. Ce symptôme est aussi
compréhensible pour un paysan que pour un citadin" (*Décrets des sens
sanctionnés par la volupté,* 1791)[40] [This green and hearty peasant
could not see Claudinette going by in the village without having his
prick immediately stand erect. That symptom is as comprehensible
to a peasant as it is to a city dweller]. A woman can question a man's
desire, and be given the most literally tangible response: "Bandes-tu
bien, mon amie? me dit-elle en appuyant sa bouche sur la mienne . . .
Pour toute réponse je pris sa main, que j'appuyai sur mon vit" (*L'Enfant du bordel,* 1800)[41] ["Are you nice and hard, my dear?" she asked
me, pressing her mouth to mine. My only response was to take hold
of her hand and place it on my dick]. With a symptom as clear as this,
there can be no doubt about the business of eroticism. There are, of
course, less rustic ways of making the point that are just as unequivocal. The "declaration" of the symptom can be described metaphorically, as in the following: "Alfonse s'enflamme à loisir. Une
sédition subite qui s'élève dans le pantalon l'oblige enfin à prendre
quelque arrangement qui puisse sauver les apparences. Cette
déclaration a été, dès le premier moment, saisie par la marquise, qui
en a pris une teinte animée dont l'effet est de la rendre d'une beauté
céleste" (*Les Aphrodites,* I:143) [Alfonse was alight. A sudden sedition
in his trousers required him to make some adjustment that might
save appearances. The declaration was grasped by the marquise from
the first, and her complexion became so bright as to create in her an
effect of celestial beauty]. "Grasping" the symptom—if I may be
allowed an appropriately crude pun—is a perfectly straightforward
thing. Even such euphemistic expressions as "désenchantement,"
whereby erection is characterized as the opposite of ensorceled impotence,[42] do little to reshape the theme, or even take away its directness: this is merely a polite way of referring to the same, singular,
forthright symptom of desire. If women are to be included in this
convenient thematic arrangement, however, and their sexuality seen
as leading from a similar strong beginning to a similar conclusion,
their physiology must be represented in such a way that their (supposedly singular) desire and pleasure is available for recognition in
the same way, at the same time, as men's.

Applying this rudimentary thematics to the bodies of women appears to twentieth-century eyes an imaginatively demanding task—
not to say a closely oppressive one.[43] Indeed, it is here that the
"truth" of late eighteenth century sexual knowledge appears intolera-

bly perverse to modern readers, for texts of this time seldom even recognize as problematic the assimilation of female body to male. The same discourse is simply used, and the same narrative economy worked out, for both sexes. A woman's desire is manifest in her erect clitoris, available for examination in a way that is parallel, if quantitatively inferior, to a man's. The heroine of *Le Rideau levé, ou L'Éducation de Laure* (1786) describes the state of male and female colleagues in exactly parallel ways: "Nous bandions tous encore, nos clitoris gonflés le démontraient aussi bien que la fermeté de leurs vits"[44] [We still had a hard-on. Our swollen clitorises showed that just as well as the firmness of their dicks].[51] The woman's desire is required to be demonstrable, for the sake of narrative, just as her pleasure must eventually come bursting forth, in the climactic discharge of female sperm.

This collapsing of sexual difference shocks modern commentators, for good reason, and may well have led many to a sense of historical estrangement. It is unfortunate, however, that the estrangement, and the critique, have often been focused exclusively on Sade, who is thus transformed from modernist hero into misogynist villain, in a way that further exaggerates the monumental, canonical status of his work. The attacks on Sade that I am about to quote are telling, coherent ones: they are merely lacking the historical dimension that might have come from acknowledging the extension of this discourse far beyond one author's work. Anne-Marie Dardigna expresses derision at Sade's representation of female pleasure, quoting some of Sade's favored utterances with exclamation marks of her own: "Certes, Juliette, Clairwil, la Dubois, la Durand, Charlotte et Olympe jouissent, mais c'est chaque fois à la manière des hommes: elles 'déchargent,' elles 'éjaculent!' "[45] [It is true that Juliette, Clairwil, Dubois, Durand, Charlotte, and Olympe experience pleasure, but they do so every time in the way that men do: they "unload," they "ejaculate!"]. Andrea Dworkin makes the same point succinctly when she says: "even in such a symptomatic detail as ejaculating sperm, which they all do—Sade's libertine women are men. They are, in fact, literary transvestites."[46] The only qualification I would wish to make in agreeing with Dworkin is that it is not "even" in such details, but precisely in such details, and in the thematic need for them, that transvestism is imposed. Pascal Bruckner and Alain Finkielkraut are more specific in relating the andromorphic semiotics of the female body to Sade's practice of climactic sexuality: "Les héroïnes qui sont citées en exemple . . . ne trouvent rien de mieux à faire, une fois parvenues à l'apogée de leur désir, que de décharger"[47] [The heroines who are held up to us as examples can only manage, when they have reached the apogee, to unload]. The fact is that there is no apogee of desire in narrative unless they are seen to discharge.

Sade, who is too often defended, is here too narrowly the focus of attack. In making him the bad guy, critics may fail to perceive the general nature of the problem. His systematic blindness to many specificities of the female body is not eccentric, but is well-supported discursively by the state of scientific knowledge at the time, as Richard Lewinsohn points out: "As late as the eighteenth century natural historians still wrote of a female semen which was emitted in coitus in the same way as the male."[48] Theories of "generation" in the eighteenth century were highly contested, and experimental evidence inconclusive, although it is doubtless the case that Sade's fictional use of scientific discourse was quite tendentious.[49] Uncertainty about what actually went on in coitus could, in any case, hardly satisfy the requirements of narrative eroticism. Accordingly, Sade, Restif, Mirabeau, and other erotic writers of the time can regularly be seen to affirm the sexuality of erection and discharge as the one true pattern of all desire and pleasure.

There is a powerfully convergent set of reasons, rational and irrational, technical and political, at work in defining these symptoms as those of female pleasure. If climactic pleasure is to function as avowal, it must display the truth of satisfied desire in utterly conclusive ways. In bringing about this moment, narrative will depend on a set of conventions whose very purpose is to deny their conventionality, and enforce their claim to corporeal immediacy. This, as Nancy Huston points out apropos of modern pornography, serves the unstated and unstatable purpose of denying the female body any possibility of withholding or counterfeiting its display: "si [les textes pornographiques destinés surtout aux hommes] insistent tant sur les signes extérieurs de ce plaisir (les cris, les yeux révulsés, les vagins inondés de 'foutre'), c'est justement parce qu'ils savent que, à la différence des hommes, les femmes peuvent feindre le plaisir"[50] [pornographic texts destined primarily for men insist so much on the external signs of pleasure (cries, eyes turned upward, vaginas full of "fuck") precisely because they know that, by contrast with men, women can fake pleasure]. Women may be stereotyped as capricious, but the intensity of pleasure must be such as to deny them room, at high moments, for any further coquettishness. They must be trapped in the radical immanence of their bodily truth. That they might still have room for mobility, for tactics, must be rendered unthinkable. Their silencing-and-confession is the routine achievement of climactic eroticism, from the late eighteenth century to twentieth-century pornography, and it is achieved all the better for not being made an

explicit aim.[51] Only very rarely is this furtive purpose even half acknowledged, as we shall see.

In "aristocratic" libertinism, it might have been acceptable for
desire and pleasure to be defined by convention, but the "natural"
eroticism of erection and ejaculation requires that its signs be the
undisputed outward symptoms of an inner truth. What climactic
eroticism needs and desires is proof. It finds this proof readily in the
bodies of men, and exacts it in kind from the bodies of women.
Ejaculated sperm gives rise to a moment of decision, not to say of
judgment: sperm is exhibit A, the substantive evidence of desire.
Indeed, at this time, the word *preuves* often serves as a distinguished
synonym for ejaculate. In *La Philosophie dans le boudoir*, Dolmancé
utters the following command: "il faut que le sein et le visage de votre
amie soient inondés des preuves de la virilité de votre frère; il faut
qu'il lui décharge ce qui s'appelle au nez" (III:456) [the breasts and
face of your friend must be drenched with the evidence of your
brother's virility. He must unload right in her face]. Ejaculating so
close to the woman compels her to attend to the demonstration. It
makes material contact coincide, in space and time, with the specta-
cle of pleasure. Insistently, this demonstration is performed right in
women's faces, and is just as often required from them in approximately symmetrical terms.

At another point in *La Philosophie dans le boudoir*, Dolmancé is con-
ducting a first lesson in sexual physiology for the benefit of his pupil
Eugénie: "Eh bien! tu le vois, Eugénie, après une pollution plus ou
moins longue, les glandes séminales se gonflent et finissent par exhaler une liqueur dont l'écoulement plonge la femme dans le trans-
port le plus délicieux. Cela s'appelle *décharger*" (III:401; original emphasis) [So you see, Eugénie, that after a more or less sustained
stimulation the seminal glands swell up and finally express a liquor
whose flow immerses the woman in the most delightful pleasure.
That is called *discharging*]. Eugénie does indeed see, in a didactic
environment, that this is how her pleasure happens, and what it is
called. As do Sade's admiring readers, who will presumably not fail to
see it again whenever it is demonstrated. They can certainly have the
satisfaction of seeing it repeatedly if they limit their attention to
erotic narrative. And it is still available for "direct" observation in *Les
Folies amoureuses d'une impératrice* (1865), where the clitoris is seen to
ejaculate in exquisite miniature: "Et tout à coup, de ce bouton
s'échappait un petit jet que mes lèvres recevaient avec ravissement,
comme la rose, le matin, est rafraîchie par la goutte de rosée . . ."[52]
[And suddenly, from this little knob, there came a tiny squirt that my
lips caught with delight, as the rose in the morning is refreshed by a

drop of dew]. This is proof positive of the woman's pleasure, delivered right under the man's nose. Mirabeau's *Hic-et-Haec* (1798) could not be more explicit, either in the demonstration or in the conclusion: "A ce mot, elle ferme les yeux, se roidit et, par la plus copieuse éjaculation, me prouve le plaisir qu'elle prenait"[53] [Hearing this, she closed her eyes, stiffened, and by the most copious ejaculation proved to me the pleasure she felt].

More modern pornographic texts, especially those of the twentieth century, have no doubt been inhibited in their demonstrations of female pleasure by the diffusion of biological notions that make such descriptions as these seem absurd, with the result that cries of pleasure, rather than material discharge, are often required to stand alone, in the climactic place, as the most decisive signs.[54] Bruckner and Finkielkraut discuss the way in which modern sexology claims to identify the orgasmic moment in the absence of clearly visible signs: "à faire entendre ce qui ne se voit pas, l'orgasme féminin accède, par un autre tour, à la lisibilité. Le bruit relaie l'image: au lieu d'émettre de la semence, la femme émet un signe; en tant qu'équivalent auditif de la décharge séminale, le cri permet le retour de la volupté féminine dans le bercail de la représentation"[55] [When that which cannot be seen is rendered audible, the female orgasm becomes readable. Sound supplants sight. Instead of emitting seed, the woman emits a sign. As an auditory equivalent of seminal discharge, the cry allows female pleasure to return to the fold of representation]. Late eighteenth-century erotic narrative was less constrained in both the visible and the audible representation of symptoms, as if to ensure that female pleasure would never slip away—Diderot's Mangogul would have said, *se dérober*—from the field of clearly perceptible and tellable phenomena. Vindication was to be had at those moments when proof came gushing forth as a mixture of cries and sperm. In *Le Rideau levé, ou L'Éducation de Laure* (1786), it happens just this way: "dans le même temps que nous mîmes à chercher le plaisir pour le savourer, Rose avait déjà ressenti quatre fois ses attraits; quatre fois ses élancements et ses transports, ses expressions: je me meurs, je décharge, nous en donnèrent des preuves certaines" (411) [While we were still setting about achieving our own pleasure, Rose had already experienced it four times. On four occasions her spurts and her delight, her expressions, "I'm dying," "I'm unloading," gave us certain proof of it].

Yet doubts can linger, despite the repeated affirmations, about the confessional nature of such ejaculations. There is a slight wavering in Restif's narrator when, in *L'Anti-Justine* (1798), he describes a woman's swoon. This ought to have been a drastic symptom of pleasure, but Cupidonnet somehow feels obliged to allow that what he has seen may not be entirely conclusive: "Pour Madeleine Linguet, elle déchargea sans doute car elle se pâma" (294) [As for Madeleine Linguet, she must have discharged, because she swooned]. Perhaps she is faking it; perhaps she has swooned out of distress. The narrator's *sans doute* can only be the mark of hopeful interpretation: it reveals just the kind of doubt that demonstrative symptoms ought to preempt. The same uncertainty is forthrightly admitted by the narrator of Nerciat's *Le Diable au corps,* who apostrophizes a whole class of women in this way: "Comédiennes de Paphos, vous frémissez quelquefois, vous vous disloquez, vous haletez, jurez, mordez: tout cela le plus habilement du monde; et, si nous avons la foi, nous devons supposer que vous avez un plaisir invincible . . ." (IV:73) [Actresses of Paphos, sometimes you groan, you thrash about, you pant, swear, and bite. All that you do most skillfully. And if we have faith, we must believe that you experience invincible pleasure]. Do "we" have faith, in fact? Maintaining confidence in the reality of women's pleasure when it is performed in stories, despite an awareness of feminine deceptive skills, enacting the certainty of climax in the midst of haunting fears or worldly scepticism: this is one of the self-appointed tasks of male-centered erotic narrative. Whatever certainty is gained here is only a local, short-term victory over its opposite. Surprisingly often, one finds in the midst of a story the grudging recognition that the symptoms of feminine pleasure require interpretation, and that this interpretation is based on a particular hypothesis: "soit que Fanny éprouvât réellement un grand plaisir, soit qu'elle n'en fît que le semblant, elle manifesta certainement, par ses paroles et par ses actes, la plus extrême félicité" (*Les Amours d'un gentleman,* 1889) [either because Fanny really felt great pleasure or because she only pretended to, she certainly demonstrated, by her words and actions, the most perfect happiness]. All that is "certain" here is that there is a recognizable display: nothing guarantees its truly symptomatic nature, despite a century of thematic insistence.

Erotic narrative is not generally able to ignore or bracket out women's pleasure, despite Sade's occasional call for this to be done.[57] In that sense, contrary to a commonplace of popular feminism, it does not just "treat women as objects," since it exacts from them the marks of a particular subjectivity. In fact, to take it one step further, this kind of story is less concerned ultimately with the precise quality of response than with the directness and reliability of its occurrence. Sade's Saint-Fond appears not to have been entirely convinced by the ostensibly conclusive displays of pleasure performed so often in his presence, for we find him alluding blackly to his doubt about what is really going on inside the women he deals with. He seems to have solved the problem in ways that Restif's, Mirabeau's, or Nerciat's heroes would not consider, by giving up any attempt to provoke expressions of pleasure, and seeking to draw out other signs that can be read with greater certainty as true symptoms: "je ne me soucie pas trop de voir les impressions du plaisir sur le visage d'une femme, elles sont si douteuses; je préfère celles de la douleur, on s'y trompe moins" (*Histoire de Juliette*, VIII:388) [I am not particularly interested in seeing marks of pleasure on a woman's face. They are too uncertain. I prefer those of pain. They are less likely to deceive]. If pleasure is to give way to pain, he says, so much the better. The real point of the action is not to serve women in any way, but to provoke a crisis that leads to the unmediated utterance of bodily truth.

I have already observed that fin de siècle writing adds little to the poetics of exclamation, although it does contribute to the high thematic seriousness of erotic utterance by surrounding it with medical discourse. Fiction of that time is also able, for this very reason, to exploit the approximate coincidence of pleasure and pain by affirming the dialectical relation of the two, and hearing the desperate cry as the echo of both at once. In *Les Cousines de la colonelle* (1880), such a sound is heard, and its significance spelled out:

> Tout à coup un cri, aussitôt réprimé, s'échappa de sa poitrine et se fondit en un soupir étouffé.
> — Ah! je souffre avec bonheur! Ah! mon bien-aimé, ah! ah! c'est le ciel . . . je suis morte, je . . .[58]

> [Suddenly a cry, immediately stifled, burst from her breast and melted into a muffled sigh.
> "Ah! I am in agony with happiness! Ah! My beloved. Ah! Ah! This is heaven . . . I am dead, I . . .]

Suffering pleasurably and finding pain in the heart of pleasure is the summum of narrative experience, and leads to the ultimate vocalization of sexuality. In fact, it produces climactic utterance as the voice of death: *le râle*, the death rattle. In *Demi-volupté* (1897), we hear "le souffle rauque de la volupté" [the hoarse voice of pleasure] as it exhales, not just the standard exclamation, "je meurs," [I am dying], already present in Crébillon, but a narrower articulation of death and eroticism, a passionate longing for death-in-pleasure: "Oh! mourir ainsi! . . ."[59] [Oh! To die like this! . . .]. The ultimate exclamation—in both senses of the word "ultimate"—becomes thus the outcome of the requirement that pleasure and pain be conclusively spoken: *le râle* is as frequent in erotic narrative of the late nineteenth century as the sigh was in the middle of the eighteenth. Its extreme nature, the fact that it stands at the threshold of death, serves as a guarantee of truth, as if the death rattle were too intense to be simulated: "Des sanglots et des râles sortent de la gorge . . . le cœur bat dans la poitrine, il bat à briser ses ressorts puissants; les jambes tremblent, usées par l'effort trop grand; la bête se meurt, la bête râle, la bête étouffe, et c'est dans une apothéose"[60] [Sobs and rattles came from her throat. Her heart beat in her breast, fit to break its powerful springs. Her legs trembled, exhausted by an effort that was beyond them. The beast was dying, the beast was in its death rattle, the beast was unable to breathe, and this was its apotheosis]. Yet nothing can ensure that *le râle* will count as definitive: nothing can prevent its becoming part of narrative and thematic routine. It cannot be so extreme, nor so decisive, as to be any more (or less) than a conventional representation, happily nestled in clichéd phrases such as the following: "le corps secoué d'un frisson de désir, elle râlait"[61] [her body was wracked by a shiver of desire, as she gave out a death rattle]. Even the theme of death cannot guarantee deadly accuracy in the representation of feminine pleasure.

The key thing, and the conventionally "certain" mark of climax, is not that the woman should experience any specific quality of feeling, but that she should cry out in extremis, and that her cry should count as confession of, and coincidence with, her bodily nature. Sophie's husband, in *Méphistophéla* (1890), knows that this is the narrative model for a successful wedding night, even as he fails to make it happen: "il obligea la vierge à subir l'intromission triomphale de l'époux. Elle ne proféra pas un soupir, n'eut pas une seule plainte. . . . Sa victoire ne s'achèverait que dans l'aveu de la défaite! Mais pas même en un cri d'horreur, pas même en un sanglot, cet aveu, il ne l'obtenait!"[62] [he obliged the virgin to submit to the triumphal entry of her husband. She did not utter a sigh, not even a single complaint. His victory would only be complete when she confessed defeat! But not in the form of a cry of horror nor even of a sob did he obtain that confession!]. It is not enough, for the male's dramatic purpose, that "intromission" should occur, however triumphantly: the proper conclusion will only be reached when his wife is provoked, by a kind of rough symmetry, to a cry of avowal. Even were this to occur, however,[63] there is likely to be doubt as to whether the utterance called forth is really the substance of truth. The whole procedure is in fact disturbed by its own close circularity, and troubled by self-defeating irony. Truth may be no more than a thematic convenience, and the language of compulsive pleasure no more than the well-disciplined sound of compulsory satisfaction, produced on cue.

From Crébillon and Diderot to the fin de siècle, there are no great rifts in the the history of exclamation, merely a long process of compaction whereby utterances that were already present in erotic fiction came to be more fully owned and integrated. The exclamation was not invented, or eventfully rediscovered, during those one hundred and fifty years. It merely gained some poetic elaboration, and took on much greater thematic density. It became in fact a privileged mark of bodily pleasure-and-pain, taking its place in the heart of narrative as a sign of expressive climax.

NOTES

After the first full citation of these novels, subsequent page references will be given in the text. All translations are my own.

1. Michel Foucault, *Histoire de la sexualité*, vol. I, *La Volonté de savoir* (Paris: Gallimard, 1976), 101.

2. Denis Diderot, *Les Bijoux indiscrets* (Paris: Garnier-Flammarion, 1968), 126.

3. Crébillon fils, *La Nuit et le moment*, in *Œuvres complètes* (Geneva: Slatkine Reprints, 1968), IX:64.

4. Gustave Colline, preface to *Le Roman de mon alcôve: Confessions galantes d'une femme du monde* (Paris: À l'enseigne du musée secret, c. 1935), 6.

5. Pietro Aretino, *Les Ragionamenti, ou Dialogues du divin Pietro Aretino*, trans. Alcide Bonneau (Paris: I. Lisieux, 1882), I:57.

6. Anon., *Vénus dans le cloître, ou La Religieuse en chemise* (Paris: Lattès, 1979), 122.

7. Jean-Baptiste Louvet de Couvray, *Les Amours du chevalier de Faublas* (Paris: Chez les marchands de nouveautés, c. 1910), I:239–40.

8. Charles Pinot Duclos, *Acajou et Zirphile*, in *Contes parodiques et licencieux du XVIIIᵉ siècle*, ed. Raymonde Robert (Nancy: Presses Universitaires de Nancy, 1987), 42–43.

9. Marie-Antoinette Fagnan, *Kanor*, in *Contes parodiques et licencieux*, 127.

10. D'Argens, *Les Nonnes galantes* (Paris: Librairie anti-cléricale, n.d.), 24.

11. Théophile Gautier, *La Morte amoureuse*, in *La France frénétique de 1830*, ed. Jean-Luc Steinmetz (Paris: Phébus, 1978), 487.

12. Andréa de Nerciat, *Les Aphrodites, ou Fragments thali-priapiques pour servir à l'histoire du plaisir* (n.p., 1925), I:41. See also Anon., *Les Libertines du grand monde* (au Palais-Royal, Chez la petite Lolotte, 1890 [1880]), 55: "he inserted his great thing into me and gave me more pleasure, sometimes so great that it made our assholes blow like clarinets." Janet Beizer, *Ventriloquized Bodies: Narratives of Hysteria in Nineteenth-Century France* (Ithaca: Cornell University Press, 1994), 45, observes that metaphoric connections between the voicebox/throat/neck and vagina/uterus/cervix are retained from antiquity well into the nineteenth century.

13. Anon., *La Nouvelle Académie des dames* (A Cythère: n.p., 1774), 77–78.

14. Michel Camus, "Les Paradoxes du discours amoureux," in *Œuvres anonymes du XVIIIᵉ siècle III, L'Enfer de la Bibliothèque Nationale V* (Paris: Fayard, 1986), 194–95.

15. Jean Marie Goulemot, preface to *La Messaline française*, in *L'Enfer de la Bibliothèque Nationale V*, 290–91.

16. Andréa de Nerciat, *Le Diable au corps* (n.p., 1803), IV:30. Original emphasis.

17. G.-C.-A. Pigault-Lebrun, *La Folie espagnole* (Paris: P. Arnould, 1889), 17–18.

18. Ernest La Jeunesse, *Demi-volupté* (Paris: Offenstadt, 1900), 211–12.

19. René Saint-Médard, *L'Orgie moderne* (Paris: Bibliothèque du fin du siècle, 1905), 120.

20. Crébillon fils, *Tableaux des mœurs du temps dans les différents âges de la vie* (Paris: Lattès, 1980), 224.

21. Anon., *Le Triomphe des religieuses, ou Les Nones babillardes*, in *L'Enfer de la Bibliothèque Nationale V*, 225.

22. Restif de la Bretonne, *L'Anti-Justine*, in *Œuvres érotiques* (Paris: Fayard, 1985), 364.

23. Anon., *Lettres galantes et philosophiques de deux nones*, in *L'Enfer de la Bibliothèque Nationale V*, 244.

24. Jean-Charles Gervaise de Latouche, *Histoire de dom Bougre, portier des Chartreux*, in *L'Enfer de la Bibliothèque Nationale III* (Paris: Fayard, 1985), 36.

25. Anon., *Amélie, ou Les Ecarts de ma jeunesse* (Brussels: Gay et Doucé, 1882), 131. The date of first publication of this novel is not known to me. It must belong in the period 1770–1790.

26. Anon., *Vénus en rut*, in *L'Enfer de la Bibliothèque Nationale VI* (Paris: Fayard, 1988), 122.

27. Félix Nogaret, *L'Arétin français, suivi des Epices de Vénus*, ed. Louis Perceau (Versailles: Aux dépens des fermiers généraux, n.d.), 23.

28. When Mme Rastard asks whether her disguise as a male is convincing, Mme Dodo replies: "My word, Madame! Looking like that, all you would need would be to say 'foutre!' and everyone would be fooled" (Crébillon fils, *Tableaux des mœurs*, 224).

29. See also Nerciat, *Les Aphrodites*, I:189: "Madame de Vaquifout was beneath the illustrious Boutavant, who was able to make her open her eyes twice and give out at the last moment a *foutre!* that echoed throughout the space." Original emphasis.

30. Cf. Marcel Hénaff, *Sade: L'Invention du corps libertin* (Paris: P.U.F., 1978), 91–92: "the cry is the presymbolic use of the voice, the voice before it is taken over by language, the voice that escapes from the body or is extorted from it in the same way as other secretions: fuck, shit, farts, blood. It is voice reduced to material flux."

31. Sade, *Œuvres complètes*, ed. Annie Le Brun and Jean-Jacques Pauvert (Paris: Pauvert, 1986–87), VI:268. Subsequent references to this edition are given in brackets in the text.

32. Jane Gallop, in *Thinking through the Body* (New York: Columbia University Press, 1988), 18, observes that "the connection between these two productions of bodily fluids—tears and arousal—points to a similarity between the sentimental (coded as feminine) and the pornographic (coded as masculine). In Sade, the difference between libertines and victims is that, in one situation, libertines get aroused whereas victims cry."

33. Alfred de Musset, *Gamiani, ou Deux nuits d'excès*, in *L'Erotisme romantique*, ed. Jean-Jacques Pauvert (Paris: Carrere, 1984), 114.

34. Anon., *Thérèse philosophe* (Geneva: Slatkine, 1981), II:24–25.

35. This is what Georges Bataille does when he imagines the force of Sade's personal bellowing as an extension of his characters': "Rose Keller, in official testimony, spoke of the abominable cries that pleasure drew from him. This feature at least makes him like Blangis. I do not know whether it is legitimate, when speaking of such frenzy, to speak simply of pleasure. At a certain level, excess takes us beyond common feelings" (*La Littérature et le mal* [Paris: Gallimard, 1967], 139–40).

36. Théophile Gautier, *Mademoiselle de Maupin* (Paris: Charpentier, 1919), 408.

37. See Peter Cryle, *Geometry in the Boudoir* (Ithaca: Cornell University Press, 1994), 9–10 and 30–31.

38. Anon., *Le Roman de Violette*, in *L'Érotisme au dix-neuvième siècle*, ed. Alexandrian (Paris: J.-C. Lattès, 1993), 524.

39. Brantôme, *Les Dames galantes*, ed. Maurice Rat (Paris: Garnier, 1965), 324–25.

40. Anon., *Décrets des sens sanctionnés par la volupté*, in *L'Enfer de la Bibliothèque Nationale VI*, 335.

41. Anon., *L'Enfant du bordel*, in *L'Érotisme au dix-neuvième siècle*, 68. See also Nerciat, *Le Diable au corps*, V:93, where the comtesse asks a similar question and receives the reply, "Have no doubt of it . . ." "And I felt at the same time," she relates, "that he was pressing against my hand something that declared the most ebullient desire."

42. See for example Andréa de Nerciat, *Félicia, ou mes fredaines* (Paris: Livre de Poche Hachette, 1976), 132.

43. Linda Williams, in her fine book, *Hard Core: Power, Pleasure, and the Frenzy of the Visible* (Berkeley: University of California Press, 1989), points to a comparable problem that arises in another domain, the medium of pornographic cinema. She refers to "hard core's utopian project of offering visual proof of authentic and involuntary spasms of pleasure" (147). A particular problem is posed by the "invisible place" of female pleasure (49), and this tends to be dealt with by "argu[ing] for the fundamental sameness of male and female pleasure" (50). Williams adds that "the articulate and inarticulate sounds of pleasure that dominate in aural hard core are primarily the cries of women" (123).

44. Mirabeau, *Le Rideau levé, ou L'Éducation de Laure*, in *Œuvres érotiques* (Paris: Fayard, 1984), 411.

45. Anne-Marie Dardigna, *Les Châteaux d'Eros, ou Les Infortunes du sexe des femmes* (Paris: Maspero, 1980), 37.

46. Andrea Dworkin, *Pornography: Men Possessing Women* (London: Women's Press, 1981), 95. A similar critique is formulated in Nancy Huston, *Mosaïque de la pornographie* (Paris: Denoël/Gonthier, 1982), 63: "No author illustrates better than Sade that [poverty of the vocabulary of female pleasure]: his libertine heroines screw and talk exactly like libertine heroes. They all say that they have 'hard ons' and 'unload,' preferably while torturing other women."

47. Pascal Bruckner and Alain Finkielkraut, *Le Nouveau Désordre amoureux* (Paris: Seuil, 1977), 71.

48. Richard Lewinsohn, *A History of Sexual Customs*, trans. Alexander Mayce (New York: Harper, 1958), 197. For a more recent analysis, see Thomas Laqueur, *Making Sex: Body and Gender from the Greeks to Freud* (Cambridge, Mass.: Harvard University Press, 1990).

49. On this question, see Lucienne Frappier-Mazur, *Sade et l'écriture de l'orgie* (Paris: Nathan, 1991), 48–59, and the unpublished thesis of Jeremy Horwood, "Sade et la génération" (B.A. Honours, University of Queensland, 1994). Cf. Jean Mainil, *Dans les règles du plaisir. . . . Théorie de la différence dans le discours obscène, romanesque et médical de l'Ancien Régime* (Paris: Kimé, 1996), 19: "What people have taken as a provocation on Sade's part was only the translation (admittedly exaggerated in quantity) of a *scientific truth* that was still widespread at the beginning of the nineteenth century." Original emphasis.

50. Huston, *Mosaïque de la pornographie*, 84.

51. My insistence, following Foucault, on the subjective discipline of confession makes me reluctant to accept Janet Beizer's metaphor of ventriloquism, of which she says: "I intend it as a metaphor to evoke the narrative process whereby a woman's speech is repressed in order to be expressed as inarticulate body language, which

must then be dubbed by a male narrator" (*Ventriloquized Bodies*, 9). I am concerned to show, in the context of erotic fiction, that it is not possible to identify separate phases of repression, forced silence, and dubbed expression. An exclamatory discipline, as a particular fictional form of Foucault's *dispositif de sexualité*, exacts certain types of expression, and claims that they come from the woman's soul.

52. Anon., *Les Folies amoureuses d'une impératrice*, in *L'Érotisme Second Empire*, ed. Jean-Jacques Pauvert (Paris: Carrere, 1985), 26.

53. Mirabeau, *Hic-et-Haec*, in *Œuvres érotiques* (Paris: Fayard, 1984), 209.

54. See Stephen Heath, *Questions of Cinema* (Bloomington: Indiana University Press, 1981), on the attempts made by pornographic cinema to deal with "the immense and catastrophic problem of the invisibility or not of pleasure. Such films use a whole gamut of pants and cries . . . to guarantee the accomplishment of pleasure" (189).

55. Bruckner and Finkielkraut, *Le Nouveau Désordre amoureux*, 81.

56. Anon., *Les Amours d'un gentleman* (Brussels: Schmidt, 1895), 57–58.

57. See Sade, *La Philosophie dans le boudoir*, in *Œuvres complètes*, III:542.

58. Anon., *Les Cousines de la colonelle* (Lisbon: da Boa-Vista, [1880]), 64–65.

59. Jane de la Vaudère, *Les Demi-sexes* (Paris: Ollendorff, 1897), 237.

60. Victorien du Saussay, *Chairs épanouies, beautés ardentes* (Paris: Méricant, 1902), 65.

61. Jean de Merlin, *La Luxure* (Paris: Bibliothèque du fin du siècle, 1905), 152.

62. Catulle Mendès, *Méphistophéla* (Paris: Dentu, 1890), 120–21.

63. In Mendès' story, it does not ever do so, because Sophie's energies are directed toward the love of other women. It is she who will later provoke from her lover Céphise the avowal of happy death (*Méphistophéla*, 446).

Textual Sex

ROSEMARY SORENSEN

Way up there near the roof of Godown No.1, Aurora da Gama at the age of fifteen lay back on pepper sacks, breathed in the hot spice-laden air, and waited for Abraham. He came to her as a man goes to his doom, trembling but resolute, and it is around here that my words run out, so you will not learn from me the bloody details of what happened when she, and then he, and then they, and after that she, and at which he, and in response to that she, and with that, and in addition, and for a while, and then for a long time, and quietly, and noisily, and at the end of their endurance, and at last, and after that, until . . . phew! boy! Over and done with!—No. There's more. The whole thing must be told.

SALMAN RUSHDIE'S ELLIPTICAL DESCRIPTION OF THE COPULATION that led to his narrator's birth in *The Moor's Last Sigh*[1] is one way of tapping into narrative desire. "It is around here that my words run out," says Moraes Zogoiby, and hands over the story to the narratee, who knows exactly which kinds of words are missing, but nevertheless feels shortchanged in the exchange. The pleasure of withheld pleasure is one that is understood by all readers and the reference is only occasionally confined to the specific pleasure of orgasm. There is always more, as Zogoiby admits with mock integrity: but as for telling the "whole thing," what kind of contract is this, and is it one that can be fulfilled?

In her essay "Narrative and the Gender Trap," Marie Maclean[2] sets the scene for my exploration here. She shows how narratives set up traps that appear to invite one reading, and then offer or enforce another kind. She makes the point that "our century is encouraging, on an unprecedented scale, new reversals" (82) and that feminism has made us aware that "we read from an ideologically and socially constructed position" (83). The extending beyond traditional audiences of the invitation to read about a specific form of desire and performance—sex—provides an exemplary focus for a discussion about how gendered narratives work in specific instances. With a characteristically ironic flourish, Marie Maclean ends her essay with this challenge: "In our new world of equal opportunity, the key of

134

Bluebeard's chamber is now available to both sexes" (83). We can talk about desire in language, and about textual seduction, skirting around sex as part of a larger process of the desiring being, which will always intersect and blur with investigations into narrative sex—the physical act described and evoked in stories. While the reversals are evident, and indeed encouraging, my premise here is that these reversals are taking place inside a chamber, as Marie Maclean suggested, and while handing out copies of the key is at least encouraging variations on the way the door is unlocked and on what goes on inside, how often, and with whom, the chamber cannot be other than what it is: a closed space. Textual sex is a limited act, so limited, in fact, that it might be impossible. It tries to happen with tenacious application, and there's plenty of evidence of it happening more and more frequently. It is even meant to happen now in traditionally chaste (salaciously coy) romances, where, of course, it has always happened, but off the page. And it is meant to happen in just about every story that is categorized as best-seller, and this indicates the first and most obvious thing that can be said about the implied readers of textual sex: they want it, and want it bad. And they want it coded: variations on the act that are a conventional blend of concrete and metaphorical images, from a masculinized perspective (which is to say, from the perspective of a desiring ego focused on an achievable, finite, but renewable desire).

How women readers are masculinized in postfeminist texts is, in part, the impetus for this exploration of sexual texts. And why there are so many pages of strained, cliché-ridden writing published to fulfil our apparent desire for sex in texts is another part. In an age that talks endlessly about good sex and bad, I am interested in what sex is doing in texts, and to whom.

My comment about best-seller sex does not hide a literary judgment. And I do not want to get into the contested area where the difference is between erotica (written by someone clever who wants to write art) and pornography (written by someone exploitative who wants to make money). Nevertheless, that the styles of sex described in a narrative conform to the styles of reading implied in the style of writing is an observation about textual classification, and textual classification comes with a weighty baggage of judgment, both literary and moral. How does a text that describes copulation, say, turn into a work of art, and why is a work of art judged differently in terms of its social and moral content? It is easy to show how pulp fiction relies on one set of rules and fashions, while the literary end of the reading list has other rules, the breaking of which is part of "literariness." This naming convention is a critical shortcut, and even though it periodi-

cally undergoes challenges to its authority, it acts as a sorting mechanism in a field that is becoming more and more crowded. And yet, in
the case of sex texts, this mechanism has resulted in an uneasiness
among some readers, who find that their reaction to the sleazy mean-
street sex (all grunts and gasps and organ-focused orgasm, with a
touch or more of violence according to the rules of the genre) is
much the same as their reaction to the arty violence of the surrealists,
or the post-surrealist nastiness of a Philip Roth. The word misogyny is
one of the shortcuts to describing what elicits this response, but in
both cases it is refuted within the very structure it is responding to.
The misogyny of the sleaze is, apparently, generic, stylized into the
narrative, and a reader understands, apparently, that this is not real
life. In the case of the high-lit sex, the sex is part of the narrator's self-
annihilation, the author's exploration of the dark side of desire, an
exposé of social rituals through a text that literalizes the metaphor of
desire—apparently. In both cases, the reader is required not only to
take a seat at a performance that is textually intimate and extraor-
dinarily focused (what other "scenes" in narrative have the need to
stay on and in skin like a sex scene?), but also to sit in a certain way:
there is, apparently, a wrong way to sit through a sex scene.

All these implied rules about the sexual text and the reader lead
me to suggest that textual sex is essentially bullying, but its bullying is
disguised. A narrator who describes his own or others' desire brought
to the surface of the body as sexual stimulation and fulfilment is a
narrator who is making a gesture of invitation to intimacy, a conventionally mono-gendered invitation. A text that signals itself as "the
confessions of" is signaling that you are going to hear things that
would shock "most people" but your reading the book initiates you
into a club, the club of intimates, the experienced. The privileged.

Reading sex is a reading contract that depends on a number of
restrictive clauses. A good example of the strength of our understanding of this pact is the reaction to Bret Easton Ellis's *American
Psycho,* which some feminists refused to read because they did not
want to be degraded by such descriptions of perverted, sadistic sex,
and masculinists refused to accept because the descriptions of sex
did not reconfirm their status as members of a desirable group.
Reading sex, the group member reaffirms his own sexual potency,
even when the sex is "bad," as in rape or degrading perversion. The
group member shows through reading that he knows about this, that
he is able to distinguish between the reality of sex and the fantasy of
sex. And since any sexual fantasy represents a strong, well-developed,
lusty, masculinized psyche, then even the bad sex is good. That I like
reading about sex is a sign that I like sex, and this means I am a

powerful male (and more recently, also a female with attitude, which is to say a post-feminist female). But what happens when the central character takes this affirmation beyond the artificial barrier that is masculine self-assurance of the primacy of sex? Where did Easton Ellis's text go that was "too far"? It went to the center of the myth itself, and it didn't refuse it, but made it manifest.

The descriptions of "sex" in *American Psycho* are the continuation of any number of pornographic narratives, from Sade to the magazine you buy wrapped in plastic at your newsagent. It makes men violent, cried the critics, it gives them ideas of how to force rats into vaginas and decapitate tramps. The absurd logic behind the complaints is that if you describe a scene of sadomasochistic sex and keep the chamber door closed, the reader knows that there is a place for these things, and the socialized human being (the reader) conforms to this truth by keeping both his reading and his violence inside the chamber. Easton Ellis broke the rules and said that the chamber was New York, and that when the reader is mad or desocialized, then the narrative keeps going out there.

The reader's position in *American Psycho,* vis-à-vis the central character and his violent sexual acts, is not complicit: in contrast to the swagger of Bataille's male narrator in *Blue of Noon,*[3] for example, Ellis's psychopath is uninterested in either teasing or pandering to, involving or coercing, or even impressing the reader—he is self-impressed, self-involved, and unable to find his reflection in anything but his own desire. The text makes the words conform to the codes of pornography (I looked at her, she did this to me, we made these noises, then this bit attracted my attention, this was happening, and then I came . . .) with the usual variations also conforming to the rules. But then the code goes all wrong, because the psychopathic sex (which means violent and unlimited except by annihilation of the object of desire) respects no limits. The group has let in a bad seed.

American Psycho is a telling exception to a rule that says sex in texts is socially acceptable, and indeed even desirable as a kind of therapy. The old belief that a masculine desire for sexual gratification can be both pandered to and assisted by representations of the sexual act has received a boost with the inclusion of women in the equation. But the belief has had the effect of either making sex in texts an inappropriate or trivial topic for analysis, or one that always develops into a discussion of desire as metaphysical, rather than physical. Sex in texts is protected from scrutiny, more often than not, because it is both beneath and above it. And it is still a common line of defense in literary criticism to attack those readers who claim such writing is uninteresting as being textual puritans whose bodies inhibit them not only in their ability to read but also in their ability to go out into the world and pleasure themselves to death, very metaphorically speaking. Sex texts are peculiarly open to becoming less texts that give information about the narrator, about writing or about the author, about society, or about any other thing at all, and to occupying a peculiar place in the modern reading universe: they tend to become all coded information about the reader. And this provides remarkable latitude for the writer to write very badly indeed.

New stories (new ways of telling) about sexual desire are uncommon. What is new is that the options for point of view and the conventions of the telling have expanded to account for the wider range of readership. Whereas Sade was for leisured males, erotica is now aimed at educated females, and the men enjoy as always a privileged position as empowered voyeur. If it weren't for the fact that critics who want to position themselves within popular culture, to rub shoulders with the real as created by mass imagery, approve of and find useful erotica written by women, many stories claimed to be feminist would sit without much bother among the traditionally masculinist model, where sperm is the holy grail and the hero's quest is a story of seeking, losing, struggling, and finally achieving climax.

The paragraph quoted above from Salman Rushdie's *Moor's Last Sigh* is a variation on the theme, using the technique of creating gaps easily filled by the reader to enjoy the joke: we all know exactly how much the telling of desire and its sexual appeasement is contained by the language available for its telling. It relies on our knowing other such narratives, and this is both its strength and its limitation. To describe copulation or any form of genital stimulation, or, if you like, any erogenous pleasure, the text is bounded by the mimetic function. Easton Ellis is a good example of a text that has minimum metaphoric function, except for the codified description of the body's sexual parts: "The two girls are facing each other—Sabrina's fucking my cock, Christie's sitting on my face—and Sabrina leans in to suck and finger Christie's small, firm, full tits. Then Christie starts French-kissing Sabrina hard on the mouth as I continue to eat her out, my mouth and chin and jaw covered with her juices, which momentarily dry, then are replaced by others."[4] The use of metaphor would expand the space, allowing the pleasure or other reactions to the sexual activity to be described more fully. Also in terms of content, the limited interest lies in a small range of variations: of characters, settings, and props. And so the color, shape, and size of the characters vary, or the narrator can increase the numbers of persons or animals or things or whatever involved in the quest for orgasm, endlessly varying the setting, the duration of the act, the accoutrements (fruit and veg is not only organically sound at the moment but also increases the options for colorific metaphor), and then, more challenging, the scope of pleasure.

Describing sexual activity in detail does not necessarily increase the possibility that the desire that prompted and supported the activity will be communicated to or understood by the reader. In fact, it would appear that it can prejudice this possibility. To put that in another way, a cookbook may make you want to go and bake a cake, but it gives you no insight into the relationship between body and mind within which appetites are constructed. Furthermore, a recipe for the preparation of a dish of offal is unlikely to make a vegetarian's mouth water. And a recipe for any extravagant or complicated dish will contain very little that communicates to readers the pleasure that they may experience when they eat it. A recipe relies on the reader's previous experience of satisfaction. A sex text works in a similar way, and yet it differs significantly.

Textual sex is predominantly constructed on conventions that presuppose a learned response from the reader. In other words, textual sex relies on a prescriptive code. But in contrast to the recipe for oral or digestive satisfaction, the recipe for sexual satisfaction presupposes not the experience but an imagining, since pornography is often fantastical in ways that, if enacted, would not lead to the kind of pleasure that the text itself offers. Text sex supplants the real thing. This is a big and difficult territory, and I am not suggesting that pleasures are not given and received à la Sade or à la Bataille or à la Masoch. There are plenty of accounts that prove otherwise (although there's the rub: the accounts are themselves sex texts). However, and briefly put, the text is able to fantasize in ways that bodies cannot enact: a page of Sade makes this clear. My point is not to say whether or not textual sex is accurate of the desire of human beings, but that it works ahead of the desire—it is provocative—rather than following that desire with a retro-description that reenacts the pleasure.

The role of the code in romance is clear. The humor in Rushdie's truncated "he did, then she did, then they both, and so on" of sexual intercourse is partly due to the familiarity of such descriptions. His narrator promises and then withdraws, as well as any romantic teaser, but what he adds is the guileless confession that he knows what he's doing, and we must forgive him for his inability to be more "honest." The narrator is a seducer, tantalizing the reader: in romance narratives and their less elliptical relations, sex narratives, the desire that is being manipulated is directly linked to sexual desire, so that the reader's desire is enacted, made visible, in the narrative.

It is in response to the restrictive codes of descriptive sex narrative

that writing about desire is replaced by a writing that attempts to be
desire. The pleasure of the text is that elusive power that cannot find
the words to describe it—or can it? What often happens with writing
that sets out to explore desire, and to manifest desire inside a narrative, to have words operate directly on the desiring body (rendering
the rational body secondary, the process of thinking about desire
secondary to the process of feeling that desire), is that the text
describes desire, even when there may be an attempt to mimic the
processes of desire on the body. The following example, from a novel
by Mary Fallon, *Working Hot,* shows how the project to "represent
sexuality in women's lives" may result in syntactical dissolution, as
though to approximate the physical and emotional dissolution of an
individual consciousness that is experienced in sex:

> . . . by lavishing love tongue fingers gentleness palm teeth
> suction chewing affection care delight stroking to the
> clitoris labia anus vagina (and don't forget the bush-walk
> between Lake Vagin and Lake Anus) by doing this
> deliberately and to delight and excess the petite venus (as
> I affectionately call it) forgets its pain and deprivation
> directly and when this is achieved there is no more call
> for the soul (the soul as we know being the gladbag as it
> were for all our unfulfilled desires everything we can't
> have) of course this technique must not be applied every
> time or when one is not in the mood
> thus the soul is sucked into the waiting mouth of the
> lover and digested . . .[5]

Elizabeth Grosz says that this is "strong and sensual writing," in which
the "rhythms follow those of lovemaking."[6] Such has been the aim of
sex texts that profited from the valorization that psychoanalysis gave
to psychic "freedom," to the sloughing off of repression and the
exploration of the unconscious, where secrets of desire had been
locked to protect them from the punishing superego.

These are sex texts that can be read, then, as functioning therapeutically, a "good thing," cleansing for readers who may have repressed
guilt and confusion—hang-ups, as they used eloquently to be
called—about their own sexuality. Or, about whether or not they
have got desiring right. The narrative is related to the "how to" text,
where the primary function of the writing is to allow a reader to apply
an action to each word or group of words: first take a bowl, break an
egg, beat the egg, add a pinch of nutmeg. . . . Because this style is
common in sex narratives, the prescriptions in pornography and
ultra-sadistic texts—and satires such as *American Psycho*—are written

"to be followed," which produces anxiety in readers who find such directives offensive or ridiculous.

As in all "how to" texts, the cause and effect are measurable. In sex texts, desire is measured—it is a quantity, not a quality, and the writer who can describe the most orgasms (a handy indicator, since it can be counted, and even given an intensity rating, like an earthquake) is, it is understood, the writer who is doing the most to release readers from their hang-ups, to give them access to their sexual feelings through the description of the sexual processes of others, and therefore to feeling desire. As the pages are turned, so are the repressions overcome, and *jouissance* enjoyed.

This "good sex" text is enjoying a revival in Western narratives. Where texts that describe sex have been either "pure sex" (yellow press pornography for male consumption, for example) or metaphor sex (the artistic misogyny of surrealism, for example), we now want good dirty consenting adult sex, described by the writer as though he or she is one side of the consenting couple or group, and the reader the other side. Only the old-style repressed reader, who is afraid of desiring, would object—so implies the publication rehabilitation of sex as a topic and theme of literature and popular fiction.

Certainly, it is hard to accuse a text of dishonesty when it displays its organs—and its desire—so openly. And yet that is just what it is: dishonest in the mechanisms it uses to entrap the reader into a relationship that appears egalitarian but is constructed on a bullying premise (again) that allows no opposition. Before I look more closely at how this bullying works, I would point out that I am very aware that this is the contractual trap of all texts, and that part of the pleasure of the text for the reader is the realization that you are giving yourself to the writer, allowing the writer access to your desire in order to make the text function. And secondly, in using such terminology, I am aware, too, that I am subscribing to the feminization of the reading position, producing a relationship that makes even the most cogent and fascinating readership studies reliant on a gendered approach to its analysis. Far from finding this a stumbling block, I think it makes the task more interesting: the attempt to understand how sex works in texts is especially seductive for someone whose experience has been that of a feminized reader. Even when awareness of that experience provokes a reaction and antifeminized reading position, the dichotomy functions as a central mechanism in the reception process. While I will cling stubbornly to my belief that the distinction between male and female readers is pretty well useless until much more efficient and much less superficial arguments are formulated, it is obvious that as a starting point for finding a way in to how a text functions the masculine/feminine dichotomy of readership positions can be very useful. That a reader who has adopted or been given a masculine reading position is going to prefer Ernest Hemingway to Jane Austen, and the feminized reader the opposite, is often given as a way to explain either socialization processes or biological necessities. This simplified difference can, instead, be used as a way to describe how and why a reader accepts or rejects the contract offered by the writer. In other words, it offers a way forward from the impasse.

The contrast between the Austen and Hemingway styles is, simplistically drawn, between thought and action, between the domestic and the out-of-doors, between individual psychology as it reflects social custom and individual heroism as it rejects social conformity. It is also between sex as suggestion and sex as conquest: in both cases, sex is a small but dominant part of the desiring being—rather like the penis is a small but dominant part of the masculine being. In the feminine text (which means the text constructed to manipulate the desires of the feminized reader), sex is implicit in all descriptions but never happens. In the masculinized text, sex is also implicit in all descriptions but it happens as though independent of, although unrelated to, this implication. Thus the Private Eye who walks the mean streets with a loaded pistol and a tough attitude will, at periodic intervals throughout his narrative progress, copulate with a female whose sexuality is a kind of stage prop that objectifies the PI's desires and therefore character. Sex is, like the low-brimmed hat, the trench coat, the endless cigarettes, the hard liquor, the physical and psychological scars on his body, a sign that informs the reader of the hero's masculinity. Men *do* sex in hard-boiled crime fiction, and women have it *done* to them, with much groaning to signify not their own pleasure but the prowess of the hero. He shoots straight and fast and always gets his target. But it's lonely on the mean streets—so the sex is lonely too. This kind of description does not try to describe anything but the physical act and the responses of the body from the masculine point of view.

For the reader, the promise of pleasure is in being allowed into a taboo territory, where sex is enacted and you are watching. When he sees and feels, you project yourself into those acts and you respond as if you were not just seeing imaginatively but actually there. How you respond to that actuality is, in the case of sex, judged and evaluated as information about your own sexuality. In no other reading process is this process of evaluation so tyrannical and so loaded in favour of the masculinized response.

It is a puzzling thing about the evaluation of reading experience that when feminized readers project themselves into the romance description—into a scenario where the preliminaries to the act are much more important and detailed than the act itself, which is often left out of the narrative entirely—this is seen as contemptible or trivial, while the masculine projection into a vicariously pleasurable situation is just *honest* need and *healthy* response. The need for orgasm—which for so long was masculinized—has, in societies dominated by masculinist ideologies, been valued as good in contrast to the need for sentiment, valued as undesirable because favored by feminized individuals. Boys were allowed to hurl abuse at girls because they had genitalia that were different, but to act in a nonaggressive manner was acting "like a girl" and discouraged. Boys were supposed to feel desire for the genitalia of girls, but simultaneously to despise that difference as inferior, while girls were not supposed even to imagine the difference.

Those polarizations of the ways in which males and females manifest desire in behavior conditioned the masculinization and feminization of individuals. And from that process, the textualization of desire proceeded in conditioned directions. A man with whom I was discussing the seductive attraction of Jane Austen's *Pride and Prejudice* (translated into film) suggested that what women mean by "sexy" differs from what men mean. When he was encouraged to go to see another film, because it was "so sexy," he realized that the three people who had thought this were all women, and that when he went to see the film he found himself frustrated by the slow pace of the narrative and the lack of "actual" sex. What defined sexy for men, he concluded, was more direct: people taking off their clothes and copulating, with a bit of a warm-up. That is sexy. For women, according to this summary, the foreplay, the postponement, and even more annoyingly, the clothed concealment of the body in a way that highlighted the nakedness beneath, is sexy. Accepting that "man" and "woman" in this context are inaccurate (since if you find one biological male or female who responds in the nonexpected way your theory is invalid—or your respondent perverse, a very restrictive conclusion) and have been replaced efficiently by "masculine" and "feminine," the difference in these definitions is simply that: *difference*. That a valorization process has rendered one "honest" and "uncomplicated" and the other "hysterical" at worst and "sentimental" at best, is part of the reason why literary value systems lauded such a lot of crap and condescended to undervalue such a lot of rich writing for so long.

So, if you agree that it is necessary to repudiate the hierarchization of the responses to textual sex as being inadequate and masculinized, you might also agree that it is necessary to untangle a knot of right-sounding prejudices that have stymied advance on the subject of how sex works in texts. Or whether sex works in texts. Or what it means to say that sex works in texts. My supposition has been that textual sex is a highly contractual activity, which uses its transgressive appearance to disguise its strict control of readers' responses by prejudging the character of that response. Why hasn't the breaking down of the taboo around sex been sufficient to break down the delimitations of the contract? It has, to some extent, but the fallacy at the core of this new permissiveness (which is to say, a new situation where contracts are negotiated between consenting individuals, not by controling regimes) is that it is possible to create a text that embodies *jouissance* by describing sexual *jouissance*. That it is possible to satisfy hunger by writing about a banquet. Or, that it is therapeutically valuable to arouse hunger by describing other people satisfying it.

One way in which writing about sex has been forced to expand its contract is through the inclusion of female protagonists. This necessarily alters the hierarchy, since a description of sex from a female point of view, and which also valorizes the responses of the female equally with that of any other participants, of whatever sex, is going to allow and demand a different, perhaps less codified, identification on the part of a reader.

> Standing in the middle of the bedroom, we take off each other's clothes.
> He has a light, fumbling brutality, which several times makes me think that this time it'll cost me my sanity. In our dawning, mutual intimacy, I induce him to open the little slit in the head of his penis so I can put my clitoris inside and fuck him.[7]

Is this erotic? It is certainly transgressive of the boundaries that define both propriety and generic expectations. To find this in the middle of a crime novel would alert the reader to more than the codified function of what is usually called a sex scene, that obligatory time-out sequence where the rules of the game are reiterated in the relationship between a hero and his desires. But this short scene (and this is it entirely) is, in fact, in the middle of a crime novel, with a detective of sorts in pursuit of the perpetrators of a murder. In Peter Hoeg's *Miss Smilla's Feeling for Snow,* this sex scene is both elliptical and explicit. It does not avoid the description of copulation, and so does not enjoy Rushdie's joke with the reader that our expectations are really only for repetition, so why should we desire the words to be written when we can write them ourselves. Hoeg uses up a whole sentence of this three-sentence scene with a psychological enigma and so feminizes his text, but even there he confounds the code because this enigma is difficult to trace to the generic norm. Even if being driven mad for love is part of the tradition of feminine stories, why should his "light, fumbling brutality" drive her mad? And since this is stated quite clearly as a "cost" to the woman narrator, it is clear that such a cost is a bargain controlled by the woman. The ambiguity of the sentence fuzzes this bargain, and immediately, with the word "mutual," she reestablishes the equality inherent in the contract: but the shock of that final image is irrevocably transgressive of all sexual norms, fictional, textual, or real.

What happens in a text when the reader is forced to fill in descriptive gaps with uncodified imaginings? Rushdie's "then he, then she, then they" is useless here, but the brutality, indeed the "light, fumbling brutality," of this text prevents a loss of meaning sufficient to make the text undecipherable. There is nothing missing from this description, because it is not a recipe that is supposed to make your mouth water as you imagine the product of the baking, but it does make you imagine the process, given the ingredients and the manner in which those ingredients are combined. If Hoeg's text transgresses the code of writing about sex, it does so by taking literally the role reversal of feminist—or antifeminine—analysis. All textual sex is controlled by the verb "to fuck," which has a masculine subject and a feminine object. Changing the pronouns is superficial without this reversal that Hoeg, with light, fumbling brutality, brings about in this one sex scene of his crime novel.

Other attempts to transgress and redefine the boundaries of text sex also aim at confounding the masculine and feminine roles, but because the information that is loaded into the verb "to fuck" is so oppressive, such attempts can lead to pastiche rather than novelty. The point here has to do with the narrative position, and if the narrative position is masculinized, then no amount of pronoun-gender-swapping is going to change the options for the reader. Either you take up the masculinized role ("I recognize and identify with the narrator's subject-position that sees sex as what provides *jouissance* for the subject, and the more pleasure I receive from the sex text, the more sexual—and valorized—I am as a subject") or you are feminized, yet again. That being feminized does not depend on your sex is the positive change that is promised in these kinds of texts that are called "feminist." But they function in similar ways to masculinist texts, and so would perhaps be better labeled neo-masculinist.

I have just skipped over what has been, in fact, the goal of this discussion: what the masculinized reader's role is, according to the textual contract. I snuck it in between parentheses in that last paragraph in a way that might suggest I am afraid of saying it up front, uncertain of my confidence in stating it. Parentheses indicate what? A loss of authorial sureness, a lack of clarity in the organization of material? If I were to sexualize this text, I might say that parentheses are the insertion into the narrative drive of a decoy to *jouissance*, not so much a false piste or a postponement but a weakening of the main thrust. In the act of intercourse, the penis is momentarily ignored while the back of the knee is examined. If textual sex worked like this, perhaps it would be neo-feminist in a way that blurred the contractual strictures sufficiently to make a reader feel free to read rather than to measure up.

NOTES

1. Salman Rushdie, *The Moor's Last Sigh* (London: Jonathan Cape, 1995), 3.

2. Marie Maclean, "Narrative and the Gender Trap," in *Narrative Issues,* ed. John Hay and Marie Maclean, special issue of *AUMLA* (Journal of the Australasian Universities Language and Literature Association) 74 (1990): 69–84.

3. Georges Bataille, *Blue of Noon* [*Le Bleu du ciel*], trans. Harry Matthews (London: Marion Boyars, 1986).

4. Bret Easton Ellis, *American Psycho* (New York: Vintage Books, 1991), 175.

5. Mary Fallon, *Working Hot* (Melbourne: Sybylla Cooperative Press, 1989), 72.

6. Elizabeth Grosz, cover note to Fallon, *Working Hot.*

7. Peter Hoeg, *Miss Smilla's Feeling for Snow,* trans. F. David (London: Harvill/Harper Collins, 1993), 171.

"Vous êtes sans doute très surpris, mon cher d'Albert . . .": Improvisation and Gender in Gautier's *Mademoiselle de Maupin*

NATHANIEL WING

MY TITLE IS TAKEN FROM A PASSAGE IN THE LAST CHAPTER OF Gautier's novel *Mademoiselle de Maupin*, from the opening lines of a letter to d'Albert, breaking off a liaison after a night of love: "Vous êtes sans doute très surpris, mon cher d'Albert, de ce que je viens de faire après ce que j'ai fait. — Je vous le permets, il y a de quoi" (370) [You are no doubt greatly surprised, my dear d'Albert, at what I have just done after acting as I did. I will allow you to be so, for your have reason] (292).[1] This quirky and unconventional novel ends with an amusing twist on narrative conventions, emblematic of a much wider set of disruptions at work throughout the text; here it is not the man who loves, leaves, and takes to the road, but rather Madeleine/ Théodore, a lover whose equivocal sexuality escapes the closure of the text, remaining undecided, a mobile mix of gender permutations. D'Albert, a central protagonist engaged in an erotic and aesthetic quest for the perfect mistress, proclaims glibly in an early chapter of the novel that he prefers women who read extensively: "on est plus tôt arrivé à la fin du chapitre; et en toutes choses, et surtout en amour, ce qu'il faut considérer, c'est la fin" (51) [we arrive sooner at the end of the chapter; and in everything, and especially in love, the end is what we have to consider] (10). The denouement, how- ever, produces very different effects from those he anticipates early on. Like the open road that Madeleine/Théodore embraces at the end of the novel, her/his sexuality remains multiple, vagrant, refus- ing closure, whether in domestic stability with either of the protago- nists, d'Albert or Rosette, a young, libertine widow, who desire her/ him or in gender categories in which Rosette and d'Albert have experienced their desires. The novel itself, similarly, deflects inter- pretive certainties and resolutions at every turn, and that, I believe, accounts for the considerable interest that it has generated among

147

readers in recent years.[2] Just as it mixes literary genres, first-person confession in pseudo-epistolary form, dialogue, aesthetic essay, and picaresque narrative, it problematizes gender, introducing a complex of gender asymmetries, producing a very considerable puzzlement in conventional categories even as it reiterates them, whether they be heterosexual, homosexual or lesbian.[3]

The novel's central theme concerns the two main protagonists' awakening to desire and to an understanding of their presumed core identities in terms of their sexuality. Gender identity and self-knowledge are linked in a manner that was to become a major topos of the century and, indeed, as Foucault and others have shown, continues as a prominent motif in a great variety of contemporary fictions and critical inquiries.[4] The quests of the two protagonists originate in moments of unquestioned heterosexual identity yet, as suggested above, produce surprising and irretrievable disruptions. For d'Albert it is a question of locating and possessing the ideal woman, to be determined unequivocally in terms of androcentric, heterosexual identity; he will gain greater self-knowledge through the palpable assuaging of his desire. In an overtly Platonic context, d'Albert frequently speculates about the ideal mistress as an abstract figure to be given sculpted form according to masculine aesthetic ideals and erotic desire: "Qui nous a donné l'idée de cette femme imaginaire? de quelle argile avons-nous pétri cette statue invisible. . . ? (63) [Who has given us the idea of this imaginary woman? From what clay have we formed this invisible statue?] (21). Madeleine's quest, on the other hand, begins with a critique of the social-sexual subservience of women and with a repudiation of the social constraints that burden them, yet she also assumes that she will attain self-knowledge and self-definition by coming to know the other. Madeleine anticipates that the project of entering the world of men disguised as a man will make available to her a knowledge of men "as they are." This protagonist assumes that in attaining that knowledge she will ground her own identity outside the traditional social schema that she has disparaged and will then reenter heterosexual relations with a secure, self-discovered identity as a woman. On one level, then, the novel can be considered as a transvestite progress narrative. Madeleine's disguise, as revealed in the first letter to her confidant, Graciosa, will permit her to hear, see and know the world of men from within: "Pauvres jeunes filles que nous sommes; élevées avec tant de soin, si virginalement entourées d'un triple mur de précautions et de réticences, — nous, à qui on ne laisse rien entendre, rien soupçonner, et dont la principale science est de ne rien savoir, dans quelles étranges erreurs nous vivons, et quelles perfides chimères nous bercent entre leurs bras!" (206) [Poor young girls that we are, brought up with so much care, surrounded in such maidenly fashion with a triple wall of reticence and precaution, who are allowed to understand nothing, to suspect nothing, and whose principal knowledge is to know nothing, in what strange errors do we live, and what treacherous chimeras cradle us in their arms!] (147). Having mastered the masculine arts of horsemanship and the sword, she begins her quest: "décidée à n'y revenir qu'avec l'expérience la plus complète" (210) [determined not to return without the most complete experience] (151). Her goal is to know the "true story" of men, not their fictions: "les femmes n'ont lu que le roman de l'homme et jamais son histoire" (210) [women have read only man's romance and never his history] (152). The terms of this quest set feminine transparency and legibility to the penetrating male gaze ("notre vie est claire et se peut pénétrer d'un regard") (211) [As for us, our life is clear and may be pierced at a glance] (152) against the socially sanctioned opacity and illegibility of male difference. Madeleine's understanding of gender identity and her role as a voyeur, however, privileges a phallic-dominated schema of heterosexuality; paradoxically, her understanding and coming to know men and, consequently, herself, by becoming a woman different from the trivial beings that she disavows, are grounded in a well-known schema of heterosexuality in which woman is constructed symbolically as absence and lack, and man is figured as being and presence.[5] Both d'Albert and Madeleine are initially situated, then, in spite of obvious differences, in profoundly similar configurations of gender, being, and knowledge. During the course of the novel, however, it is revealed that transvestism, by linking gender identities and ontological being to performance, situates core identities as effects of surface, of performance, and thus produces vigorous and often exhilarating disruptions of heterosexuality, considered conventionally as a dyadic construction of "male" and "female."[6] This puzzlement of androcentric heterosexuality and the various anxious or exhilarating effects of its disruption are the subjects of this study.

Though never fully acknowledged by the protagonists of the text and never assumed by an extradiegetic narrator, gender in *Mademoiselle de Maupin* can be understood as a performativity, not the self-defining core of being that proves so elusive to certain characters in the novel.[7] A performative utterance in speech act theory is a discursive practice that produces what it names and, as Derrida suggests in his writings on Austin and the problems of performatives and iterability, succeeds because it repeats a coded or iterable utterance, as when I launch a boat, or open a meeting. Performative citation is a complex affair in this novel, involving not only d'Albert's anxious meditations on the constraints of the heterosexual code, but also transvestism, theatrical performance, and the unnamed errancy that escapes at the end of the novel. The text raises the question of how citation operates in producing the subject as originator of her/his effects as a consequence of dissimulation or theatricality.[8] The novel also suggests the potential open-endedness of gender performatives and the extent to which gender differences are effects of negotiations that are necessarily susceptible to reconfiguration.

If, as Ross Chambers has shown so insightfully, many early modernist texts are characterized by the fogs of melancholy that scramble identities and blur discourses,[9] this early modernist text, exceeding its male protagonist's predictably anxious surprise about his availability to nonheterosexual desire and about the uncontrolled errancy of Théodore/Madeleine's sexuality, produces euphoric and giddy multiplicities that are very different from those that inhabit the fogs of ennui. This euphoric difference is all the more effective because it repeats, as citation, aesthetic and gender codes that it reconfigures and supplements.

The opening section of the novel, the first five chapters, combines a libertine plot of erotic conquest with aesthetic meditations on beauty and desire that alternate between classical models and an emergent romantic ideal as d'Albert speculates on his quest for the elusive perfect mistress.[10] Although d'Albert shares with the typical *mal du siècle* hero an abundance of passion and a perceived lack of being that yearns for fulfillment in an ever-retreating object, he also professes to know what he wants: the coincidence of the ideal and the material in perfect love, or more simply, a woman who would be as much his own as his favorite horse: "une maîtresse tout à fait à moi— comme le cheval" (48) [a mistress—a mistress quite my own—like the horse] (7).[11] D'Albert's playfully fatuous discussion of his inability to be satisfied with any given type of woman—young girls, mothers, widows, candid virgins, or coquettes, etc. (chapter 2)— attributes his failure to a general human defect, the inability to find the material realization of the ideal.

"Ce que je cherche n'existe point . . . Cependant, si la femme que nous rêvons n'est pas dans les conditions de la nature humaine, qui fait donc que nous n'aimons que celle-là et point les autres, puisque nous sommes des hommes, et que notre instinct devrait nous y porter d'une invincible manière?" (63) [What I seek has no existence . . . Yet if the woman of our dreams is impossible to the conditions of human nature, what is it that causes us to love her only and none other, since we are men, and our instinct should be an infallible guide?] (21). These unexceptional speculations on the discrepancy between need and desire are of greater interest, however, when we consider how blatantly they assert a context predetermined by andro-centric categories, equivalent to the "naturel" [instinct]. "Human nature" and the inadequacies about which d'Albert meditates turn out to be pervasively heterosexual and male: "En vérité, je crois que l'homme, et par l'homme j'entends aussi la femme, est le plus vilain animal qui soit sur terre" (60) [In truth, I believe that man, and by man I also understand woman, is the ugliest animal on earth] (17). All configurations of the heterosexual ideal in d'Albert's specula-tions center upon the figure of the masculine, and one might observe that this is hardly surprising in a narrative of erotic conquest, whose principal protagonist is a brilliant, if ironically presented, alter-ego of the male writer. I will examine briefly these figurations of the andro-centric heterosexual ideal and the narrative in which it is imperfectly realized, the affair with Rosette, then turn to d'Albert's projected identification with woman and his thoughts on what he calls the *monstrous*. The desires that animate the protagonist and the various figures that draw him toward them, as he says, like a satellite around a planet, or a compass needle responding to magnetic polarity, have as their subtext a heterosexual, male-dominated matrix. These se-quences, however, lead the reader, or at least this reader, to speculate on how the text reveals the precariousness of the heterosexual norm as a constructed regulatory system and thereby invites questioning of its legitimacy as a quasi-permanent symbolic structure.[12]

As d'Albert reflects on his affair with Rosette, when he becomes "l'amant en pied de la dame en rose" [the established lover of the lady in rose] in chapter 3, he professes that he is unable to take possession of her as a mistress, which he defines as living through another, assimilating the other to the self: "Jamais personne autant que moi n'a désiré vivre de la vie des autres, et s'assimmiler une autre nature; — jamais personne n'y a moins réussi" (92) [Never has any-one desired so strongly as myself to live the life of others, and to assimilate another nature; never has anyone succeeded less in doing so] (46). This unrealized desire is specifically linked at the end of chapter 3 to an idealization of the other and to d'Albert's inability to embrace the "real": "Cette tension acharnée de l'oeil de mon âme vers un objet invisible m'a faussé la vue. Je ne sais pas voir ce qui est, à force d'avoir regardé ce qui n'est pas, et mon oeil si subtil pour l'idéal est tout à fait myope dans la réalité" (81) [This intense strain-ing of the eye of my soul after an invisible object has distorted my vision. I cannot see what is for my gazing at what is not; and my eye, so keen for the ideal, is perfectly near-sighted in matters of reality] (37).

The persistent ideal of the feminine, never attained, turns out to be a narcissistic figuration of the self: "Peut-être aussi que, ne trouvant rien en le monde qui soit digne de mon amour, je finirai par m'y adorer moi-même, comme feu Narcisse d'égoiste mémoire" (82) [Perhaps, too, finding nothing in the world worthy of my love, I shall end by adoring myself, like Narcissus of egotistical memory] (38).[13] Within a quite conventional erotic narrative recounting a witty and playful affair with a sophisticated and ironic mistress, d'Albert's desire excludes the other, though not in the terms that he professes, as in a passage in which he likens himself to a drop of oil in a glass of water, "repoussant invinciblement toute alliance et toute mixtion" (93) [. . . the oil can never mix with it] (48). According to now-familiar scenarios of specularization and assimilation, the other that d'Albert claims to seek is desirable only as a double of the one or as assimilated by the one. This is true even in apparently transgressive moments, as when d'Albert says that he wishes to be a woman: "j'aurais préféré d'être femme . . . et aux instants de plaisir j'aurais volontiers changé de rôle, car il est bien impatientant de ne pas avoir la conscience de l'effet que l'on produit" (95) [I would have preferred to be a woman . . . and at particular moments, I would willingly have changed my part, for it is very provoking to be unaware of the effect that one produces] (50). The sought-after pleasure, projected as becoming the female other, would be the consequence of masculine pleasure objectified. The other is a reiteration of the masculine, as is stated ironically at the conclusion of chapter 3, if one reads the statement in the light of my remarks above: "la femme ôtée, il me reste du moins un joli compagnon, plein d'esprit, et très agréablement démoralisé" (105) [putting the woman on one side, there remains to me at least a pretty companion, full of wit, and very agreeably demoralized] (59). D'Albert's heterosexual schema preserves an imaginary dyadic structure of gender and, like all regulatory norms, it is based on exclusion. The homoerotic implications of specular desire, as in the passage quoted above alluding to Narcissus, or the "pretty companion," or any hint that the boundaries configuring the exclusions might be unstable or contingent, are recuperated here by the protagonist's repeated assertions of an androcentric heterosexuality. All imagined roles affirm the heterosexual masculine, consuming the feminine in the masculine, as in d'Albert's lyric allusion to the Ovidian hermaphrodite: "Comme l'antique Salmacis, l'amoureuse du jeune Hermaphrodite, je tâchais de fondre son corps avec le mien; je buvais son haleine" (96) [Like the ancient Salmacis enamoured of the young Hermaphrodite, I strove to blend her frame with mine; I drank her breath] (50–51); and in another passage, "L'âme de Rosette était entrée toute entière dans mon corps" (100) [The soul of Rosette had entered in its integrity into my body] (54). The figure of the Ovidian hermaphrodite haunts this narrative, reappearing in d'Albert's musings on pre-Christian desire and the lures of homoerotic beauty in antiquity (chapter 5) and in key scenes in which heterosexual gender identity is represented as most menaced by homoerotic desire; I will discuss its resonances in greater detail later, but one can observe here that the sexual "completeness" of the hermaphrodite is an allegorical figuration of the one, a desired wholeness that is invariably androcentric at its root. There is also a curious residue of melancholy here, which can be linked to the incorporation of homosexual desires, in d'Albert's fantasy in an episode in chapter 3 in which he muses upon his inabilities to experience sexual delight other than as an extension of himself (94). He imagines himself as a spectator in the scene of his own erotic activities: "Mon âme, assise tristement, regardait d'un air de pitié ce déplorable hymène où elle n'était pas invitée" (96) [My soul, seated mournfully, gazed with an air of pity on this lamentable marriage to which she was not invited] (51). This melancholy is closely associated with d'Albert's passive heterosexuality and merits examination, for it can be linked later in the novel to his anxious and fascinating awakenings to desires that can only be understood as homoerotic. Melancholy is intimately tied throughout the text to heterosexual male gender identity and to its disturbances. Judith Butler, in *Gender Trouble* and *Bodies That Matter,* reading Freud's "Mourning and Melancholia" (1917) and "The Ego and the Id" (1923), makes the extremely suggestive claim that melancholy is constitutive of all heterosexual identity. Following Freud, melancholy is understood as the effect of an ungrieved loss; gender melancholy is "an attachment to and a loss and refusal of the figure of femininity by the man."[14] Melancholia, in Freud's sense, is "a sustaining of the lost object/other as a psychic figure with the consequence of heightened identification with the Other, self-beratement and the acting out of unresolved anger and love."[15] Butler suggests that this process of internalizing lost loves becomes pertinent to gender formation, since the incest taboo produces a loss of a love-object for the ego: the "ego recuperates from this loss through the internalization of the tabooed object of desire."[16] Heterosexual melancholy in d'Albert's musings throughout the novel, then, can be understood as an incorporative fantasy, taking in an object that he refuses to relinquish, a fantasy that retains not only the mother but also the father, in an unyielding homoerotic attachment.

The arrival of Théodore de Sérannes, the persona adopted by

Madeleine, provides d'Albert with a way out of his melancholy by disrupting an erotic attachment between Rosette and d'Albert in which heterosexual romantic intoxication ("Rosette est soûle de moi, comme je suis soûl d'elle" (125) [Rosette has had enough of me as I of her] (76) is revealed to be quite intolerable: "elle est assommante d'esprit, de tendresse et de complaisance, elle est d'une perfection à jeter par la fenêtre" (124) [she is wearisome with wit, tenderness, and kindness; she is perfect enough to be thrown out of the window] (76).[17] Prepared by the impossible intimacy of a heterosexual tête-à-tête, d'Albert is astonished by Théodore's arrival, for Théodore is the embodiment of beauty: "Cette beauté excessive, même pour une femme, n'est pas la beauté d'un homme" (187) [Such beauty, even for a woman, is not the beauty of a man] (130). This description hints at a loosening of the oppressive dyadic gender schema of the first chapters of the text, a loosening that occurs later in the novel following the performance by the major protagonists of *As You Like It* and continues in the final pages of the novel. These shifts in the boundaries of gender identities occur not simply because d'Albert is so obviously drawn to a figure whom he takes to be a man but, in a more powerful sense, because gender here is associated with an undefined supplement.[18] That supplement, as we will see, opens gender to the exclusions that have up till this point in the novel served to define the masculine heterosexual self, and it proves to be very destabilizing in its effects. It is not until the staging of the play, however, later in the novel, with its linking of identity and gender to theatricality and performance, that the possibility of radically different and mobile configurations of gender will be advanced.

Théodore/Madeleine's narrative begins in a manner very similar to d'Albert's, as indicated in my discussion above. Théodore is a *mal du siècle* hero, very like d'Albert, highly sensitive, melancholic, pursued by desires s/he is incapable of assuaging, haunted by indeterminacy, as a dialogue between Rosette and Théodore reveals: "Ah si je pouvais savoir ce que je veux; si l'idée qui me poursuit se dégageait nette et précise du brouillard qui l'entoure; si l'étoile favorable ou fatale apparaissait au fond de mon ciel . . . si je savais où je vais, dussé-je n'aboutir qu'à un précipice" (161) [Ah! if I could know what I want; if the idea which pursues me would extricate itself clear and precise from the fog that envelops it; if the fortunate or fatal star would appear in the depth of my sky; . . . if I knew whither I am going, though I were only to come to a precipice!] (108). The effects of Madeleine's disguise in the pages preceding the central episode of the staging of *As You Like It* are worked out both for her and for d'Albert within an only slightly disturbed heterosexual schema of desire and subject positions. Madeleine wishes to know the world of men from within by disguising herself as a man, to observe for herself a masculine transparency that would be equivalent to the transparency that she says defines the role of women: "Nous autres, notre vie est claire et se peut pénétrer d'un regard. Il est facile de nous suivre de la maison au pensionnnat, du pensionnat à la maison" (211) [As for us, our life is clear and may be pierced at a glance. It is easy to follow us from our home to the boarding-school, and from the boarding-school to our home] (152). Her strategy of knowing men by appropriating a male role and acting as a voyeur within a male world is indeed transgressive initially insofar as it is a forced entry of an excluded difference within the borders of male activities—drinking binges at an inn (chapter 10), duels (chapter 11, 14), mastery of horsemanship, and the like. But prior to the pivotal reenactment of Shakespeare's play, neither Théodore nor d'Albert go all the way to embrace a sexual otherness that displaces an overbearing heterosexual model. Each strains the limits of heterosexuality, however, and thereby exposes the fragility of configurations of gender that each had presumed to be so firmly in place.

The sequence of narrative presentation plays a crucial role in differentiating between d'Albert and Théodore/Madeleine regarding a dominant, though disturbed, heterosexuality. D'Albert's narrative of his desire for Théodore/Madeleine, in chapters 7, 8, and 9, precedes the account of the play, and is resumed after the play in a single chapter (13). Madeleine/Théodore's narrative, however, is more radically divided and more complex in its narrational perspectives, containing the initial episode alluded to above, which is recounted before the play, and a second analeptic narrative sequence in two chapters following the play (14 and 15), one preceding and one following d'Albert's resumed narrative in chapter 13. Madeleine thus narrates from a double perspective events that occur between that early sequence and the play. Madeleine tells most of her narrative—her near seduction of or by Rosette, her wounding of Rosette's brother who had discovered Rosette and Théodore in bed, her arrival at the château where she rejoins Rosette and meets d'Albert and where the play is staged—after the play itself, thus from a perspective of greater knowledge about her desires and her gender identities than when she engaged in the events recounted. Like her gender, her story is split and her narrational voice multiple. D'Albert, however, tells the story of his desire before the play and only regains a narrative voice in a single chapter in which he asserts that the play has permitted him to *resolve* the enigma of Théodore's gender: "je vous ai vue dans le costume de votre sexe . . . vous êtes femme, et mon amour n'est plus répréhensible" (319) [I have seen you in the costume of your sex . . . you are a woman, and my love is no longer reprehensible] (248). D'Albert's certainty, of course, is based on a complex of disguise and fiction, yet that does not deter him from reinstating a normative model of gender, even as it has been effectively disrupted and displaced.

D'Albert's account of his attraction for Théodore is presented as an investigation into the mystery of his/her gender (is he a woman? I am in love with a man who must be a woman, etc.) in which the only alternatives are heterosexual male or female, or abject sexuality referred to as "monstrous." In chapter 8, d'Albert confesses that, as he speculates on Théodore's sexual identity, his own sexuality has become an enigma: "en vérité, ce que j'éprouve depuis quelque temps est d'une telle étrangeté que j'ose à peine en convenir devant moi-même. Je t'ai dit quelque part que j'avais peur, à force de chercher le beau et de m'agiter pour y parvenir, de tomber à la fin dans l'impossible ou dans le monstrueux" (177) [in truth, what I have experienced for some time is so strange, that I can scarcely dare to acknowledge it to myself. I told you somewhere that I feared lest, from seeking the beautiful and disquieting myself to attain it, I should at last fall into the impossible or monstrous] (121).

The enigma of his desire, though it puts in question stable heterosexuality and thus exceeds known sensations and intelligibility, is nonetheless formulated in terms that reinstate binary gender relations, however puzzlingly disrupted: "C'est la plus déplorable de toutes mes abérations, je n'y conçois rien, je n'y comprends rien, tout en moi s'est brouillé et renversé; je ne sais plus qui je suis ni ce que sont les autres, je doute si je suis un homme ou une femme; j'ai horreur de moi-même, j'éprouve des mouvements singuliers et inexplicables . . ." (184) [It is the most lamentable of all my aberrations, I cannot comprehend it at all, everything is confused and upset within me; I can no longer tell who I am or what others are, I doubt whether I am a man or a woman, I have a horror of myself, I experience strange and inexplicable emotions . . .] (128). While implicitly revealing the fragility of d'Albert's own gender identity, his descriptions of Théodore, observed in a melancholy pose at his window, reveal the very fluidity and mobility of the signs and boundaries that mark the terms of gender identity. "Avec ses longs cheveux que la brise remuait doucement, ce cou de marbre ainsi découvert, cette grande robe serrée autour de sa taille, ces belles mains sortant de leurs manchettes comme les pistils d'une fleur du milieu de leurs pétales, — il avait l'air non du plus beau des hommes, mais de la plus belle des femmes, et je me disais dans mon coeur: — C'est une femme oh!

c'est une femme" (187) [With his long hair stirred softly by the breeze, his marble neck thus uncovered, his ample robe clasped around his waist, and his beautiful hands issuing from their ruffles like the pistils of a flower from the midst of their petals, he looked not the handsomest of men but the most beautiful of women, and I said in my heart—"It is a woman, oh! it is a woman" (130); "Cette beauté excessive, même pour une femme, n'est pas la beauté d'un homme . . . — C'est une femme, parbleu, et je suis bien fou de m'être ainsi tourmenté. De la sorte tout s'explique le plus naturellement du monde, et je ne suis pas aussi monstre que je le croyais" (187) [Such beauty, even for a woman, is not the beauty of a man, . . . It is a woman, by heaven, and I was very foolish to torment myself in such a manner. In this way everything is explained in the most natural fashion in the world, and I am not such a monster as I believed" (130).

"Natural" explanations of desire and gender fail, however, as d'Albert's speculations return consistently to the conundrum of Théodore's "true" gender identity and of d'Albert's enigmatically "monstrous" desire. Of course, it is the very category of the "natural" that is at stake here. D'Albert's reasoning operates according to a logic that recent critics have explored from both philosophical and psychoanalytic perspectives.[19] Gender is said to be explained by nature or biology, while the symbolic configurations of gender are, in fact, applied to nature and constitute nature as a category and as a set of symbolic configurations.[20] What Butler refers to as the "substantive effect of gender" "is performatively produced and compelled by regulatory practices of gender coherence."[21] The "natural" explanation that d'Albert seeks, grounded in perceivable differences, is an effect of performative signification.[22]

In the final pages of the novel, Madeleine/Théodore professes to be neither woman nor man, having too much or not enough of one or the other sex to adhere to fixed, binary, gender identities. There are crucial scenes preceding these emancipatory revelations, however, in which Madeleine describes her awakening desires for Rosette in terms of disruptions of dyadic heterosexual roles. In two episodes, Rosette draws Madeleine into a comic-erotic encounter, an unintended consequence of Madeleine's travestied identity as Théodore. Having fallen in love with Théodore, Rosette lures him into a rustic cabin, in a seduction scene that is interrupted "fortuitously" by her brother's dog and by her brother. In the second episode, Rosette's exasperated desire later leads her to Madeleine's bedroom, where she enters her bed. At a crucial moment, the couple is again interrupted by the intrusion of Rosette's brother . . . resulting in a duel between Madeleine/Théodore and Alcibiade in which Madeleine/

Théodore triumphs and hastily departs. These scenes provide voyeuristic titillation for the reader in the representation of an arousal
to lesbian desire ("je l'aimais réellement beaucoup et plus qu'une
femme aime une femme") (310) [I did really love her very much and
more than any woman loves a woman] (240), while denying its possibility through reiterations of Théodore/Madeleine's incapacity "to
be" and "to do" as the heterosexual male that Rosette assumes that
she is. Prohibitions against same-sex desire are strained, as Madeleine
describes in detail Rosette's voluptuous body and her arousal and
draws out a description of Madeleine's own arousal; yet the prohibitions are embraced throughout, in the very terms in which the scene
is narrated and the erotic is evaluated (290–91, 294). Madeleine
speculates on the enviable pleasures of men who are said to actively
possess and dominate women, while women remain passive: "cette
réflexion me vient que les hommes étaient plus favorisés que nous
dans leurs amours, que nous leur donnions à posséder les plus char-
mants trésors, et qu'ils n'avaient rien de pareil à nous offrir . . . Nos
caresses à nous ne peuvent guère être que passives" (296) [the reflection occurred to me that men were more favoured in their loves than
we, seeing that we gave them possession of the most charming trea-
sures while they had nothing similar to offer us . . . Our caresses can
scarcely be other than passive, and yet it is a greater pleasure to give
than to receive] (228). While declaring herself to be no longer
woman and not yet man (297), she reasserts key components of
androcentric heterosexuality, alluding to her "viriles pensées" (288)
[manly thoughts] (220), as opposed to feminine "précieuses niais-
eries" (288) [affected nonsense] (221), and by the quite blatant
ascription to woman of a lesser status and of passive roles. In the
scene when Rosette arrives uninvited and scantily dressed to
Madeleine/Théodore's bedroom on a moonlit night, Théodore is
restrained from pursuing "des idées singulières (326) [strange ideas]
(254) by constantly recalling the constraints imposed by the disguise,
speculating "peut-être aurais-je fait quelque *vaine et folle tentative* pour
donner un semblant de réalité à l'ombre de plaisir que ma belle
amoureuse embrassait avec tant d'ardeur" (326) [(had I not dreaded
the betrayal of my incognito) I should have given play to Rosette's
impassioned bursts, and should, perhaps, have made some vain and
mad attempt to impart a semblance of reality to the shadow of pleasure so ardently embraced by my fair mistress] (254). This passage
overtly denies to the protagonists the ultimate satisfaction of
orgasmic pleasure, and thus remains within the literal limits of heterosexual identities. Rosette is presumed to seek satisfaction from a
man and that satisfaction is presumed to rely on a (missing) phallic

organ. Madeleine's enactment of that desire would be an "empty," "mad effort" ("une vaine et folle tentative"). The material stability of dyadic heterosexuality, however, is set in a disarray not unlike that of Rosette's passionately disordered garments. The kernel theme of the scene, that of mistaken identity, is staged in a way that suggests from several perspectives that any assumption of a stable, materially grounded gender identity is phantasmic. The comic dissymmetry between gender codes here and "real" gender identities suggests the constructed nature of all such codes. On the one hand, Madeleine/ Théodore's gender is caught up in travesty, a performance enacted by an avowedly equivocally gendered persona; on the other hand, Rosette's pleasure is presented as very real, produced necessarily by her phantasmic identification of the other: "cette ombre de plaisir que ma belle amoureuse embrassait avec tant d'ardeur" [the shadow of pleasure so ardently embraced by my fair mistress] (254). In these passages, the novel can be said to have it both ways, straining the limits of heterosexual decorum and prohibitions while evoking desires represented as nonheterosexual. Heterosexual prohibitions are reiterated at every turn, however, and same-sex desire is denied the finality of a narrative/erotic climax. In its descriptive detail and in its reiteration of terms alluding to the violation of heterosexual norms ("Ma situation devenait fort embarrassante et passablement ridicule") (299) [My situation was becoming very embarrassing and tolerably ridiculous] (230), this scene offers voyeuristic pleasures to the reader, while both denying and affirming the transgressive character of the activities: "cette scène, tout équivoque que le caractère en fût pour moi, ne manquait pas d'un certain charme qui me tentait plus qu'il n'eût fallu" (299) [the scene, equivocal as its nature was for me, was not without a charm which detained me more than it should have done] (231). Beyond the overtly contained titillating transgressions, however, the scene affirms in many ways the precariousness and constructed nature of all gender identities, preparing Madeleine's final moments in the narrative. In short, the scenes both assert components of heterosexual identities and dismantle them at the same time. It is also worth noting that the threat of violence, symbolic or "real," at the heart of the dynamics of heterosexual identities, the threat of castration, takes a curious turn in the bedroom episode. Though Rosette's brother violently interrupts the scene, offering the guilty Théodore the conventional resolutions of revenge and death or marriage, it is a travesty of the law that prevails, for Madeleine/Théodore practically kills the brother, avenger of family order and guardian of the continuity of heterosexuality. Madeleine retreats, to reemerge in the final pages of the novel to engage alternative configurations of sexuality and of desire. The alternative to the heterosexual construct grounded in the threat of castration that Madeleine/Théodore's actions will propose at the end of the text is the constant disrupton of gender equilibriums that castration is burdened with assuring.

In the final pages of the novel, Madeleine/Théodore's relation to binary sexuality is asserted as either inadequate or excessive: "En vérité, ni l'un ni l'autre de ces deux sexes n'est le mien, je n'ai ni la soumission imbécile, ni la timidité, ni les petitesses de la femme; je n'ai pas les vices des hommes, leur dégoûtante crapule et leurs penchants brutaux: — je suis d'un troisième sexe à part qui n'a pas encore de nom: au-dessus ou au-dessous, plus défectueux ou supérieur: j'ai le corps et l'âme d'une femme, l'esprit et la force d'un homme, et j'ai trop ou pas assez de l'un et de l'autre pour me pouvoir accoupler avec l'un d'eux" (352) [In truth, neither of the two sexes are mine; I have not the imbecile submission, the timidity or the littleness of women; I have not the vices, the disgusting intemperance, or the brutal propensities of men: I belong to a third, distinct sex, which as yet has no name: higher or lower, more defective or superior; I have the body and soul of a woman, the mind and power of a man and I have too much or too little of both to be able to pair with either] (271). While d'Albert professes to be relieved that his desires for Théodore are not eccentric and, as he says, monstrous, having assured himself of Théodore's "true identity" as a woman, Madeleine/Théodore embraces plural gender identities in an open ended process of disguise and performance. Her/his "monster" is the chimera: "Ma chimère serait d'avoir tour à tour les deux sexes pour satisfaire à cette double nature: car le vrai bonheur est de se pouvoir développer librement en tous sens et d'être tout ce qu'on peut être" (353) [My chimera would be to have both sexes in turn in order to satisfy this double nature: . . . for true happiness consists in the ability to develop freely in every direction and to be all that it is possible to be] (271). The wholeness alluded to here does not imply a completion of self by the addition of gender identities, as in the Platonic androgyne myth, or in a synthesis producing a third term, but, I believe, something quite different. Théodore/Madeleine embraces a social/sexual identity ("*in every direction*") that never fully inhabits itself, that is characterized by constant rearticulation, transformation, and supplementation.

The play, a staging of As You Like It recounted by d'Albert in chapter 11, is a pivotal point in the novel, a *mise en abyme* of the situation of the protagonists, as critics have noted. It affords d'Albert an opportunity to understand Théodore/Madeleine's gender as multiple and mobile, emerging through the roles that he/she assumes, yet d'Albert chooses, rather, a deluded "proof" of her identity as a woman.[23] Referring to his earlier anguish over his desires for Théodore as unspeakable, monstrous, *insensés*, he now finds authorization for his passion in the "proof" afforded by Théodore's costume and performance in the role of Rosalind. Identity here, of course, is in d'Albert's own words, a "frail house of cards" (255). He comes to know "true" gender as a performance of a fiction of a disguise. Because Théodore's role in the play parallels that which d'Albert speculates has been assumed in life, a woman playing a man who adopts in the play a persona of a man playing a woman, as Rosalind disguised as Ganymede plays Rosalind in *As You Like It*, d'Albert assumes that he has penetrated the mystery of Théodore's identity. His understanding will be flawed in many ways, as this passage suggests: "L'image qui jusqu'alors ne s'était dessinée que faiblement et avec des contours vagues, le fantôme adoré et vainement poursuivi était là, devant mes yeux, vivant, palpable, non plus dans le demi-jour et la vapeur, mais inondé de flots d'une blanche lumière; non pas sous un vain déguisement, mais sous son costume réel; non plus avec la forme dérisoire d'un jeune homme, mais avec les traits de la plus charmante femme" (256) [The image which, till then, had shown itself only feebly and with vague outlines, the phantom that I had worshipped and vainly pursued was there before my eyes, living, palpable, no longer in twilight and vapour, but bathed in floods of white light; not in a vain disguise, but in its real costume; no longer in the derisive form of a young man, but with all the features of the most charming woman] (192). Retrieving the image of his desire, a "real woman" beneath the clothes of a man, d'Albert settles upon a "real costume," as though, paradoxically, a signifying surface designated a material core identity in this complex of disguise and theatricality. His understanding is flawed in at least two ways. D'Albert's "failures" are exploited in the novel to produce an exhilarating dispersal of sexual possibilities and mobility of desires, into which d'Albert himself is drawn. First, d'Albert has participated in understanding gender, as presented in the play and as figured by Madeleine/Théodore, as the effects of a desiring fantasy "materialized" on costumed surfaces, enactments of fictions of desire. This complex and elusive understanding of gender mutability, which d'Albert naively denies, heightens the futility of his quest for "proofs" of stable identities in matters of gender and desire. Second, he misapprehends Théodore/Madeleine's sexuality as though it were linked to an originative identity, failing to see the possibilities of multiple-gendered identities and the mobile configurations in which he is engaged. If, as I have suggested, gender is a citing of the symbolic law, a performativity, reiterated and produced as law by the citations it is said to command, d'Albert and Madeleine/Théodore assume very different positions regarding this process.[24] D'Albert anxiously reassumes a binary heterosexual discourse through role-playing, through the *mise en abyme* of the character's own situation in the play, the aim of which is to deny its own status as performance by masquerading as the natural. Madeleine/Théodore, however, affirms a virtually open-ended dynamics of citation. The performance of *As You Like It* reveals that the gendered subject is identified by the gendered role that it performs; these performances are always reiterations of coded behavior assumed by a subject in a process through which the subject is formed. Thus the novel suggests that the production of the subject as originator of his or her effects—that "real" identity that d'Albert anxiously seeks for himself and for Théodore/Madeleine—is a process of ordinarily dissimulated citation that both drag and theatrical performance make explicit.

The narrative denouement in the novel, the satisfaction of d'Albert's aesthetic/erotic quest, Madeleine's "gift" of her virginity, her "metamorphosis" from "girl" to "woman," (365) is recounted by a third-person narrator in chapter 16. In its very traditional aspects, releasing simultaneously erotic and hermeneutic tensions, when all things come together, as it were, this chapter quite subtly prepares the jolt, the unresolvable puzzlement of the last pages of the text, alluded to at the beginning of this study. In chapter 16, having received no response to a desperate letter to Théodore declaring his love, d'Albert commits a further and equally foolish indiscretion by writing and sending a second letter; he then prepares to throw himself in a river, when he is stayed unexpectedly by a restraining hand: "La main était emmanchée au bout d'un bras qui répondait à une épaule faisant partie d'un corps, lequel n'était autre chose que Théodore/Rosalinde, Mademoiselle d'Aubigny, ou Madeleine de Maupin, pour l'appeler de son véritable nom" (360) [The hand was at the extremity of an arm which corresponded to a shoulder forming part of a body, which was nothing else but Théodore-Rosalind, Mademoiselle d'Aubigny, or Madelaine de Maupin, to call her by her real name] (284). While this passage reiterates multiple identities, d'Albert and Madeleine/Théodore initially address each other in their roles of Rosalind and Orlando; Madeleine/Théodore asserts that she is Rosalind only at night and can be Théodore only by day, d'Albert remains deluded by his passionate urgency to know and to possess. In the final pages d'Albert has before him an unveiled body that conforms to his ideal of beauty and that is also real and palpable.

"Tout était réuni dans le beau corps qui posait devant lui: — délicatesse et force, forme et couleur, les lignes d'une statue grecque du meilleur temps et le ton d'un Titien. — Il voyait là, palpable et cristallisée, la nuageuse chimère qu'il avait tant de fois vainement essayé d'arrêter dans son vol . . ." (366) [Everything was united in the beautiful form standing before him—delicacy and strength, grace and colour, the lines of a Greek statue of the best period and the tone of a Titian. There he saw, palpable and crystallized, the cloudy chimera that he had so often vainly sought to stay in its flight . . .] (289).

Both the idealist aesthete and the lover will be satisfied (366–68). Madeleine plays out her role as a virgin, announced in an earlier description of her initial project, who will finally know heterosexual satisfaction, and, as the passage makes abundantly clear, will enjoy it repeatedly throughout a long night of love. The links between gender, knowledge of self and other, are also underscored. As initiator into orgasmic sex, d'Albert appears confirmed in his heterosexual mastery and prowess: "Le divin moment approchait, un dernier obstacle fut surmonté, un spasme suprême agita convulsivement les deux amants, — et la curieuse Rosalinde fut aussi éclairée que possible sur ce point obscur qui l'intriguait si fort" (367) [The divine moment approached. A supreme spasm convulsed the two lovers, and the curious Rosalind became as enlightened as possible on a matter which had so deeply perplexed her] (290). The narrator coyly observes that decorum prohibits him from revealing the number of these "lessons" and "enlightenments" (367). Here, however, as throughout, stable resolutions, whether they be erotic, psychological, or narrative, are fleeting and illusory and the gendered subject remains as plural as the several names of the intervening Madeleine/Rosalind/Théodore suggest. The play of plural identities is further complicated in the final pages of the text, of course, since Rosalind leaves a sleeping d'Albert to enter Rosette's chamber in an episode that is never described. The figure that emerges from Rosette's room subsequent to the night of love with d'Albert is Théodore. Oddly, the only core identity missing in these final narrative episodes is Madeleine de Maupin who, presumably, would be the subject of d'Albert's desire, the woman who had served as the body for his dreams (370).

It is one of the many ironies of the erotic encounter between d'Albert and Rosalind in the penultimate chapter, that in d'Albert's hyperbolic male sexual performance, as he gives her repeated "lessons" (the word in the text) in sexual ecstasy (367), the male protagonist remains so apparently untouched by the narrative's revelations

about the performativity of all gendered subjectivity. As he reinstates
his own heterosexual masculinity, so tempted by Théodore, he ig-
nores the foreclosed boundaries that he has himself been led to
encounter and that are, indeed, embraced by the very body that he is
caressing. D'Albert may have arrived at the final chapter of his own
erotic narrative, safely reinserted in his assumed heterosexual identity, but the novel has added an erotic encounter between
Madeleine/Théodore and Rosette from which the voyeuristic gaze
has been excluded; the reader can only conjecture about the permutations of gender that are played out behind that closed door. As I
noted at the beginning of this discussion, the narrative refuses
closure, as Madeleine/Théodore resumes her/his wanderings, leaving behind a letter and a considerable puzzlement for d'Albert. The
writer, whose voice does not assume any of her/his several names,
affirms: "Vous aviez envie de moi; vous m'aimiez, j'étais votre idéal;
fort bien. Je vous ai accordé sur le champ ce que vous demandiez; il
n'a tenu qu'à vous de l'avoir plus tôt. J'ai servi de corps à votre rêve
. . . Maintenant que je vous ai satisfait, il me plaît de m'en aller—qu'y
a-t-il de si monstrueux?" (370) [You desired me, you loved me, I was
your ideal; — very well, I at once granted you what you asked; it was
your own fault that you did not have it sooner. I served as a body for
your dream as compliantly as possible . . . Now that I have satisfied
you, it pleases me to go away. What is there so monstrous in this?]
(292). The writer of the letter, though consistently gendered grammatically as feminine, specifically maintains the conundrum of plural
and equivocal gender identities and does not provide an identifying
signature, refusing both by narrative act and narrational inscription
to give a name or a stable identity to the desiring subject.

The final words of Gautier's novel are an imperative to d'Albert
and Rosette to love each other. While overtly inciting restoration of
the heterosexual couple, this passage delightfully activates further
spirals of desires and identities: "Aimez-vous tous deux en souvenir
de moi, que vous avez aimée l'un et l'autre, et dites-vous quelquefois
mon nom dans un baiser?" (373) [Love each other well in memory of
me, whom both of you have loved, and breathe my name sometimes
in a kiss] (294). What name are we to suppose that Rosette and
d'Albert might properly attach to that memory?

NOTES

1. Théophile Gautier, *Mademoiselle de Maupin* (Paris: Éditions Garnier, 1966). All
French quotations are from this edition. English translations are from: Théophile

Gautier, *Mademoiselle de Maupin*, trans. unidentified (New York: Random House, n.d.). Page references are incorporated into the text.

2. See Pierre Albouy, "Le Mythe de l'androgyne dans *Mademoiselle de Maupin*," *Revue d'histoire littéraire de la France* 72, no. 4 (juillet-août, 1972): 600–608; Michel Crouzet, "Gautier et le problème de 'créer,'" ibid.: 659–87; Marjorie Garber, *Vested Interests: Cross-Dressing and Cultural Anxiety* (New York: Harper, 1993), 73–75; Rosemary Lloyd, "Rereading *Mademoiselle de Maupin*," *Orbis Litterarum* 41, no. 1 (1986): 19–32; Kari Weil, "Romantic Androgyny and Its Discontents: The Case of *Mlle de Maupin*," *Romanic Review* 78, no. 3 (1987): 348–58.

3. The motif of transvestism in this novel activates a questioning of binary sexual oppositions, and of binarity in general, by introducing a third term that destabilizes the categories of "male" and "female," as Marjorie Garber notes in *Vested Interests:* "The 'third' is that which questions binary thinking and introduces crisis—a crisis which is symptomatized by *both* the overestimation *and* the underestimation of cross-dressing. But what is crucial here . . . is that the 'third term' is *not a term*. Much less is it a *sex*, certainly not an instantiated 'blurred' sex as signified by a term like 'androgyne' or 'hermaphrodite,' although these words have culturally specific significance at certain historical moments. The 'third' is a mode of articulation, a way of describing a space of possibility. Three puts in question the idea of one: of identity, self-sufficiency, self-knowledge" (11). While cross-dressing is certainly a central motif in Gautier's novel, it alone does not bear the burden, as I will show, of a multifaceted questioning of gender identities.

4. Michel Foucault's *Histoire de la sexualité: La Volonté de savoir* (Paris: Gallimard, 1976) demonstrates the intimate link in investigations, descriptions, and regulations of sexuality in the late eighteenth century and throughout the nineteenth century between sexuality and innermost subjectivity and self-knowledge. Gautier's novel can be seen as part of a widespread "incitement" and *mise en discours* of polymorphous sexuality (Foucault, 21), that reaches with considerable vigor into several domains in the late nineteenth century: pedagogy, medicine, demography, and, of course, literature. The particular attention accorded throughout the nineteenth century to the formation of the category of perversion is of special relevance to our discussion, since former moral categories, such as debauchery or excess, associated with specific practices, are replaced during the course of the century by medical technologies that seek to define the individual himself or herself as a subject (Foucault, 156). This motif haunts Gautier's novel, as both the threat of the "monstrous" and an exhilarating temptation of polymorphous sexuality proscribed by heterosexual codes.

5. On "feminine lack" in phallocentric systems of representation, see Luce Irigaray, *Speculum de l'autre femme* (Paris: Éditions de Minuit, 1974), and, especially, the essay entitled "Pouvoir du discours, subordination du féminin," in *Ce sexe qui n'en est pas un* (Paris: Éditions de Minuit, 1977), 67–82.

6. Marjorie Garber, *Vested Interests*, 16–17, discusses "transvestite effects" as producing a "category crisis," a failure of definitional distinction. "The binarism male/female, one apparent ground of distinction (in contemporary eyes, at least) between "this" and "that," "him" and "me," is itself put in question or under erasure in transvestism, and a transvestite figure, or a transvestite mode, will always function as a sign of overdetermination—a mechanism of displacement from one blurred boundary to another" (16).

7. See Judith Butler, *Gender Trouble: Feminism and the Subversion of Identity* (New York and London: Routledge, Chapman and Hall, 1990), 24–25, 134–41, and *Bodies That Matter* (New York and London: Routledge, Chapman and Hall, 1993), 12–16:

"The forming, crafting, bearing, circulation, signification of the sexed body will not be a set of actions performed in compliance with the law; on the contrary, they will be a set of actions mobilized by the law, the citational accumulation and dissimulation of the law that produces material effects, the lived necessity of those effects as well as the lived contestation of that necessity. "Performativity is thus not a singular 'act,' for it is always a reiteration of a norm or set of norms, and to the extent that it acquires an act-like status in the present, it conceals or dissimulates the conventions of which it is a repetition" (12).

8. Butler, *Bodies That Matter*, 13.

9. Ross Chambers, *The Writing of Melancholy: Modes of Opposition in Early French Modernism*, trans. Mary Seidman Trouille (Chicago and London: University of Chicago Press, 1993).

10. Kari Weil's excellent article, cited above, "Romantic Androgyny and Its Discontents," discusses the opposition between classical ideals of beauty and an emerging romantic aesthetic ideal, linked respectively to the figures of the androgyne and the hermaphrodite.

11. For an extensive study of the *mal du siècle* hero in novels of the first half of the nineteenth century, see Margaret Waller, *The Male Malady: Fictions of Impotence in the French Romantic Novel* (New Brunswick, N.J.: Rutgers University Press, 1993).

12. Butler, *Bodies That Matter*, "The Lesbian Phallus," 57–91, demonstrating that "the hegemonic imaginary constitutes itself through the naturalization of an exclusionary heterosexual morphology" (91), proposes possible alternatives to the heterosexual imaginary.

13. See Sarah Kofman, *L'Énigme de la femme: La Femme dans les textes de Freud* (Paris: Galilée, 1980), examines the role of male narcissism in the object choice of a narcissistic woman. Kofman (66) asserts that, in loving the narcissistic woman, the male projects upon her a portion of his own narcissism, which he had appeared to have abandoned.

14. Butler, *Gender Trouble*, 57–72; *Bodies That Matter*, 234–36.

15. Butler, *BodiesThat Matter*, 234.

16. Butler, *Gender Trouble*, 58.

17. In a study of several prose poems by Baudelaire, "On Certain Relations," in *The Limits of Narrative: Essays on Baudelaire, Flaubert, Rimbaud, Mallarmé* (Cambridge, London, and New York: Cambridge University Press, 1986), 19–40, I discuss the violent effects produced by encounters with feminine difference when it is conceived in terms of an ideal of a perfect union of thought and sentiment. The poem "Portraits de maîtresses" has clear affinities with these passages in Gautier's text.

18. The passage in which d'Albert confesses that he loves a man begins: "Cela est ainsi. — J'aime un homme, Silvio. — J'ai cherché longtemps à me faire illusion; j'ai donné un nom différent au sentiment que j'éprouvais, je l'ai vêtu de l'habit d'une amitié pure et désinteressée; j'ai cru que cela n'était que l'admiration que j'ai pour toutes les belles personnes et les belles choses; je me suis promené plusieurs jours dans les sentiers perfides et riants qui errent autour de toute passion naissante; mais je reconnais maintenant dans quelle profonde et terrible voie je me suis engagé" (185) [It is so. I love a man, Silvio. I long sought to delude myself; I gave a different name to the feeling that I experienced; I clothed it in the garment of pure and disinterested friendship; I believed that it was merely the admiration which I entertain for all beautiful persons and things; for several days I walked in the treacherous, pleasant paths that wander about every waking passion; but I now recognise the profound and terrible road to which I am pledged] (128).

19. See, for example, Butler, "The Lesbian Phallus," in *Bodies That Matter*, 57–91.

20. Butler, *Gender Trouble*, 7.

21. Ibid., 24.

22. Butler, *Bodies That Matter:* "the materialization of norms requires those identificatory processes by which norms are assumed or appropriated, and these identifications precede and enable the formation of a subject, but are not, strictly speaking, performed by a subject . . ." (15).

23. Garber, *Vested Interests*, 73–75, discusses the central psychological and narrative role of the performance of the play and several aspects of the "conundrum of gender indecidability" realized by its performance in the novel.

24. See Butler, *Bodies That Matter*, 14.

Makeup and Mirrors: Writing on the Face in Colette's *La Vagabonde*

JULIE SOLOMON

THE CONCLUSION OF COLETTE'S *LA VAGABONDE* IS MOST OFTEN READ as positive: the heroine chooses creativity and freedom over the subservience of patriarchal marriage, while the narrator frustrates readers' expectations that the happy ending of the love story will involve the lovers being united at last. However, a reading that concentrates on the corporeal and the visual highlights more complex tensions. *La Vagabonde* begins with a mirror scene, and continues, as the novel progresses, to thematize the heroine's perception of her own appearance, and the meaning of that appearance. In a sense, the entire novel will be spent in trying to answer the questions posed by the face in the mirror, and to decide whether the critical judgments of the painted woman are justified. Who is looking at Renée? Who has the power to define who she is? To what extent is her identity predicated upon her existence in the visual? In examining these questions, this study will posit a more ambiguous reading, and attempt to show that the conclusion is also a defeat. If Colette suggests an alternative to the heterosexual happy ending, her analysis is far from utopian. She shows that the masquerade of gender, and the endless mirrorings of the scopic regime are formidably powerful in the ways that they limit options, for women in particular, and in the undeniable pleasures that they furnish.

We will begin by studying Renée's relationship to various mirrors, both literal looking glasses and characters who functions as mirrors for her. Whether the mirror is seen as a redoubtable judge or a tool for self-awareness, her positions within the scopic regime are mapped as the novel progresses. In a second movement, then, we will explore the ways in which the heroine takes charge of her appearance through the use of makeup and other elements of the feminine masquerade. Colette highlights the advantages and disadvantages, the pleasures and discomforts, of such attempts to control one's place in the visual. She undermines both feminist and misogynist analyses of the uses of the masquerade, and at the same time shows the limits of its power. Finally, as the notion of the "real face" becomes less and less defensible, we will study the relationship between the woman's body as object and as subject of representation and desire. Perhaps the quest for authenticity can only take place within the play of the fictional.

THE MIRROR SCENE

Renée Néré, divorced from her philandering husband, has stopped writing novels, and now works in the music hall as a dancer and mime. In the opening scene of *La Vagabonde,* she sees herself in her dressing room mirror, barely recognizable in her exaggerated stage makeup. The glass seems to represent a powerful and implacable presence that obliges her to face "truths" she would rather avoid. Renée's reflection is distanced through the use of the third person and the inversion of the gaze: "cette conseillère maquillée qui me regarde" (5) [that painted mentor who gazes at me (from the other side of the looking glass)].[1] The woman before the mirror describes a painted face that is looking at her. She concentrates on the make-up, rather than any corporeal features beneath the vivid colors. The painted counselor has "de profonds yeux aux paupières frottées d'une pâte grasse et violâtre. Elle a des pommettes vives, de la même couleur que les phlox des jardins, des lèvres d'un rouge noir, brillantes et comme vernies" [deep-set eyes under lids smeared with purplish greasepaint. Her cheekbones are as brightly colored as garden phlox and her blackish-red lips gleam as though they were varnished]. The image does not seem to be painted onto a surface: the makeup simply *is* the face.

"Elle me regarde longtemps, et je sais qu'elle va parler" (5) [She gazes at me for a long time and I know she is going to speak to me]. The mirror criticizes Renée for her solitude and marginality, and suggests that she has lost her identity in changing her life this way, but she finally admits that the face in the mirror is her own: "C'est pourtant bien moi qui suis là, masquée de rouge mauve, les yeux cernés d'un halo de bleu gras qui commence à fondre" (7) [There's no getting away from it, it really is me there behind that mask of purplish rouge, my eyes ringed with a halo of blue greasepaint beginning to melt]. As Renée accepts to identify herself with the made-up face and its harsh criticisms, her sense of self seems in danger of dissolution: "Vais-je attendre que le reste du visage aussi se délaie? S'il n'allait demeurer, de tout mon reflet, qu'une coulure teintée, collée à la glace comme une longue larme boueuse?" (7) [Can the rest of my face be going to melt also? What if nothing were to remain from my whole reflection but a streak of dyed color stuck to the glass like a long, muddy tear?]. As the greasepaint melts it seems to fuse with the skin and flesh, so that its disintegration entails that of the face itself. The scene does not end with a "vanity." The melting makeup simply reveals an absence. When all that is left is a tear of viscous greasepaint sliding thickly down the mirror, both the *je* and her cruel counselor will apparently have disappeared entirely. The makeup becomes a caricatural emblem of the sticky, fusional dangers of the feminine.

Who, then, is this adviser who lies in wait for Renée on the other side of the mirror? Jenijoy La Belle suggests that women who recognize a great deal of judgmental power in the mirror often identify it as a male gaze. She posits a "continuum between what women perceive in the glass and what the masculine world creates."[2] Thus, for one character she studies: "The mirror is not just a tool by which one sees one's appearance; the whole revery of herself being looked at by many men evolves out of her looking in a mirror. This mature woman acts out the adolescent performance of trying to please the glass and of becoming both male spectator and female actor."[3] However, as Francette Pacteau points out, our narcissistic relation to self-image is founded in the ambivalences of the mirror stage. As such, it involves, for men and women, pleasures both of looking and of being seen: "The subject sees itself, as a picture, from the vantage point of the other; the pleasure is fundamentally scopophilic."[4] In *The Symptom of Beauty,* Pacteau argues for "Freud's notion of the fundamental duality of the drive, the coexistence of passive exhibitionistic and active scopophilic tendencies in men as well as in women."[5] While these transactions of the gaze are not always pleasurable, *La Vagabonde* would tend to corroborate Pacteau's analysis. Colette's works are replete with women who give a great deal of power to the mirror, but I wish to argue that it is not gendered male in a simple sense.

The aging women in *Chéri* and *La Fin de Chéri*[6] are as quick to see signs of each other's withering beauty ("flétrissures") as they are their own. Their companionship and support are always barbed with these rivalries: "Elles se connaissaient depuis vingt-cinq ans. Intimité ennemie de femmes légères . . . , amitié hargneuse de rivales à l'affût de la première ride et du cheveu blanc" (7) [They had known each other for twenty-five years. The hostile intimacy of women of easy virtue . . . , the aggressive friendship of rivals always on the lookout for the first wrinkle or gray hair].[7] Women in Colette are rivals, even in friendship, unless they are safely beyond beauty and desire.[8] They are uncompromisingly aware of the dictates of beauty, as applied to themselves and to others. A woman's ability to evaluate feminine appearance is a skill she needs to survive.

Even though Renée's practiced eye assesses other women's charms, there is not the same sense of rivalry that we find later in the *Chéri* books. Most of the judgmental observations concern her own appearance. And yet the idea of the younger rival will play an important role in the evolution of Renée's feelings about Max and her eventual decision to leave him. An out-of-focus photograph of her suitor's tennis partner comes to represent the figure of the younger woman who will inevitably distract his interest as Renée ages. "Je ne sais pas son nom, je vois à peine son visage, renversé sous le soleil, noir, avec une grimace joyeuse où brille une ligne blanche de dents" (222) [I do not know her name, I can hardly see her face, turned up to the sun, and dark, with a cheerful grin revealing a shining line of white teeth].

Even if the rivalry between women is less developed here than in *Chéri*, the tone more elegiac, the mirror is nonetheless a woman, representing the critical and competitive gaze of women on each other and themselves. And when the mirror speaks, it is a judgmental and authoritative Mother. The "wise" double in the mirror in fact speaks unhelpful messages that limit Renée's options. She declares that a woman of thirty-three years who is alone is a scandal and a failure. And yet, later in the novel, the "pitiless mentor" insists that the hope of falling in love again is illusory, for true love occurs only once in our lives: "rien ne compte, en amour, hormis le premier amour" (146) [nothing counts, in love, except the first love]. The apparent contradiction between these two adages is resolved if we read the adviser (Colette's term is "conseillère") as representative of a conventional view of love. She—Renée herself—in fact reproaches Renée with defying social convention by leaving her husband. "Pourquoi es-tu là, toute seule? et pourquoi pas ailleurs?" (6) [Why are you there, all alone? And why not somewhere else?].

The mirror-counselor can be compared with Renée's ex-sister-in-law, Margot, another adviser who deals in "unvarnished truths." While she provides Renée with both material and emotional support, Margot does not represent an encouraging role model: a mother-figure offering only cold comfort. With her short gray hair, apparently beyond sexuality, and immune to desire, she lavishes her maternal feelings on a brood of ungrateful and sickly lapdogs. Margot generously includes Renée among her charges, giving her a monthly stipend, and advising her on her health. Margot's "mirror" tells a different story from the painted counselor. She does not deal in how Renée *should* be, but in how she is, presenting a bleak analysis of the

options open to women outside marriage. She bluntly recognizes
Renée's sensuality, and anticipates that the younger woman will be
unable to resist its urges, that she will throw away her freedom for
sexual pleasure and a comfortable place in the world. "Chatte écha-
udée, tu retourneras à la chaudière" (67) [Burnt child though you
are, you'll go back to the fire], she predicts. The French phrase
compares the heroine's predicament to that of a scalded cat, an apt
animal metaphor, for Margot is here the voice of Colette's theory of
"the female," according to which "biological" urges make women
naturally disposed to accept their submissive relationship to men.[9]

For the "female," the eyes of the man literally replace the mirror.
Renée fears indeed that seeing herself through Max's eyes will lead to
illusions about her appearance: "Ta ferveur, qui me convaincra, qui
me rassurera, ne me conduira-t-elle pas à l'imbécile sécurité des
femmes aimées? Une ingénue maniérée renaît, pour de brèves et
périlleuses minutes, en l'amoureuse comblée, et se permet des jeux
de fillette, qui font trembler sa chair lourde et savoureuse" (223)
[Will not your fervor, if I let it convince and reassure me, lead me into
the fatuous security of women who are loved? I have seen satisfied,
amorous women in whom, for a few brief and dangerous minutes,
the affected ingenue reappears and allows herself girlish tricks that
make her rich and heavy flesh quiver]. Later, the danger of lover as
mirror is expanded still further. If she traveled with Max, she would
see the world only through the speculum of his eyes: "les plus beaux
pays de la terre, je refuse de les contempler, tout petits, au miroir
amoureux de ton regard" (247) [I refuse to see the most beautiful
countries of the world microscopically reflected in the amorous mirror of your eyes].

"Tu as vieilli" (151) [You've got older], observes Margot in a concerned but somewhat medical tone, as Renée is about to confess her
attachment to Max. This alarming remark saps the narrator's confidence in her appearance, and brings her to hide her tear-stained face
with a veil. Only a woman who is beyond sexuality could note such a
loss calmly. The sexual woman needs the (impossible to maintain)
narcissistic assurance that she is a beautiful picture. "It is essentially *in
anticipation* that we insistently strive towards a corporeal ideality, in
the face of the slow but certain degradation of what Laura Mulvey has
termed the 'entropic body.'"[10]

In the last part of the novel, Renée is away from Max, on a theatrical tour. She enthusiastically abandons the demoralizing preoccupation with her appearance that Max's courtship has accelerated and
intensified. When she occasionally comes upon her face in a mirror,
she no longer encounters the critical judge of her imperfections.

These mirrors are themselves imperfect. Dirty and provincial, haphazardly encountered in a restaurant, train, or hotel room, they are without redoubtable powers. "Je risque pour m'occuper un arrangement éphémère de la table à écrire, j'ouvre le buvard, entre le miroir-chevalet et le bouquet de narcisses, je cherche un semblant de home" (236) [I . . . try a temporary arrangement of the writing table, opening the blotter between the cheval glass and the bunch of narcissus; I'm trying to make the place look like home]. Here, the heroine as writer balances between the mirror and the mythical flowers. The self-conscious irony of this precarious "arrangement" is a *mise en abyme* of the "solipsistic" nature of her writing. Renée plays out her role as narrator, and acknowledges that her narcissism is not only the question explored in her text but in effect the source of her self-descriptive narrative. The overdetermined image undoes itself, and points elsewhere: if the writer and her text play out her self-mirrorings with such insistence, she calls attention to difficulties that concern more than one woman.

I Am a Picture

La Vagabonde contrasts two different practices of makeup. As a tool of trade, stage make-up is worn by both men and women, who are equally concerned with techniques of painting their faces and bodies and who enjoy it in an almost fetishistic way. Street make-up, on the other hand, is clearly marked as feminine, and constitutes a narcissistic attempt to hide a woman's age and preserve her sexual attractiveness. However, it quickly becomes apparent that this distinction cannot be maintained.

Brague, Renée's mime partner and trainer, is proud of his face-painting ability. The narrator finds his obsessive precision with nuances of color admirable, if a little ridiculous: "Brague hausse les épaules sans répondre, absorbé par le fignolage de ses sourcils, qu'il dessine en violet foncé parce que 'ça fait plus féroce.' Il a un certain bleu pour les rides, un certain rouge orangé pour le dedans des lèvres, une certaine ocre pour le fond du teint, un certain carmin sirupeux pour le sang qui coule, et surtout un certain blanc pour les masques de Pierrot 'dont je ne donnerais pas la recette à mon propre frère!'" (40) [Brague shrugs his shoulders without answering, so intent is he on the tricky job of making up his eyebrows; he paints them dark violet because "that gives a fiercer look." He has a particular blue for wrinkles, a particular orangy-red for the inside of lips, a particular ochre for makeup base, a particular syrupy carmine for dripping blood, and above all a particular white for Pierrot masks, "the recipe for which," he avers, "I wouldn't give to my own brother!" There's no denying that he makes very skillful use of this multi-colored mania of his, and it is the only absurdity I know of in this intelligent, almost over-conscientious mime]. Throughout the novel, we see various performers using mirrors to apply their makeup, adjust their costumes, and perfect their movements. These work-manlike and matter-of-fact masquerades suggest that alienation of self from self-representation (Rimbaud's famous *je est un autre*) is no more than a daily chore for actors, quite distinct, perhaps, from the problematic rehearsals and masks of daily life.

And yet, we never lose sight of the fact that Brague's ferocious makeup suggests the content of his mime pieces. In *L'Empryse*, Renée plays a scornful woman who has betrayed her husband. Brague's character beats her in a jealous fury and throws her to the ground.[11] *La Dryade* seems to be another scenario of sexual violence. Brague's persona, a lubricious faun, rescues a vaporous nymph from a terrify-ing "Old Troglodyte." His choreography, like the costumes and makeup, draws upon and exaggerates stereotyped gender roles.

In the theater, all the performers are masquerading, and the audience is defined as knowing, or believing, that the actors are not the same as the roles they play. In this sense, her stage makeup protects Renée within the circle of her performance, like the footlights that demarcate the heightened space of the stage, or the costume, how-ever flimsy, that turns the dancer's nakedness into a draped and painterly nudity.[12] Renée takes pleasure in performance. The text describes both a kinesthetic pleasure in movement and corporeal mastery, and a visual pleasure in being an object of the appreciative gaze. These are mirror-stage, narcissistic pleasures, scopophilic and exhibitionistic at once.

But the traditional view of actresses as little different from pros-titutes undermines the illusion. By hypnotizing herself into the vi-sual, Renée tells herself that nothing is real but her own dancing, in effect "disavowing," refusing to recognize, the real social position and reputation of the actress. As Nancy Miller shows, the gendered power relations between Renée and her public make the enthusiastic cheers of the male audience an example of "interpellation."[13] Each performance becomes a struggle between the reading that she desires to communicate, and that includes her talent and pleasure, and the much more crude judgments of her audiences, which re-spect neither her person nor the artistic mastery of her performance. The spectators are concerned with their own desires: they complain to the management if Renée's costume does not fall off to show her breasts as much as usual, and they miss no opportunity of grabbing at her body if she is obliged to walk by them to reach the stage. They write her letters attempting to arrange a rendezvous, expecting to have easy access to the sexual favors of a woman who displays her body on the stage. Colette's narrator is aware that there are two economies of pleasure at work in Renée's performance. To the extent that the footlights separate performer from audience, the two can be played out without incidence on each other, but it seems that in fact the audience's pleasures are always threatening to cross these boundaries. The dancer's work is read as a woman displaying her body for the eyes of men. While only Max succeeds in penetrating her private life, every man in the audience expects access to this offered body.[14] The feeling of inviolability of the woman in makeup is illusory: "The narcissistic fantasy of an inviolable second skin can only be sustained if it is recognized as such by the other; and in order to be recognized, it must first be acknowledged . . . [as] a surface that cannot be penetrated by any means, including sexual means."[15]

Returning home after her performance, Renée continues the confrontation with her mirrored face. Upon removing her stage makeup, she observes her "real face," and analyzes her good points and faults dispassionately. Her insistence upon the need for long hours of soaking and scrubbing to remove the garish colors implies a process of purification. After the dressing room, we have, as it were, the undressing room, after *maquillage, démaquillage:* "Me voilà donc, telle que je suis!" (13) [Behold me then, just as I am!]. But she does not in fact expose this perhaps real self to others. For Renée, in her daily life, makeup is almost as necessary as clothing for her to feel at ease in the visual.

Baudelaire uses the term "fragile beauty" in his essay "Éloge du maquillage" ("In Praise of Makeup").[16] Makeup not only makes beauty divine, but "consolidates" it. He speaks of "les pratiques employées dans tous les temps par les femmes pour consolider et diviniser, pour ainsi dire, leur fragile beauté" (9) [those practices that have always been used by women to consolidate and, as it were, to make divine, their fragile beauty].[17] Women's carnal beauty, even (indeed specially) heightened and idealized with makeup, will not in fact endure like a statue or a painting. Only when the passage of time is discretely bracketed may the beautiful woman become a window on the eternal, a figure of mediation allowing man access to a higher plane of being. "Qui ne voit que l'usage de la poudre de riz . . . a pour but et pour résultat de . . . créer une unité abstraite de couleur de la peau, laquelle unité . . . rapproche immédiatement l'être humain de la statue, c'est-à-dire d'un être divin et supérieur?"[18] [Who cannot see that rice powder is used . . . with the aim and the result of banishing those blemishes that nature has outrageously sown on the complexion, and creating an abstract, skin-colored unity which, like that produced by a stocking, immediately makes the human being more like a statue, that is, a divine and superior being?] As long as woman may be seen as a timeless icon, the anxiety of mortality may be disavowed.

The image of the statue derives much of its piquancy from the fact that women are of mortal flesh. The reference to "fragile beauty" shows that Baudelaire does not completely forget the repression involved in the transcendental impulse he claims is inherent in makeup and fashion. But neither does he directly address or develop this question. "Éloge du maquillage" concentrates on the successful masquerade, and on the benefits it brings to the male spectator of feminine adornment. In *Le Deuxième Sexe*, Simone de Beauvoir will use the Baudelairean opposition between "nature" and "artifice" to present her analysis of makeup. She goes on to draw out the relationship between the feminine masquerade and social attitudes to women's aging and death. "Plus une femme est jeune et saine, plus son corps neuf et lustré semble voué à une fraîcheur éternelle, moins l'artifice lui est utile; mais il faut toujours dissimuler à l'homme la faiblesse charnelle de cette proie qu'il étreint et la dégradation qui la menace. . . . C'est sur le corps de la femme, ce corps qui lui est destiné, que l'homme éprouve sensiblement la déchéance de la chair"[19] [The more a woman is young and healthy, the more her new and glowing body seems promised to eternal youth, the less she has need of artifice; but woman must always hide from man the carnal weakness of this prey he holds in his arms and the degradation which threatens it. . . . Life itself, though it be dressed in the most attractive forms, is always inhabited by old age and death. . . . It is on the body of woman, this body that exists for him, that man feels so keenly the decay of the flesh. . . . The old woman, the ugly woman, are not only without charms; they provoke hatred mixed with fear].

In *La Vagabonde*, and even more keenly in *Chéri* and *La Fin de Chéri*, Colette explores the effects of this positioning of woman as the bearer of mortality. Her texts will not allow us to forget that the joyous misrecognition of beauty (our own, or that of another, there is little difference from this point of view) is fleeting. The anger directed at women by both men and women for failing to be ideally and always beautiful is perhaps at the root of the accelerated aging process experienced by Colette's characters.

Renée's adoption of everyday makeup reminds us of the contemporary discourse on face-paint in women's magazines and advertising slogans. It seems to fit with our knowledge that Colette herself set up shop at one time to sell cosmetics and teach her customers how to use them. In an article on contemporary makeup advertising, Judith Goldstein develops the notion of a "female aesthetic community" where women learn to see their own and each other's face with a critical eye, and to use makeup in order to realign their appearance as closely as possible with the cultural ideal.[20] This analysis, while treating a much later period, is helpful for our reading of Colette in that it insists on the way in which women look at each other and themselves rather than waiting passively to be looked at by men. Goldstein emphasizes the modernist acceptance, exemplified by Baudelaire's praise of makeup, that we consciously construct our appearance.

Renée repairs her makeup, while Max waits to see her: "Poudrer mes joues, rougir mes lèvres, et disperser d'un coup de peigne les cheveux bouclés qui cachent mon front, c'est une besogne machinale, rapide et qui ne demande pas même le secours du miroir. On fait cela comme on se brosse les ongles, par convenance plutôt que par coquetterie" (136–37) [To powder my cheeks, redden my lips, and comb out the tangled locks that hide my forehead is a rapid mechanical task that does not even need the help of a mirror. One does it as one brushes one's nails, more for manners than vanity]. But in spite of this claim, it is clear that Renée resorts to makeup when she feels in danger of violation. Max is at some level aware of this, for he is dismayed that she wishes to powder her nose when they are alone. It is not a signal of availability to other men, as he feigns to fear, but a self-protective mask: "Pour qui voulez-vous mettre de la poudre, à cette heure-ci? — Pour moi, d'abord. Et puis pour vous. — Pour moi, ce n'est pas la peine. Vous me traitez en homme qui vous courtise" (119) [Whoever d'you want to put powder on for, at this hour? — For myself, in the first place. And then for you. — There's no need to bother on my account. You treat me like a man who is paying court to you].

Like the trainers in Goldstein's makeup videos, Colette's narrator holds the discourse of the "scopic régime": "A quoi bon mirer, devant lui, les flétrissures d'un visage qui perd l'habitude d'être contemplé au grand jour? Un adroit maquillage de crayon brun, de koheul bleuté, de raisin rouge ne suffisait-il pas, hier comme tous les jours, à attirer l'attention sur les yeux et la bouche, les trois lumières, les trois aimants de mon visage? Point de rose sur la joue un peu creuse, ni sous la paupière que la fatigue, le clignement fréquent ont, déjà, délicatement guillochée" (130) [What would be the sense of examining, in front of him, the blemishes of a face that is losing the habit of being looked at in daylight? And what could my mirror have taught me, since yesterday, as on all other days, a skillful makeup of brown pencil, bluish kohl, and red lipstick managed to draw attention to my eyes and my mouth, the three lights, the three loadstars of my face. No rouge on my rather hollow cheeks, nor beneath the eyelids that weariness and frequent blinking have already delicately chequered]. But unlike the makeup videos discussed by Goldstein, which end with a freeze-frame image, Renée's gaze on the face is aware of passing time: "à quoi bon?": "Son aveuglement me refuse le droit de changer, de vieillir, alors que tout instant, ajouté à l'instant écoulé, me dérobe déjà à lui" (217) [In his blindness he will not admit that I must change and grow old, although every second, added to the second that is fleeting, is already snatching me away from him].

In a letter to Max, she describes traveling by train through the country where she grew up, and reflects on the loss of her adolescent beauty. "Et qu'aimez-vous en moi, maintenant qu'il est trop tard, sinon ce qui me change, ce qui vous ment, sinon mes boucles foison-nant comme un feuillage, sinon mes yeux que le koheul bleu allonge et noie, sinon la fausse matité d'un teint poudré? Que diriez-vous si je reparaissais, si je comparaissais devant vous, coiffée de mes lourds cheveux plats, avec mes cils blonds lavés de leur mascaro . . .?" (199) [And now that it's too late, are not the things you love in me the things that change me and deceive you, my curls clustering as thick as leaves, my eyes that the blue kohl lengthens and suffuses, the artifi-cial smoothness of my powdered skin? What would you say if I were to reappear, if I appeared before you with my heavy, straight hair, with my fair lashes cleansed of their mascara . . .?]. For Renée, the face she now wears, whether made-up or not, is not her true face. David Le Breton suggests that: "Vieillir, pour beaucoup d'occidentaux, c'est perdre peu à peu son visage, et se voir un jour sous des traits étrangers avec le sentiment d'avoir été dépossédé de l'essentiel. . . . Et pourtant palpite le souvenir d'un visage perdu, le visage de référ-ence"[21] ["for many westerners, aging is the equivalent of gradually losing one's face, of one day seeing oneself with unfamiliar features and with the feeling of having been dispossessed of something essen-tial. . . . And yet the memory still stirs of a lost face, the face of reference]. Le Breton's face of reference must be understood in relation to the ideal face, which is part of the ego ideal. How I think I look may be closer to or more distant from how I wish I looked, or think I could look. But the image sought in the mirror is perhaps always the ego ideal, loved for its perfection (however each individual may construe that perfection), and detested for its impossibly unattainable . . . perfection! Discussing Virginia Woolf's story "The New Dress," Pacteau explains: "She went to the party *as* a picture, an 'object of the look' certainly, but at the same time *her own picture—the one at the core of herself*, a charming girl. A moment of joyous misrecognition."[22]

Renée's street makeup at once veils and announces her aging, and she will refuse to marry Max in part because of the impending loss of her beauty. Her choice of independence is not, then, an unmixed victory, for it contains the bitter recognition of women's cultural definition. Renée believes that as she ages, her desire is becoming excessive, and clearly fears the consequences of acting on it: "Imagine-moi belle encore et désespérée, enragée dans mon armure de corset et de robe, sous mon fard et mes poudres, sous mes fragiles et jeunes couleurs. . . . J'atteins—tu le sais!—l'âge de l'ardeur. C'est celui des imprudences sinistres" (223) [Imagine me, still beautiful but desperate, frantic in my armor of corset and frock, under my makeup and powder, in my young, tender colors. . . . I am reaching—you know it—the age of ardor. It is the age of fatal imprudences].

Nancy Miller claims that the fear of losing Max as she ages reads largely as an excuse that he will understand. "Renée rehearses a refusal comprehensible to Max's masculinity; a classically feminine insecurity about appearance."[23] However, Renée *is* concerned about the role of aging and appearance in heterosexual love scenarios. Her rewriting of the story, and her desire for freedom are real, but so is her acknowledgment of the social meaning of an aging woman's face and body. Her understanding of the necessity and futility of makeup undermines her choice, shooting it through with mortal vul-nerability. Thus, the feminist triumph of her decision to eschew mar-riage with Dufferein-Chantel is in reality also a feminist defeat. Renée puts aside her real sexual desires in recognition of the social conse-quences of corporeal aging for women.

To a limited extent, Colette's novel moves toward what we think of as a contemporary, playful, and practical view of makeup. The discourse defining ornamentation as feminine, and castigating women for vanity and narcissism in general, and for wearing makeup in particular, has a long history. While there have been times and contexts where both men and women wore makeup, and while its condemnation in Western cultures has not been uniform across class, period, or nationality, such judgments are familiar, recurring, and powerful.[24] And yet, Renée chooses to keep both her paint boxes. Expressed against the guilt so often attached to the "painted woman," her affirmation requires courage. The deft rapidity of her makeup skills both on and off the stage is the same, and recalls the fluidity she values in her writing. Further, her awareness that it is in fact impossible to present an undisguised face precludes the suggestion that her acceptance of makeup implies no more than a desperate stopgap: "Il n'y a pas de déguisement sans coquetterie et il faut autant de soins, autant de vigilance, pour s'enlaidir à toute heure que pour se parer" (125) [There is no disguise without coquetry, and it needs as much care and vigilance to make oneself ugly all the time as to adorn oneself].

LE VISAGE MOBILE

In *La Vagabonde,* Renée's music hall work may be seen to prevent her from continuing her career as a novelist, but in another sense dancing comes to represent a kind of writing: "She turns these suggestive performances into celebrations of movement, of rhythm and beauty—all the qualities of her writing."[25] But if we look for a similar development in the meaning of makeup as the novel progresses, we must acknowledge that "writing on the face" never becomes writing in the way we sense, or hope, it might, for it remains tied to femininity and the economy of the masquerade. There seems, indeed, to be an opposition between the mobility of expression and creation, and the defensive stasis of makeup: "Deux habitudes m'ont donné le pouvoir de retenir mes pleurs: celle de cacher ma pensée, et celle de noircir mes cils au mascaro" (23) [Two habits have taught me how to keep back my tears: the habit of concealing my thoughts, and that of darkening my lashes with mascara]. It would seem that whether makeup represents the attainment of ideal beauty, or a defensive veil, it is incompatible with the facial gymnastics of authentic feeling. Max compares Renée's rapid and unrestrained writing to her "mobile face," "surmené par l'excès d'expression" (222) [exhausted from expressing too much].

Susan Gubar has pointed out that since women are culturally defined as the objects of representation rather than the subjects of it, their creative output has tended to be limited to "feminine" domains such as personal writing of various sorts, homemaking arts, fashion, makeup, and dance.[26] In all these forms, the subject of the creative act is also its object. The woman makes her own life or self into a work of art. Such a restriction limits the fictional distance between what women (re)present and what they are, and the analogy between the

woman artist and the woman of loose morals follows, as both are
selling their "selves." Colette makes explicit the relationship between
Renée's self-presentation in her dancing, her experience as model
for her ex-husband's paintings, and her self-assurance when naked
before a lover. Her pride in this beauty and in her control over it is a
rebellious stance in the face of this logic.

The opposition between authentic expression and the defensive
masquerade does not finally preclude a reading of makeup as writing, however. For *La Vagabonde* moves beyond confession, and makes
a claim to fiction—and "creative expression" is linked to seduction,
and to lying. Adolphe Taillandy's only genius is for lying (28). Pleas-
ing his clients by representing them as more beautiful than they
really are, "il voit blond, résolument" (27) [he resolutely sees everything in a rosy light]. The stereotyped lie of his paintings seduces the
society ladies who model for them, and procures not only a lucrative
income but a series of mistresses: "Je ne veux pour modèles que des
maîtresses, et pour maîtresses que mes modèles" (28) [I want no
models but my mistresses, and no mistresses but my models]. Taillandy can provide women with the seductive illusion of unchanging
beauty, of being a perfect picture.

Traditionally, the right to make images of women rests with men,
and the pleasure of women is in being the picture. Even Renée's
allies, Brague and Hamond, participate in this economy. Brague is
Renée's trainer and choreographer: she represents a medium for his
expression. Hamond is an artist, and on occasion observes Renée
with a measuring, painterly eye. Max goes further, laboriously reducing her face to an idiosyncratic hieroglyph, "un petit dessin géométri-
que lisible pour moi seul" (160) [a little geometric design that con-
veyed something to me alone]. He claims the right to name her:
"vous ne serez plus Renée Néré, mais Madame Ma Femme!" (214)
[you will no longer be Renée Néré but My Lady Wife] and define her:
"Ses yeux vigilants vont et viennent rapidement, de mes paupières à
ma bouche, de ma bouche à mes paupières, et semblent lire mon
visage" (123) [His watchful eyes dart rapidly from my eyelids to my
mouth, from my mouth to my eyelids, and seem to read my face].
Further, it is clear that he does not recognize the same right or ability
in her, reacting with amused impassivity when she describes his
character. His eyes seem to say: "Mon souci n'est pas que vous me
connaissez tel que je suis: créez votre amoureux à votre guise, et c'est
après—comme un maître retouche et refait l'œuvre médiocre d'un
élève chéri, c'est après que, sournoisement, peu à peu, j'y mettrai ma
ressemblance!" (122) [My worry is not that you should know me as I

am: create your admirer according to your liking, and afterwards, as a master touches up and re-does the mediocre work of a beloved pupil, I will quietly introduce a better likeness] (p. 93, translation modified). The existence of Renée's narrative suggests that Max's confidence in the masculine prerogative was misplaced. But his self-assured claims are particularly galling to Renée, who delights in her own dexterity and facility of expression, and observes her suitor's distinct lack of talent in this area. "Il écrit simplement, mais cela se devine, sans facilité" (202) [He writes simply but obviously not with ease].

We could thus see makeup, as it is often seen, as something that men do to women, in that women feel obliged to present themselves as paintings, if they are to be seen by men. But must a woman rebel against makeup, then, if she desires to be a subject of the mimetic and aesthetic gaze? No, in fact. For this path only circles back to the personal, the illusion of authenticity.

When she encounters a doe in the forest, Renée explicitly compares her appearance to the animal's: "ses longs yeux, allongés encore d'un trait brun—comme les miens—exprimaient plus d'embarras que de peur" (182) [her long eyes, made longer still by a brown line—like mine—expressed more embarrassment than fear]. Renée's perception of her own eye makeup as a lie is at once forgiven and condemned by the comparison—the brown rim around her eyes is naturalized by the similar markings on the doe, but at the same time indicted because, unlike the animal's, it is painted on. She thus exposes her identification with nature as a fiction, as writing.

Renée's return to writing is based on fiction and masks at least as much as upon self-knowledge and "authenticity." Her letters are a combination of confession, denial, and hedging. "Que faire? . . . Pour aujourd'hui, écrire, brièvement, car l'heure presse, et mentir" (219) [What shall I do? For today I'll write—briefly, for time is short—and lie to him]. She dreams of an unadorned, honest writing (that one might call *écriture démaquillée*): "Écrire sincèrement, presque sincèrement! J'en espère un soulagement, cette sorte de silence intérieur qui suit un cri, un aveu" (222) [To write sincerely, almost sincerely! I hope it may bring me relief, that sort of interior silence that follows a sudden utterance, a confession]. But just as she is aware that it is impossible to present a "true," unprepared face, so the text admits the self-protective functions of fiction, and the possibilities of play between the mask and its wearer. In the end, the masquerade is indeed a form of writing, a space of expression (however conflicted), and a necessary defense (however vulnerable).

Conclusions

Renée's rejection of Max, and her choice of independence, writing, and adventure does not mean that she has overcome and gone beyond the mirror. In a sense, it represents the mirror's victory over her, for she rejects her suitor at least in part because of beauty's inevitable defeat at the hands of time. However, insofar as the mirror represents the "conseillère maquillée" [painted mentor], speaking woman's necessary silence, her great vulnerability, her sexual needs, her fragile mortality (somehow more mortal than men)—and the passive subservience to husband and social place that the latter justifies—Renée does go beyond the logic of the glass.

Her choice of writing, and the powerful seduction of the road, of performance, do not suggest that Renée is destined to emulate Margot's model of the husbandless life. It is true that love and sexuality are coded as life, against the death imagery of solitude, but Renée paradoxically experiences the cold winds of independence as invigorating and challenging, while warmth and sensuality betray an unmistakably regressive quality: a certain cloying and oppressive liquidity. This tension, then, between going beyond the logic of the mirror in one sense, and submitting to the harshness of its consequences in another, is what constructs the ambiguity of the novel's conclusion.[27]

Notes

1. *La Vagabonde* was originally published by Ollerdorf in 1911. The edition cited in this essay is Colette, *La Vagabonde* (Paris: Livre de Poche, Albin Michel, 1988). Here I have used Enid Macleod's translation (London: Penguin, 1960); unless otherwise indicated, all other translations are my own.

2. Jenijoy La Belle, *Herself Beheld: The Literature of the Looking Glass* (Ithaca: Cornell University Press, 1988), 26.

3. Ibid., 29.

4. Francette Pacteau, *The Symptom of Beauty* (Cambridge: Harvard University Press, 1994), 149.

5. Ibid., 149.

6. Colette, *Chéri* (Paris: Calmann-Lévy, 1920); *La Fin de Chéri* (Paris: Flammarion, 1926).

7. Colette, *Chéri*, 27.

8. It should be noted that for Colette women who are not "feminine" are seen as virilized. They include those who are too old and no longer sexually attractive (Léa in *La Fin de Chéri*), those who repress their sexuality or are unattractive (Margot), and in general those who are not subject to the humiliating needs of "the female" for men's sexual attention.

9. Christina Angelfors, *La Double Conscience. La Prise de conscience féminine chez Colette, Simone de Beauvoir, et Marie Cardinal,* Études romanes de Lund, 44 (Lund, Sweden: Lund University Press, 1989), 30–48.

10. Pacteau, *Symptom of Beauty,* 189.

11. *The Pursuit* seems to be a transposition of the mime that Colette performed with Georges Wague: *La Chair (Flesh).* For more details, see Joanna Richardson, *Colette* (New York: Franklin Watts, 1984), 39–40. Of course, the mimes and dances described in *La Vagabonde* also suggest contemporary influences such as Loïe Fuller, Isadora Duncan, and Diaghilev's *Ballets russes.*

12. See Kenneth Clark's distinction between the naked and the nude in *The Nude: A Study in Ideal Form* (Princeton: Princeton University Press, 1956), and Anne Hollander's chapter "Nudity," in *Seeing through Clothes* (New York: Avon, 1975).

13. Nancy K. Miller, "Woman of Letters: The Return to Writing in Colette's *The Vagabond,*" in *Subject to Change: Reading Feminist Writing* (New York: Columbia University Press, 1988), 242–43.

14. Colette suggests that male performers may also be read as feminized, and thus sexually available, most notably through the figure of Stéphane-le-danseur.

15. Pacteau, *Symptom of Beauty,* 156–57.

16. Charles Baudelaire, "Éloge du maquillage," in *Œuvres complètes,* ed. Claude Pichois (Paris: Gallimard, Bibliothèque de la Pléiade, 1976), 2: 714–18.

17. Ibid., 717.

18. Ibid.

19. Simone de Beauvoir, *Le Deuxième Sexe,* 2 vols. (Paris: Gallimard, Idées, 1949), 1: 219–20.

20. Judith L. Goldstein, "The Female Aesthetic Community," *Poetics Today* 14, no. 1 (1993): 143–63.

21. David Le Breton, *Des Visages. Essai d'anthropologie* (Paris: Métailié, 1992), 12.

22. Pacteau, *Symptom of Beauty,*190; my emphasis.

23. Miller, "Woman of Letters," 253.

24. See, for example, J. Howard Bloch, *Medieval Misogyny and the Invention of Western Romantic Love* (Chicago: University of Chicago Press, 1991); Marcia L. Colish, "Cosmetic Theology: The Transformation of a Stoic Theme," *Assays: Critical Approaches to Medieval and Renaissance Texts* 1 (1981): 3–14; Jacqueline Lichtenstein, "Making Up Representations: The Risks of Femininity," *Representations* 20 (1987): 77–87; Naomi Schor, *Reading in Detail: Aesthetics and the Feminine* (New York: Methuen, 1987).

25. Erica M. Eisinger, "*The Vagabond:* A Vision of Androgyny," in *Colette: The Woman, the Writer,* ed. Erica Mendelson Eisinger and Mari Ward McCarty (University Park: Pennsylvania State University Press, 1981), 98.

26. Susan Gubar, "'The Blank Page' and the Issues of Feminine Creativity," in *Writing and Sexual Difference,* ed. Elizabeth Abel (Chicago: University of Chicago Press, 1982), 73–93.

27. Marie Maclean's influence on my career and thinking cannot be overstated. I miss her mentoring greatly, and feel keenly the loss of all that she could have continued to write and say to us. I would also like to express my gratitude to Gerald Prince, Lucienne Frappier-Mazur, Lance Donaldson-Evans, Ross Chambers, Jean-Marc Kehrès, and Gwendolyn Wells for suggestions and comments on versions of this paper.

HAIR—And How to Do It

ANNE FREADMAN

On 30 May 1917, we could say, taking a leaf out of one of Virginia Woolf's essays and just changing the date a little, human character really did change.[1] They were all having their hair cut. Well, the women were, while their menfolk had their backs turned, engaged as they were in the important warrior pursuits of the day. It was not unlike Penelope and her lovers, when you think about it. Odysseus off at the Trojan War, she warding off the galloping hordes at home. She was weaving a tapestry, and Freud tells us that weaving and plaiting may be the only contribution women have made to the history of civilization. We plait, he tells us, our pubic hair—symbolically, of course—in an unconscious representation of our penis envy.[2] So Penelope, wise girl that she was, wove during the day and unwove at night, fraying and separating, frustrating the desire of the penis, turning its telos back upon itself. But the women of the early twentieth century just cut it off, and when the men came back from the war, wounded, limping, traumatized beyond belief at the destructive powers set to work by the modern masculine imagination, they found these women unrecognizable in their short skirts and their short hairstyles, their free and suddenly athletic bodies striding around the streets of Paris, their sense of purpose unmistakable as they signified in their very person what had become the modern world.[3]

Colette wrote a lot during this period, of men who no longer desire their wives or the mistresses they had left behind, and women who have lost control of the arts and the practices of femininity. I shall have more to say about her as I proceed: she is the chronicler, and Coco Chanel is the practitioner whose importance, if not to "the" women's movement, at least to "women's movement" we should remember in a mantra every morning. But I want to show you some pictures before I come to the words of this story, pictures that are sometimes photographs, and sometimes the wonderful graphic art of the early years of *Vogue*. And before I get to them, let me call to mind the image of Virginia Woolf: the portrait of the three Stephen sisters

185

of 1896 with their center parts and their hair drawn back at the nape
in the thick Edwardian chignon that is shown so clearly in the portrait of Virginia of 1903, the long hair that is sometimes, in the early
thirties, drawn back in combs, and that becomes the wispy, rather
untidy little bun of her later years. Virginia Woolf strode, certainly,
with her long bony body so clearly at ease in its cardigans and flat
shoes, and she may have had her hair trimmed, as we used to say, to
keep the ends healthy. Over time, it was most certainly shortened, its
coiffure simplified to diminish its Edwardian luxuriance, but it was
never bobbed or shingled. Marie Maclean, too, always wore her hair
long, fashioned over the years in different styles of chignon, her tall
frame lovingly draped in jerseys and fine stuffs. This choice, to wear
the hair short or long, "up" or loose, parted, fastened, fringed or
curled, this choice became possible with some version of the Lacanian slash, on 30 May 1917. It is a slash, if I might put it this way, that
weaves together several strands of social and aesthetic history to write
with the bodies of women the text of a certain modernism.

We can start the narrative of change with an image of Colette with
Willy. The change is aesthetic: it can be watched in a kind of geometry, a play of volumes in space (fig. 1).

Fashionable attire for the 1909 races displays the hourglass body,
itself designed by three-dimensional triangular shapes (fig. 2).

Note the proportions, the very large hat, the enormous coiffure
that must be needed to support it.[4] We can see the same sort of thing
in pictures from Vogue covers of 1909 (figs. 3 and 4).

For women who wished to take advantage of the greater opportunities for professional careers that were beginning to open up at
the turn of the century, the hat was at once a sign of respectability
and a nuisance. Colette herself, for example, worked as a journalist,
sometimes trying her hand at street reporting. On 2 May 1912, she
joins the crowd "après l'affaire de la rue d'Ordener," pushing her way
through to get a better view.[5] Only the gentlemen of the press were
allowed beyond the police cordon, she is told, and even if she is a
reporter, "anything wearing a skirt" should keep to its assigned place
("tout ce qui porte une jupe doit rester ici tranquille," 610). Then she
is abused by a woman for the size of her hat. Somebody guffaws, and
offers her his trousers.

Dressed as a grande bourgeoise, her behavior is that of a member
of the public in one of the popular theaters that she knew so well:

L'exécrable esprit spectateur s'empare de moi, celui qui mène les
femmes aux courses de taureaux, aux combats de boxe et jusqu'aux pieds
de la guillotine—l'esprit de curiosité qui supplée si parfaitement au réel

Fig. 1: Colette with Willy. © Bibliothèque Nationale de France

Fig. 2: Fashionable races attire (1909).

courage . . . Je piétine, je plie le front pour me garder des rafales de poussière . . .

"Mais, madame, si vous croyez que c'est commode d'y voir quelque chose à côté de quelqu'un qui remue autant que vous!"

C'est ma sévère voisine, la mère de famille . . .

[The abominable attitude of the spectator takes hold of me, the spirit which drives women to bullfights, to boxing matches and right to the very foot of the guillotine—that sense of curiosity which so perfectly replaces real courage . . . I shift around, I squint to avoid the great gusts of dust . . .

Fig. 3: Large hats and big coiffures from *Vogue* (1909). F. Earl Christy © Vogue,
Condé Nast Publications Inc.

Fig. 4: Large hats and big coiffures from *Vogue* **(1909). Vivien Valdaire © Vogue, Condé Nast Publications Inc., H. Heyer © Vogue, Condé Nast Publications Inc.**

"Really, Madam, how do you reckon I'd see anything alongside someone who moves about as much as you!"
That was my stern neighbor, a family lady . . .

This woman—described in passing as being "en cheveux," that is,
bareheaded—complains that Colette simply doesn't have the appropriate manners for the occasion:

"Ça ne serait pas la peine qu'on soye là depuis 9 heures ce matin pour
que vous vous mettiez devant moi au dernier moment! Une place gardée,
c'est une place gardée. D'abord, quand on a un si grand chapeau, on
l'ôte!"
Elle défend son "fauteuil d'orchestre" avec une autorité qui cherche—
et trouve—l'approbation générale. J'entends derrière moi des cris
rythmés de: "Chapeau! Chapeau!", des plaisanteries qui datent des revues
de l'année dernière, mais qui prennent ici une étrange saveur quand on
songe à ce qui se passe là-bas . . . (611–12)

["One hardly stakes out a place at nine o'clock in the morning to have
you intrude in front of me at the last minute! A spot taken is a spot taken.
To begin, when one wears a hat of such proportions, one takes it off!"
She defends her seat in the stalls with an authority which looks for —
and finds— general approval. Behind me I hear chants: "Hats off!", jokes

as stale as last year's revues but which turn particularly pointed here when one thinks of what is happening over there . . .]

Appropriate manners? Women did not take off their hats in an audience; this is a rule for the *haut de forme*. She counts her curiosity as feminine, but is putting it to the service of a masculine profession; she is dressed as a bourgeoise, but she is in the crowd; she is kept in her woman's place by the police, and reprimanded for not conforming with masculine public manners, by a woman. She never gets to see the event for which she came, and the story ends up being about the multiple class and gender contradictions of the "new woman" who was precisely, at this moment in history, trying to work out what her place "in the crowd" could be. She is kept in check by the forces of law and order, her gender role being defined for the policeman by her skirt and for the woman beside her, by her hat. If we count the skirt and the hat as the signs of the practical problem that would need to be solved, then the first would be solved by the short hemline and the invention of trousers for women, and the second, by the pillbox or the cloche. Both would occur within the decade. But before women could wear the cloche, they would have to have their hair cut.[6]

Colette herself was pitilessly satirical about the cloche.[7] Women were unrecognizable beneath them, even their husbands had to examine their earrings to be sure they were greeting the right woman, and they developed permanent squints from having one eye blinkered. But let us leave Colette with her nostalgia for the flowered and feathered confection, and return to the hair that held it in place.

The women who wore these very large hats represent high Paris fashion; let us look at simpler women, the middle- and even the working-class versions of the hairstyles that will disappear.

Although she is a working-class girl, the milliner from a 1912 cover of *Vogue* wears her hair such that she can model the hats for her customers (fig. 5).

Chanel, too, started her career in millinery. A 1910 portrait of her shows her hair piled up, worn in much the same fashion as the milliner's, presumably for the same purpose (fig. 6).

These are working women. Their counterparts in the respectable but modest middle classes often wore their hair so that it was built up around the face, and fastened in a chignon on the crown of the head. The portrait of Madame Matisse, known as "The Green Line" and a sculpted head of Jeannette, from 1910 show how Matisse models hair as volumes on the head, that change with his exploration of the plastic properties of the shapes themselves (figs 7 and 8).

Fig. 5: A milliner's attire in *Vogue* (1912). © Vogue, Condé Nast Publications Inc

Fig. 6: Portrait of Chanel (1910).

Fig. 7: Matisse, "The Green Line" (1905). © Henri Matisse, 1905/Les Héritiers Matisse. Permission of VISCOPY Ltd, Sydney 2000.

But I have digressed from my shop girl; in *Vogue*'s version in 1914 she is neatly and modestly dressed, with her hair in a chignon just like Woolf's, marvelously decorative, the very image of a deeply mysterious erotic knot, the promise of a woman's own undoing (fig. 9).

The same chignon appears on both a portrait of Cléo de Mérode and on a nude from 1921 by Erna Lendvai-Dirckson (figs. 10 and 11);

Fig. 8: Matisse, "Jeannette" (1910). © Henri Matisse, 1910/Les
Héritiers Matisse. Permission of VISCOPY Ltd, Sydney 2000.

Fig. 9: *Vogue* cover (1914). George Plank ©Vogue, Condé Nast Publications Inc.

Fig. 10: Portrait of Cléo de Mérode

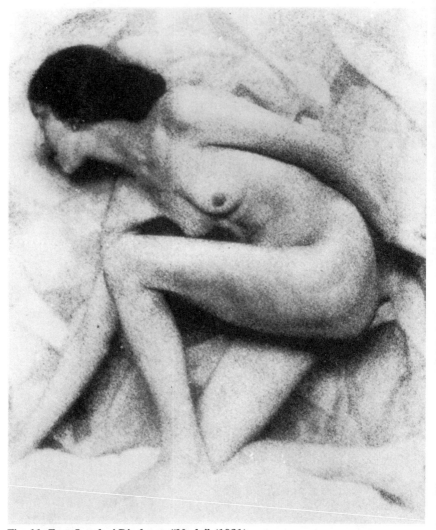

Fig. 11: Erna Lendvai-Dirckson, "Nude" (1921).

it reappears, loosened, in a picture from 1906 by Robert Demachy (fig. 12).

The chignon returns, quite undone this time, in a Man Ray photograph from 1929, where the hair is a metonym for woman herself (fig. 13). Matisse's 1932 illustration for Mallarmé's "La Chevelure," works in a similar fashion (fig. 14).

A woman's hair is her crowning glory, we were taught even when I was young. Sido, Colette's mother, was distraught when she learned

Fig. 12: Robert Demachy, "Perplexity" (1906). © The Royal Photographic Society
Collection, Bath, England. Web Site http://www.rps.org

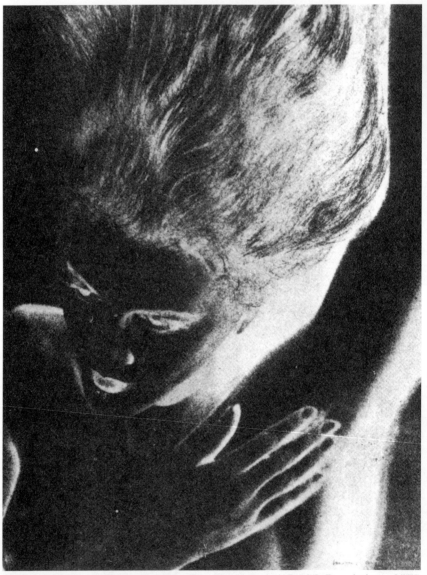

Fig. 13: Man Ray, "Woman". © Man Ray Trust, Paris/ADAGP. Permission of VIS-COPY Ltd, Sydney 2000.

Fig. 14: Matisse, "Tresses." © Henri Matisse, 1932/Les Héritiers Matisse. Permission of VISCOPY Ltd, Sydney 2000.

that Colette's hair had been cut. It was "my masterpiece," she said. Nicole Ward Jouve comments that "Perhaps the women in that period had to cut it, as they all did . . . because the weight of men's images had become too heavy to carry."[8]

Hair is a wonderful subject for photography, because of its tricks with form and surface, because of the way it moves and plays in the light, but technical considerations such as these are a distraction from its fetishistic value. I could show you hundreds of photographs of women more or less naked, in which the hair is the focus of the erotic gaze. Robery Demachy's "Untitled" (1900), surely a picture of Baudelaire's "La Chevelure," could be used to sum up the whole series (fig. 15).

This story, of hair and how to undo it, is just a way of putting us in the picture. When women cut their hair, this particular narrative knot was much more thoroughly undone than Penelope's tapestry, or the odd chignon. The event, which was certainly dramatic, was noted in the intimate chronicles of the day. It has a date, 30 May 1917: "In the last few days [writes Paul Morand], the fashion has become for women to wear their hair short. They're all doing it: Madame Letellier and Coco Chanel in the lead . . ."[9]

The Chanel Morand is referring to can be seen in two images of the early 1930s. Images of the Coco Chanel of the early 1930s referred to by Paul Morand, are cited in Charles-Roux's text of 1989, *Chanel* (figs. 16 and 17).

When Colette writes her splendid portrait of Chanel, she describes her at work, and significantly, she describes her as sculpting: "Mademoiselle Chanel est en train de sculpter un ange de six pieds," she writes, "Chanel travaille des dix doigts, de l'ongle, du tranchant de la main, de la paume, de l'épingle et des ciseaux, à même le vêtement . . ." [Mademoiselle Chanel is sculpting a six foot angel, Chanel works with all her fingers, with her nails, with the side of her hands, with her palms, with pins and scissors, directly on the garment . . .] sometimes on her knees, not in reverence, but adjusting the cut of the fabric, its fall around the body. Chanel's focus is on this body that she is molding; Colette's is on the body of the sculptor: "Cet entraînement professionnel du corps la laisse mince, un peu creusée par la fatigue." But she starts with the hair:

> de par l'énergie butée, la manière de faire face, d'écouter, par l'esprit de défense qui, parfois, lui barricade le visage, "Chanel" est un taureau noir. La touffe sombre, frisée, apanage des taurillons, retombe sur son front jusqu'à ses sourcils et danse à tout mouvement de sa tête.

> [in her obstinate energy, the way in which she confronts things and listens, in her defensive attitude which, at times, shuts off her face, "Chanel" is a black bull. A curly dark tuft, typical of the bull-calf, falls over her forehead and down to her eyebrows, dancing around with every movement of her head.]

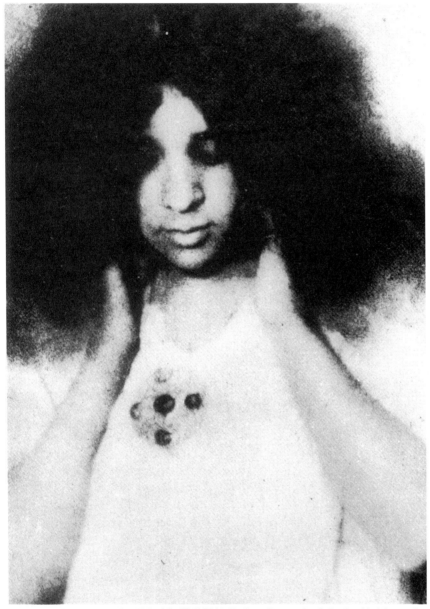

Fig. 15: Robert Demachy, "Untitled" (1900). Robert Demachy © La Société française
de photographie

Fig. 16: Photograph of Chanel (early 1930s).

Fig. 17: Photograph of Chanel (early 1930s).

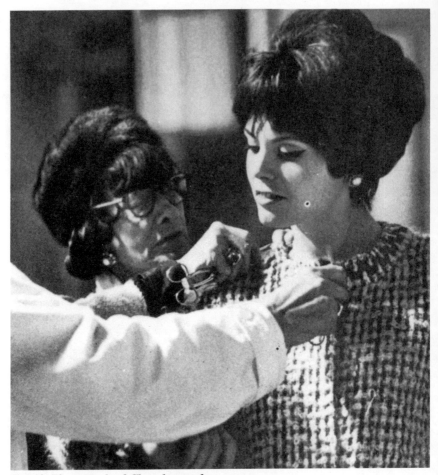

Fig. 18: Photograph of Chanel at work.

There exist several photographs of Chanel at work, often, in her later years, wearing the soft beret that became her personal signature; some of these images—dating from the period following the temporary eclipse imposed by the war, and the rise of Dior—bring her into the era of my own youthful memories of fashion (fig. 18).

Such photographs display the close working relationship between Chanel and her client; her own hair is cut as it always had been, left to fall naturally around her face, and it contrasts markedly with the teased, bouffant hairstyle of the sixties. It makes you wonder what we thought we were doing, doesn't it, especially when you think of what we called the "beehive," perched precariously like a false memory of the 1890s, grossly disproportionate with the mini-dresses that it crowned. When Chanel launched the bob to go with her slim, short designs, it was the classical proportions that made the look instantly recognizable as elegant, despite the radical break with previous styles.[10]

In 1916, Chanel had published her first revolutionary designs in *Harper's Bazaar*. The hat is still large, and would remain so for another year, but the design foreshadows the flapper of the 1920s. Notice that the body takes its compositional line, and its proportions, from the sloping horizontal of the shoulders, and is designed as a vertical arrangement of rectangles. This is clearly apparent in another Chanel design from 1926, in which everything is smaller, the lines simpler, and the proportions governing the body are given by the rule of three (figs. 19 and 20).

The body has become its own size, and the head is proportioned accordingly. Short hair, short hemlines, and indeed, sometimes fringes with fringed hems and bodices; the hair is treated as a fabric, moving with the head, but never obscuring it or weighing it down. Chanel's use of soft fabrics, the jerseys in particular, and this discovery of the properties of free short hair, allow the body to define its place in space from the inside, rather than from the outside. Designs by Lepape and Plank among others, featured in *Vogue* in the four years following the end of the First World War, show a body whose relation with space is not defined by its padding, as a relation of protection, confinement, or disguise (figs. 21, 22, 23, and 24).

Rather, such a body is defined primarily by its skeleton and its muscles, interpreted by textures—flesh, fabric, hair—that become progressively lighter, transforming the corporeal into the tactility of the air it inhabits. It does not have "a" place, and its weightlessness is a sign not only—although importantly—of the sense of joy that came with the end of hostilities, but also of dreamt vistas of emancipation. But what of its extreme youthfulness? Recall the portrait of Colette in the style of the young Madame Villars, and contrast the dignity of her position, the learned adultness of her bearing, with these imaginary women who are looking as young as possible, barely sexually mature. Short hair signifies the child, and it is the story of Colette herself that tells us so.

In the last two years of the Great War, middle-class women in Paris not only cut their hair, threw away their corsets, wore loose trousers at home, and started to smoke: they also organized hospitals and am-

Fig. 19: Chanel design in *Harper's Bazaar* (1916).

Fig. 20: Chanel design (1926).

Fig. 21: Lepape design in *Vogue* (1918). Lepape © Vogue, Condé Nast Publications Inc.

Fig. 22: Lepape designs in *Vogue* (1919). Lepape © Vogue, The Condé Nast Publications Ltd.

Fig. 23: Plank design in *Vogue* (1921). George Plank © Vogue, Condé Nast Publications Inc.

Fig. 24: Lepape design in *Vogue* (1922). Lepape ©Vogue, Condé Nast Publications Inc.

bulance services, orphanages, and other relief agencies. They had jobs, responsible jobs, that kept them out of the house all day; they were taking a policy and administrative responsibility that had heretofore been in the hands of politicians and generals, delegated sometimes to doctors. The change in roles is set out with startling clarity in Colette's pair of novels, *Chéri* and *La Fin de Chéri*, books that have their notoriety primarily as risqué stories of a young man with an older woman, not as social documents.[11] Chéri, handsome, rich, irresponsible, and spoiled, has had his sexual initiation at the hands of Léa, a wealthy—and beautiful—cocotte of middle age and luxurious tastes. He is, moreover, thoroughly attached to her, passionately in love, and his mother and her friends, including Léa, count this a danger. They marry him off to a wealthy young woman of good family, and hope that the problem will be solved. He leaves for the war, and returns after it to find his mother and his wife engaged in the kind of work I have described, much too busy and fulfilled in their new lives to give him the pampering he needs. His masculinity is the problem. Never in doubt before the war—in fact, automatically affirmed by their femininity—it now needs redefining on other bases. This is a task of which he is constitutionally incapable. He is depicted, in fact, in a parodically feminine role after the war, idle, requiring various forms of sensual gratification that leave him perpetually unsatisfied, his desires ill-defined and his life entirely directionless. Eventually, as the crisis develops, he decides to visit Léa: she has discarded her corsets, she is dressed in serge and jersey instead of silk and satin, she has put on weight, and she feels wonderful. "Ça me va, les cheveux courts?" [Does my short hair suit me?] she asks him, and he replies only with a pained "négation muette" [silent negative].[12] This is the end of the "old man" (Chéri kills himself at the close of the book) and the beginning of the "new woman," and it was, genuinely, a widespread and a very deep crisis.

So what is *Vogue* saying about all these self-assured, confident women, carving out for themselves a role in the public sphere? It was representing them as *children*. Willy, Colette's husband, had given them the lead, nearly twenty years previously, and the figure on these *Vogue* covers known as Lepape's little redhead, almost certainly owes something to the image, apparent in publicity photographs of the period, that Willy fabricated for Colette for entirely commercial purposes. I quote Nicole Ward Jouve's account of this episode:

> What marks the whole period between 1900, the date of publication of *Claudine at School*, and 1906, when Colette and Willy separated, is a riot of publicity, engineered by Willy round the character of Claudine. He made

Colette pose as Claudine, twinned by Polaire, a fiery, wasp-waisted *pied-noir* actress who played Claudine on stage. Both girls were dressed in black school-blouse (i.e. tunic), round white collar, booties, with short hair: Colette's 1.57m tresses had been cut. . . . With modern advertising genius, Willy exhibited his Claudine, the girl who was supposed to have given him the material for the books he was supposed to have written and that were signed Willy: "This child has been most precious to me," he would say, laying his soft hand on Colette's head . . .[13]

Neither of two other portaits of Colette, the first taken at the age of fifteen with extraordinary plaits and the second with her hair cut, shows the child that was fabricated by Willy, and both show the very adult *personnage(s)* that Colette forged out of his exploitation (figs. 25, 26, 27, and 28).

It is important to note, however, that it is in hairdressing, in particular, that the child-woman can be transformed again. Modernism is characterized, as we know, by ever more rapid changes in fashion, and hairstyles are no exception. Indeed, it is the very phenomenon of fashion that undermines this attempt to infantilize women, reducing it to a mere style by replacing it, toward the end of the '20s, with the severely cut shingle, the geometrical look with its corners and its sharply defined lines, sleeked down on to the head. A series of images from *Vogue* shows how the sculptural nakedness of this look depends entirely on bone structure: women no longer have heads of hair, they have heads. The similarity of the hairstyles of the man and the woman in the first image, is quite remarkable (figs. 29, 30, 31, and 32).

This image, as I have hinted, is a sculptural interpretation of the female form, it is not a painting or an ornament. It discovers the hard inner structure. When hairdressing looks for the beauty of the head itself, it is inspired, I believe, by Brancusi's "The Muse," of 1912 (fig. 33).

This is what it looks like, but what does it mean? The social history of women in this period is well known: it is evoked by mentioning such things as the movement for women's suffrage, the opening of the universities and of professional training to women, the demise of domestic labor, and the upheaval of the war. Women took to the new styles without hesitation, not only because they signified emancipation, but because they provided its physical enablement. It is hard for us now to remember how liberating it must have been to be able to do your own hair, and dress and undress on a whim or in a hurry. We are, of course, talking about upper-class women, here; but we are also talking about a moment, an act, in which they gave up the signs of

Fig. 25: Publicity photograph featuring Colette. © Bibliothèque Nationale de France

Fig. 26: Publicity photograph featuring Colette. ©
Agence Violet

Fig. 27: Photograph of Colette with plaits. © Agence Violet

their visible and physical difference from their less privileged sisters. It was Chanel, I remind you, who gave currency to costume jewelry, if she did not in fact invent it. If you must own real gems, she used to say, leave them in the bank; don't use them to display your wealth upon your persons.

This might be the social and the cultural value of the new fashions, but we were talking about hair, and surely, I hear you asking, hair has a deeper, more symbolic significance? "*Lovely, lovely hair. And such a mass of it. It had the colour of fresh fallen leaves, brown and red with a glint of yellow. When she did it in a long plait she felt it on her backbone like a long*

Fig. 28: Photograph of Colette with hair cut. © Bibliothèque Nationale de France

Fig. 29: *Vogue* image by Marty (1923). André E. Marty © Vogue, Condé Nast Publications Inc.

Fig. 30: *Vogue* image by Benito (1926). Benito © Vogue, The Condé Nast Publications Ltd

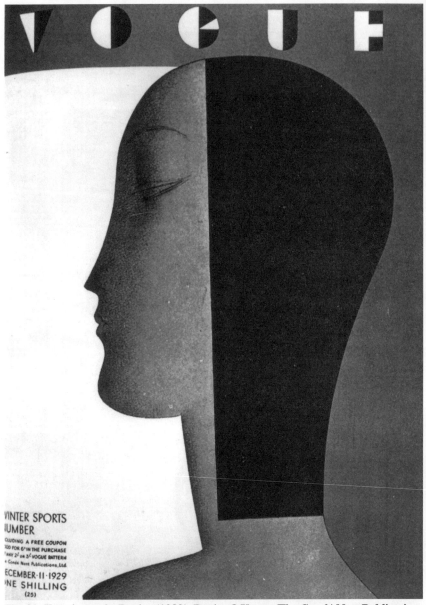

Fig. 31: *Vogue* image by Benito (1929). Benito © Vogue, The Condé Nast Publications Ltd

Fig. 32: Photograph of Mrs d'Erlanger in Vogue (1923) © *Vogue*, The Condé Nast
Publications Ltd

Fig. 33: Brancusi, "The Muse" (1912). Photograph by David Heald © The Solomon R. Guggenheim Foundation, New York

snake. "[14] Language, and literature, may take us closer to this dimension.[15]

Louisa May Alcott published *Little Women* in 1869, well before the period that concerns me directly.[16] The hair-cutting episode in it is both portentous, and an echo, probably, of the meanings that had become associated with the figure of the woman writer through the scandalous life of George Sand, among others. But when Jo March has her hair cut, it is not an act of rebellion. It is a sacrifice, and the discussion she has with her sisters and her mother turns on the contradiction between hair seen as a valuable asset for a girl's femininity, and the hair seen as a commodity, valued for its sale price. Jo sells her hair for $25.00, to "do something for father" (210). Father is wounded and ailing as a result of his military activities, and "doing something for him" means restoring him to health and strength. The threat to Father's masculinity is parried by the sacrifice of daughter's femininity; but Father, as it turns out, never has patriarchal power in this household, never even has much presence, and it is the tomboy Jo who takes his place. One is tempted by the thought that it is her decision to cut her hair that gives her possession and mastery over the symbol of phallic power, but the discussion of it among the women occults this, interpreting the fearsome act as a loss. More than that, it is an amputation, the loss of a nose or a limb, and hence, a castration:

> As she spoke, Jo took off her bonnet and a general outcry arose, for all her abundant hair was cut short.
> "Your hair! Your beautiful hair!" "O Jo, how could you? Your one beauty."
> As everyone exclaimed, and Beth hugged the *cropped head* tenderly, Jo assumed an indifferent air . . . (210).

> "What made you do it?" asked Amy, who would as soon have thought of *cutting off her head* as her pretty hair.
> "I felt wicked, and was bound to have some *money if I sold the nose off my face to get it.*" (211).

> "I will confess . . . I felt queer when I saw the dear old hair laid out on the table, and felt only the short, rough ends on my head. It almost seemed as if *I'd an arm or a leg off*" (212; emphases added).

There is no doubt that hair, long hair, is a phallic fetish, and that the drama of its cutting is generated by the anxiety of castration. Furthermore, it appears to be quite indifferent whether the hair belongs on a woman's head or on a man's. When Dalilah cuts

Sampson's hair, the pillars of the temple simply collapse; and there is a taboo among certain groups in Thailand against allowing women to cut men's hair or to barber them. But judging by the way the modernist haircut becomes a story, exactly the same effects are provoked by the cutting of women's hair. Freud himself, in his *Leonardo Da Vinci* of 1910, refers to "coupeurs de nattes," an expression glossed by the editors of the Standard Edition as meaning "perverts who enjoy cutting off females' hair." He writes that these people "play the part of people who carry out an act of castration on the female genital organs," and Barthes, telescoping this reference with the one about weaving and plaiting, suggests that "to cut the braid is to sketch the castrating gesture;" but he means men, not women.[17] Hair is a deeply ambiguous boundary, both garment and body, inside and out, exactly that part of the body that can be given away or stolen, both an object and a site of exchange. An excrescence that mirrors, in reverse, the penetration of the sexual act, hair is a substance that goes deep. To cut it is exactly the opposite, and hence the same, as to braid it, because both acts signify it as the site at which sexual identity is asserted as difference. In the heterosexual imagination, it may well be the very site of the heterosexual, a boundary that is both one thing and the other, a *différance.*

Three years before Coco Chanel turned short hair into a style, Caryathis, a dancer with the Diaghilev company with whom Chanel had studied dance for a while, "cut off her thick tresses in a fit of pique, tied a ribbon round them, and left them hanging from a nail in the home of a man whose ardor she had failed to arouse."[18] Her first appearance in public with her bobbed hair and her square fringe was at the opening of *The Rite of Spring,* a scandalous evening on all counts. But by ten years later, the haircut had lost its power to act as a sacrifice or a loss, or even as an aggressive act in a private sexual dynamic. It had become a style, a fashion, a rule of conformity, and if women are at a loss, as Colette sometimes claims that they are, to express their femininity in this new fashion, then the culture of women, their conversations, would have to invent ways of meeting the challenge. We severely misrepresent what Chanel did to this end, if we think of her as masculinizing women's clothes. Everything she did was an interpretation of the possibilities in men's clothes, their fabrics, the very kind of garments, for the use of the female form: she feminized men's clothing. Femininity, and feminine sexuality, were not lost; they were transformed.

If the young Marcel at a party *chez* Guermantes lamented the thin figures and sleek heads of the young women with whom he was mixing, well, it was his problem, not theirs. At least, this is the way Léa sees it, when she reproaches Chéri for his neurasthenic nostalgia.[19] Proust was charting loss and inventing the role of memory for the modern age, but the women of the period were inventing the possibilities of the exhilarating changes that their persons were signifying. The Duchesse de Clermont-Tonnerre, who was the model for the Duchesse de Guermantes, and who is mentioned in passing in *La Fin de Chéri* as likely to spoil the local bistro by making it fashionable, visited Gertrude Stein in 1926. In a gesture more theatrical than the defensive gesture of Jo March,

> she took off her hat and her hair was cut short. She said to Gertrude, "What do you think?" Gertrude said "It suits your head." "That is what you will have to come to," said the Duchess of Clermont-Tonnerre. That night, Gertrude said to Alice "Cut it off." "Cut it off," she said and I did."
>
> Alice took two days cutting Gertrude's hair. She did not know how to go about it so it got shorter and shorter. And the shorter it got, the better Gertrude liked it. Previously she had worn it long and "wound in an ancient fashion" (Souhami, 217–18).

Notice that it is Gertrude, as we might have known she would, who understands the move from "suiting your face" to "suiting your head," who understands, that is to say, that it is sculpture that is giving the rules, not painting. Picasso got upset, because she no longer looked like his portrait of 1905–6, while Pavel Tchelitchev decided not to paint her, because she no longer looked like his aunt.

Two photographs of Gertrude show her before and after she "had it cut off (the inset image shows the Duchess) (figs. 34 and 35). Matisse's "The White Fox" features something approximating the Duchess's waves, while his "Henriette II" shows a similar head, sculpted (figs. 36 and 37).

Alice's perplexity at the daunting task before her indicates that an art, and a whole profession based on it, would have to be invented. Jo March, we recall, had her hair cut by a barber. Women's hairdressing, and with it the industry and the commerce of "hair-care products," came into being as a result. The conversations that we now take for granted, about good and bad haircuts, about good and bad experiences with hairdressers and shampoos, about not having time to get a haircut, about hair in general and the way it mediates our whole relation with the world, our self-presentation, and our confidence, these conversations date from the times of our grandmothers, but no earlier. We do well to remember that the judgments that roll so easily off our tongues, about whether someone's hair suits her or not, must have been very rare during the reign of the head of hair; before this

Fig. 34: Photograph of Gertrude Stein with long hair (1907). © Beinecke Rare Book and Manuscript Library, Yale University.

century, it was the quality of hair that we would have noticed, like the quality of skin and the color of eyes and teeth, natural assets or defects that could be more or less modified by the arts of adornment.

But this thing about hair, and the money we spend on it! and how it has changed our lying down and our getting up! I still remember people reciting the rule of brushing the hair with one hundred

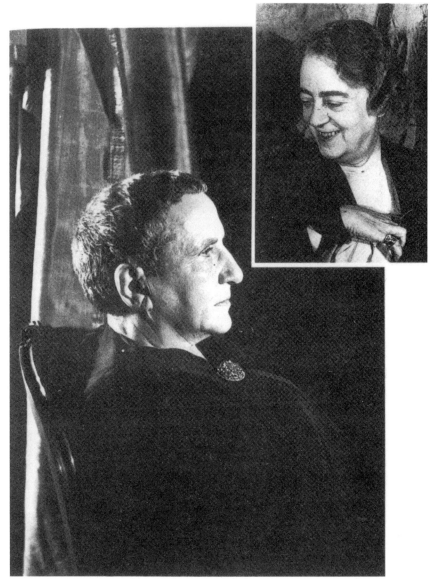

Fig. 35: Photograph of Gertrude Stein with inset of the Duchess of Clermont-Tonerre. © Beinecke Rare Book and Manuscript Library, Yale University.

Fig. 36: Matisse, "The White Fox". © Henri Matisse, 1922/Les Héritiers Matisse. Permission of VISCOPY Ltd, Sydney 2000.

strokes before bedtime,[20] but it was already a relic in the '50s, producing, with short, curly hair like mine and my sister's, the horrid mixture of oil and electricity that we avoided at all costs. In those days, when I was a girl, one of my grandmothers still wore her hair long, braided, and "wound in an ancient fashion" about her head. These people brushed their hair, if not one hundred times a night, at

Fig. 37: Matisse, "Henriette II". © Henri Matisse, 1927/Les Héritiers Matisse. Permission of VISCOPY Ltd, Sydney 2000.

least fifty, to make sure the oil got down into the ends to stop them splitting. That is also how I remember Marie Maclean when I first met her in 1969. A photograph shows my grandmother in 1914, with an infant—my father—on her knees; when she aged, she became small and stooped, but her hair remained abundant and snow white (fig. 38).

Marie was tall and statuesque, and her hair barely showed a thread of white for all that time, although it thinned, I believe, during her illness. My grandmother had her hair cut after my grandfather died, and my memories of watching her brush it and braid it for sleeping, then pin it around her head in the morning, date from this time of mourning, when she was staying in our home. The women of the family always thought of it as tragic, her strong, abundant snow-white hair, brutally cropped at the nape of her neck, and yes we did, just like Jo's sisters, think of this as a loss and a mutilation. But for her, after a life-time, it was a freedom.[21]

For Marie Maclean, braids and chignons were simply the choice of a style that suited fine, straight hair, but for my grandmother the persistence or the retrieval of the ancient fashion can be explained by recourse both to class parameters, and to the effects of the Depression. It costs a lot to go to the hairdresser, and long, braided hair is a frugality. Recipe books from the early and midcentury often contain household hints, and many of these are concerned with care of the hair. I don't know how often one washed one's hair a hundred years ago, but there is some indication that it may have been standard practice to wash it about once a month, at least in cold climates. In the '50s, we washed our hair once a week, and there were natural products we could use to give it extra shine: an egg, but not too often, because it was too rich. Flat beer was also highly recommended. But recent developments have seen the invention of the everyday shampoo, and the plethora of conditioners, waxes, and oils that reverse its depleting effects. These are of course traditional remedies, but sold in quantities and used with a frequency unthinkable in former days. There is an art and a lore of hair, time and money spent upon it, that would have amused Colette, who wrote in 1924 that the fashionable young woman of her day was lazy, with her hairstyles and dresses that didn't need changing for a whole day of varied social activities. What was wrong with a bit of *saine coquetterie*? she asks. This style of elegance was a false economy of time and of money:

> Que rêve-t-elle? Etre habillée et parée, comme elle dit, "une fois pour toutes." Elle a cru, en coupant ses cheveux, qu'elle s'éveillerait le matin, coiffée une fois pour toutes. Mais le coiffeur veillait, maître des guiches,

Fig. 38: Photograph of Estella Freadman holding her son (1914).

émondeur de la nuque, détenteur d'un certain pli près de l'oreille, et je connais mainte libérée qui déjà gémit: "Ah! c'est assommant . . . Il faut que je me fasse tailler tous les quinze jours . . . Et mon pli ne tient pas, derrière l'oreille . . . (II/p.1121).

[Of what does she dream? Of being dressed and bedecked, as she says, "once and for all." By cutting her hair, she thought she would wake up in the morning with her hair done once and for all. But the hairdresser was keeping watch, master of love locks, pruner of the nape, controller of a certain wave close by the ears, and I know many a liberated lady who already moans: "Oh! It's so tedious . . . I have to have it trimmed every fortnight . . . And my wave won't stay behind my ear . . .]

There is a hesitation between two words in this passage: once it is "couper," to cut, but the second time it is "tailler," to trim. This is the word used for pruning plants: the feathers and the flowers of the hats, and then the hair itself.[22] But "cut it off" was what Alice Toklas heard, and that is what she did, because they were "all doing it." What Chanel created, and Paul Morand and the duchess make us understand—but Caryathis did not—is this "all" that dictates fashion. It is a mechanism of conformity, and hence of banalization. The story of the modernist haircut is remarkable, not because it stirred the dramas of the deep, but because it has been so rapidly and so thoroughly integrated into our daily lives. As I have argued, this is largely a function of its action, not just as sign or representation, but as a material condition of the emerging practicalities of women's lives. The ordinariness, and the all-pervasiveness, of the cultural practices associated with this cut are not the drama-charged rituals of circumcision, nor do they resemble the half-secret cruelties of castration or clitorectomy. They are very like the tending practices of horticulture. Think on this, because the unconscious may be more determined than determining, may simply have less power in, and over, women's culture, than we have been used to think.[23]

NOTES

Every effort has been made to locate copyright holders for the images reproduced in this chapter. The author and publishers would like to thank the following for permission to include material: The Bibliothèque Nationale de France (figs. 25, 28); F. Earl Christi © Vogue, Condé Nast Publications Inc. (fig. 3); Vivien Valdaire © Vogue, Condé Nast Publications Inc., H. Heyer © Vogue, Condé Nast Publications Inc. (fig. 4); Vogue, Condé Nast Publications Inc. (fig. 5); Henri Matisse © Les Héritiers Matisse and VISCOPY Ltd, Sydney 2000 (figs. 7, 8, 14, 36, 37); George Plank © Vogue, Condé Nast Publications Inc. (figs. 9, 23); Robert Demachy © The Royal Photographic Society Collection, Bath, England. Web Site *http://www.rps.org*

(fig. 12); The Man Ray Trust, Paris/ADAGP and VISCOPY Ltd, Sydney 2000 (fig. 13); Robert Demachy © La Société Française de la Photographie (fig. 15); Lepape © Vogue, The Condé Nast Publications Ltd. (figs. 21, 22, 24); Agence Violet (figs. 26, 27); André E. Marty © Vogue, Condé Nast Publications Inc. (fig. 29); Benito © Vogue, The Condé Nast Publications Ltd. (figs. 30, 31); d/Langer © Vogue, The Condé Nast Publications Ltd. (fig. 32); David Heald © The Solomon R. Guggenheim Foundation, New York (fig. 33); The Beinecke Rare Book and Manuscript Library, Yale University (figs. 34, 35). We also thank the Office of Research and Postgraduate Studies at the University of Queensland for their generous support in meeting copyright fees.

1. Virginia Woolf, "Mr Bennett and Mrs Brown," in *Collected Essays,* edited by Leonard Woolf (London-Chatto and Windus, 1966–69), vol. III.

2. Sigmund Freud, *New Introductory Lectures on Psychoanalysis, The Standard Edition of the Complete Psychological Works of Sigmund Freud,* translated and edited by James Strachey et. al. (London: The Hogarth Press and the Institute of Psychoanalysis, 1953), vol. XXII, 132.

3. For an account of this moment in terms of the politics of emancipation, see Mary Louise Roberts, "Samson and Delilah Revisited: The Politics of Women's Fashion in 1920s France," *American Historical Review* 3 (June 1993): 657–84.

4. These hats were known as "Gainsborough hats," and were a recent fashion, imported from England in the 1880s, at the same time as lawn tennis for ladies. The reference to painted portraits is significant, in view of the modernist move to a sculptural aesthetic that I discuss below. So is the coincidence with tennis, for sporting images came to signify the modern woman, and were often used for advertising the flapper fashions of the 1920s.

5. "Dans la foule," in *Les Heures longues; Dans la foule,* Colette, *Œuvres complètes,* édition publiée sous la direction de Claude Pichois, Bibliothèque de la Pléiade (Paris: Gallimard, 1986), tome II.

6. Before the cloche, the pillbox seems to have made a brief appearance. It was to have its greater success much later, in the 1950s. There is a portrait of a woman wearing a pillbox by Matisse, "La Tocque de goura," held by the Wadsworth Athaneum, Hartford, Connecticut, which is dated(?)1918 (see the Matisse catalogue, cited below, fig. 80).

7. Colette, "Chapeaux" in *Le Voyage égoïste, Œuvres complètes,* tome II (Paris: Gallimard, 1986), 1149–52.

8. Nicole Ward Jouve, *Colette* (Brighton: Harvester Press, 1987), 95.

9. Paul Morand, Diary, quoted in Charles-Roux, *Chanel* (London: Collins Harvill, 1989), 164.

10. "Commentators were understandably discouraged by the newcomer [Chanel]. She bore no resemblance to anything, having—at least in their eyes—no memory and no tradition. She was an absolutely new woman, a woman whose dress was *without allusion.* Pointless to interrogate her. The rules of the game had been deliberately muddled." Charles-Roux, *Chanel,* 157. I write "instantly" because the first of the revolutionary designs was greeted in *Harper's Bazaar* as "Chanel's charming chemise dress," but the design had little success in Paris until 1920.

11. Colette, *Œuvres complètes* (Paris: Gallimard, 1986), tome II & tome III.

12. Ibid., 224.

13. Lachgar, *Album Colette* (Paris: Editions Henri Veyrier, 1983), 64, 80.

14. Katherine Mansfield, *Prelude,* in *Short Stories,* selected and introduced by Claire Tomalin (London: Everyman's Library, 1983), 126.

15. The fetishistic value of hair is the subject of Maupassant's *La Chevelure,* which

236 ANNE FREADMAN

was drawn to my attention while I was working on this material by Gale MacLachlan and Ian Reid's reading of that story, "Framing the Frame: Maupassant's *La Chevelure*," *Canadian Review of Comparative Literature/Revue Canadienne de Littérature Comparée* 22 (June/Juin 1995): 287–99.

16. Louisa May Alcott, *Little Women* (London: J.M. Dent & Sons Ltd; New York: E.P. Dutton & Co., Inc. 1948 (1955)), "The Children's Illustrated Classics."

17. Roland Barthes, *S/Z*, trans. Richard Miller, preface by Richard Howard (London: Jonathan Cape, 1975), 160.

18. Charles-Roux, *Chanel* (London: Collins Harvill, 1989), 126.

19. Colette, *La fin de Chéri, Œuvres complètes* (Paris: Gallimard, 1986), 221.

20. I had never heard of the 300 strokes of Janet Frame's Malfred Signal (*A State of Seige*, Sydney: Angus and Robertson, 1990 [1996]), who also wears her hair wound in plaits about her head.

21. Not quite a lifetime, in fact. I had been under the impression that my grandmother never changed her hairstyle, but this is not the case. Her eschewal of high fashion did not, it seems, date from her girlhood, and she seems to have taken a youthful pleasure in modest stylishness when her means permitted. There is a family photograph taken on the day of my great-grandparents' golden wedding anniversary; the date is 1923. My grandmother, by this time well into her thirties, sits on the far right of the group, wearing a dark satin short dress with a long rope of pearls, her feet in fashionable shoes with ankle straps—the very image of the smart young flapper. She has her hair bobbed, and my father's memory of her is with this hairstyle; he had, to my distress, forgotten the plaits wound around her head. My grandparents were very severely affected by the Depression, and I guess now, without any supporting documents, that she allowed her hair to grow again at that time and kept it that way for the whole period of the midcentury. This would explain why the cutting of her hair in the '50s was so undramatic for her: she'd done it before, at the very time and in the very way that I have attempted to describe.

22. Prior to the invention of the steel pen "tailler une plume" used to be a necessary preparatory step for writing.

23. My thanks to Jennifer Craik, for the protracted loan of some lovely picture-books; to Margaret Maynard, for sharing her valuable scholarship; to Juliana De Nooy for finding me the "coupeurs de nattes"; to Joe Hardwick and Andrew Munro who have assisted me indefatigably and with meticulous care; to Alfredo Martínez and the students of RM401 (1995) for a first opportunity to develop the material that has become this "hairpiece"; to the members of the Lyceum Club of Brisbane for a second opportunity, for their warm interest, and for their memories, and to the "Bold" Conference—organizers and participants, for a third opportunity, which gave me a lot to think about. Particular thanks, too, are due to Fleur Freadman, for finding the photograph of my grandmother.

The present essay was completed before the appearance of Stephen Zdatny's article, "The Boyish Look and the Liberated Woman: the Politics and Aesthetics of Women's Hairstyles," *Fashion Theory* 1, 4 (December 1997): 367–97. Zdatny, whose focus is on the economics of hairdressing and the social history of the new styles, points out that "short hairstyles and the *risqué* new clothes that accompanied them had been around before the war," dating them at least to 1908. I am grateful for the historical precision of Zdatny's work, and I accept his down-to-earth conclusion that women were emancipated primarily to "spend their own money." His objections to cultural studies methods in fashion history do not, however, shame me into repressing this attempt to contribute something towards an answer to "what did it mean?"

to
Anxious Reading

Eric Michaels's *Unbecoming* and the Death of the Author

ROSS CHAMBERS

Death is the sanction of everything the storyteller can tell. He has borrowed his authority from death.

—Walter Benjamin

WHAT FOLLOWS—A READING OF ERIC MICHAELS'S AIDS DIARY, *Unbecoming*—is abstracted from a book-length study of AIDS diaries as a genre[1] and poses the question of how to read them: I ask, that is, about the relation between their structures of address (which posit textual "survival") and the fact of "survivorhood" that inevitably colors the consciousness of a reader. Because the reading of *Unbecoming* originally formed part of a larger, more articulated argument, I must first rehearse here a couple of key points that contextualize it.

The first of these concerns the nature of witnessing discourse and the character of autobiography when it has a witnessing function. Like, say, teaching, translating, interpreting, and whatever it is politicians do, witnessing is mediating. In spite of phrases like "eyewitness account" or "direct report," there is no form of witnessing that is not a *representation* of some sort (and so a product of representational technology); consequently, although witnessing is nonfictional and referential in mode, it remains subject to rhetorical effects, on the one hand, and to reading and interpretation, on the other. This means that the question of reading AIDS diaries is not—as someone with a sense of the magnitude of the AIDS disaster might hastily assume—a trivial one: their success as an act of witness depends ultimately on their reception. To put my sense of the matter briefly from the start, the writing of AIDS diaries in general is designed to challenge complacent reading, and their successful witness is therefore measurable in terms of readerly anxiety. But we have no theory of anxious reading, and one of the ways in which *Unbecoming* must count as an extraordinary text is its unusual degree of explicitness, and hence its helpfulness, in this regard.

One reason why AIDS diaries appear direct in their reporting of the personal and social nightmare that is a case of AIDS is that, although they are autobiographical (and as such may contain passages of reminiscence), they are not written in the retrospective perspective of memory that is associated with the classical forms of autobiography. More particularly, for conventional autobiography's (re)construction of a life and its significance through narrative, they substitute a chronicle—whose structure and rhythm are accommodated, of course, to the simple, painful wisdom of mortal illness, known as "living each day for itself"—and a chronicle of disintegration, a day-by-day account of unbecoming. In this sense, they are oriented toward the daily realities of living (of living with AIDS), and so to speak grafted on to them, while nevertheless remaining subject to all the constraints and effects of representation, which means— among other things—that AIDS journals (some of which are in video form) are peculiarly comparable in their rhetorical effect with the mode of TV broadcasting and video representation known as the "live." They are a bit like home movies, if you will, that reach us, as readers, from a certain zone of personal, medical, and social disaster.

The "live," of course, is precisely *not* the living (although the living is what it is about); nor, however, is it the "canned." What it lacks with respect to the canned—a certain controlled perfection—is precisely what it gains from its contact with the living: a certain proclivity to disorder, a tendency for things to get out of control, a messiness that can be tinged with the deathly associations of entropy (disintegration, unbecoming), at the same time as it marks the incontrovertible presence, within the live, of something living. On TV, though, the most frequent accidents associated with live broadcasting seem to derive less from the living (in the form of fluffs and bloopers, or even natural disasters like the night the live broadcast of a baseball game was interrupted by the San Francisco earthquake), than from the intrusiveness of the mediating equipment itself: a camera catches someone holding a clipboard, or another camera, within the same frame as the live image, or we catch a glimpse of a roll of cables. In AIDS diaries, too, the "equipment" gets similarly foregrounded, although not necessarily accidentally so, through reference to questions of representation (writing, video technology); so that in this case the means that convert the living into the live are specifically thematized (as opposed to their inevitable but, I suppose, unintended and undesired thematization in live broadcasting). They thus come to figure, ambiguously, as death-dealing and reductive with respect to the life they represent—in conformity with a very ancient logocentric understanding of representation and representational technologies—but also as the indispensable means by which a dying author can continue to make a claim on life and the living, and in particular can seek a certain mode of survival through the production of a text. The living that is AIDS (a form of dying) can be converted into a certain prospect of survival by becoming the live of an AIDS journal. But that textual survival has a condition.

For a generation now, the phrase "the death of the author" has done duty as theoretical shorthand for the insight that the writing subject through whose agency a text gets produced does not and cannot exercise control over the many significations a text may generate in the contexts in which it is read. There is, in other words, a textual subjectivity not reducible to the writing subject's intentions, desires, understandings, or will. AIDS journals, by literalizing the theoretical metaphor, give the insight unexpected and disturbing poignancy: it is, in this case, really necessary for someone to die so that, as Benjamin puts it, a text can be "telling,"[2] *borrowing its authority*, not (unspecifically) from "death," but from the actual death of its author. If an author is performing an act of witness in recording his own death from AIDS ("his" because AIDS journals are overwhelmingly written, for obvious socioeconomic reasons, by gay men), he necessarily casts the survivorhood of a reader, charged with realizing the textual subjectivity, as the key to the only form of survival that is available to the act of witnessing his death will interrupt. Much work is therefore performed in and by the texts as part of their attempt to ensure, through their structures of address, the reading on which the survival of their project depends. But actual readings can never be fully determined by textual address-structures (which form part of the object of reading): between the writing subject and the reading subject there is inevitably (because definitionally) a gap—troped theoretically as the death of the author—a gap that defines the reader's "freedom" with respect to the textual determinations and makes of the difference between the "survival" posited by the death the author undergoes (a survival imagined in terms of continuity) and the actual "survivorhood" (manifesting discontinuity) the reader enjoys the sign of a fundamental, because foundational, paradox: the death that makes survival through reading possible simultaneously makes the survival dubious, both inadequate and questionable.

In the texts themselves, the key figure for these implications of the death of the author—as a condition of survival that is itself predicated on a survivorhood the text cannot control—is the trope of AIDS symptoms (notably the lesions of Kaposi's sarcoma) as *the writing of the author's body*. This body-writing is a writing that is destined to die, so that what will survive the death of the body, by a kind of relay effect, will be another writing, *the writing of the author's text*. The two writings are assumed to be equivalent; yet they are obviously known to be different. Textual writing is not the same as body-writing because it is a representation thereof, and indeed body-writing is in fact not a reality independent of text, but itself the product of textual figuration. The supposed relay of body-writing by authorial writing (text) has the same structure, then, as the relay of subjectivities—authorial to textual—posited by the death of the author: in each case there is a kind of necessary illusion that masks the absolute primacy of textual writing over body-writing, and of reading over writing. But that illusion, as I've just called it, nevertheless constitutes a kind of scenario of survival that the texts frequently evoke, or gesture toward, even as, in other respects, they display understandable anxiety about the issues of writing, of readability, and of readership. Thus, Eric Michaels, at the outset of his diary (the very first entry), alludes to the lesions that have begun to appear on his body as "morphemes," and records a certain sense of relief. "As if these quite harmless looking cancers might, when strung together, form sentences which would give a narrative trajectory, a plot outline, at last to a disease and a scenario that had been all too vague" (23). Seropositivity is a kind of limbo (and there are no diaries of seropositivity); the appearance of symptoms announcing the death of the author predicts at last a scenario which (I extrapolate) is a scenario of textual survival, purchased, at the price of the author's dying, by the transcription of bodily writing into "sentences" that will remain available for future reading. But the question remains: what exactly can a text that borrows its authority from death achieve? And what relation can there be between its author's project and the readings on which its survival depends?

That latter question, to the extent that it troubles a text (which, I want to show, is certainly the case in *Unbecoming*), can also, obviously—although it may not—trigger anxiety in the reader as well. Given their inescapable knowledge of the author's death, readers of AIDS journals are necessarily conscious, to some degree, both of the magnitude of the responsibility they have inherited and of the structural reasons why such responsibility can be assumed only in ways that feel inadequate, insufficient, and inappropriate. To such readers, the act of reading feels like an act of mourning (since, in particular, they are conscious of the degree to which their *continuation* of the authorial project of witness is disabled by the fact of the author's death); or else it feels like an act of burial (since the very possibility of reading is predicated on the disappearance of the author as an agency capable of having a say in the production of meaning). Thoughtful readers, therefore, can be expected to oscillate between the two types of questions that, not coincidentally, define the phenomenon known as the survivor guilt: "Did I do enough to keep the other/the author alive?" and "Did I kill the other/the author?" And in the case of AIDS this latter question is not necessarily a mere figment of the mourning imagination or a melodramatic overstatement, since there is a sense in which all AIDS mortality can be said to have been caused by social indifference (or worse), and a sense, therefore, in which all of us survivors, by virtue of not having effectively resisted that indifference, are complicitous with it, and so complicitous in causing deaths that might otherwise not have occurred. The anxiety of the reader of an AIDS diary is not "merely" theoretical, therefore; it corresponds to something that is readable in every AIDS journal: the feeling of vulnerability the authors display, grounded in their sense that, as AIDS patients, they have been socially classified as *expendable*[3] and that they are being killed by being allowed to die.

Which brings us (my second main point) to the politics of AIDS journals—specifically a gay politics, since authorship of such journals has so far been limited to gay men (indeed, very largely to middle-class, white gay men)—and to the key question: why, when symptoms appear, do so many AIDS-infected authors turn to their word processors or cameras and start a journal? why do they choose to die writing, to *die as authors?* I have already begun here to answer this question, in part by referring to AIDS diaries as acts of witness, and in part by invoking the social vulnerability and the sense of their "expendability" that AIDS writers demonstrate. Writing, clearly, is a response to that vulnerability, one that takes the form of choosing, not simply to disappear (as "expendability" requires), but to make the author's disappearance into a socially and politically meaningful act (an act of witnessing). The distinction implied by the existence of AIDS journals, in other words, is clearly one between *dying*—dying passively, because one is allowed to die, as expendable—and staging one's death as the *death of the author,* so that it can have discursive consequences. The AIDS journal, then, is the genre of writing that has arisen, historically, as a site where the staging of an author's death acquires the valence of an act of resistance, and more specifically of antihomophobic witness.

For AIDS is an infectious disease, but it is not at all contagious; AIDS patients, however, who are themselves highly vulnerable to infections, discover that they are often treated more as a threat to other people than as someone whose own life is in danger. Thus Eric Michaels, for instance, found himself hospitalized in an infectious diseases

ward, as if it were more important to isolate him from others than to
protect him from the diseases to which, given his badly impaired
immune system, he was dangerously vulnerable. Gay people are ac-
customed to the homophobic myth that produces homosexuality as a
socially contagious "disease," something that you can somehow pick
up just by being around someone who is gay; so the myth of the
contagiousness of AIDS has little mystery for them. It clearly signifies
that AIDS is being conflated with the homosexuality of which it is
taken to be an indicator. (Thus, in the spring of 1995, a group of gay
activists—not AIDS patients—invited to the White House were met
at the door by security men in face masks and rubber gloves.) And, as
a consequence, the medical vulnerability of which AIDS sufferers are
rightly conscious—the vulnerability to opportunistic infection—
easily becomes conflated with another form of vulnerability, which is
the vulnerability of gay men to the contagious social disease known as
homophobia. No one who lives in a homophobic society can escape
"internalizing" homophobia to some degree, but the vulnerability of
gay AIDS sufferers to internalized homophobia is immeasurably increased because of their exposure to patterns of avoidance behavior
that they observe in other people, caregivers, friends, people on the
street. They thus know themselves to be doubly and indistinguishably
stigmatized, as AIDS sufferers *and* as gay men; and—for them as for
the many other AIDS sufferers who are members of socially stigmatized groups—AIDS turns out to involve a double whammy. The
outcome of this consciousness on their part can be a form of despair
in which their sense of social pariah-hood (of being simultaneously
shunned and treated as expendable) is, in the end, inseparably inter-
twined with the fatal implications of their diagnosis. Such despair
leads to suicide.

On the face of it, suicide would be a rational option on the part of
any person faced not only with certain death but with a probably slow
and protracted, albeit usually intermittent, dying, complicated by
peripeteia that are both uniquely distressing in their medical manifestations and regularly accompanied by social effects ranging from
hypocritical avoidance to overt hostility. But the point is that, given
the social context in which AIDS is experienced, suicide cannot be
regarded by a gay AIDS sufferer in a more or less neutral way, as a
rational response. It necessarily signifies (whether in fact or by un-
sympathetic interpretation) that one has yielded to the social esti-
mate of one's value as an expendable person and succumbed to the
self-hatred of which despair is the sign and internalized homophobia
the cause. In this understanding, suicide becomes a form of murder,
which of course must be resisted. The decision to stay alive, and to

die of AIDS, and to write one's dying in the form of an AIDS diary, corresponds then to the further desire to ensure that one's dying be read and understood as the rejection of homophobia—a deliberately chosen alternative to suicide—that it in fact signifies. That is, it corresponds to the desire, not just to reject homophobia, but to bear witness to one's rejection of homophobia, even to the point of choosing a very difficult death over a relatively easy one.

Address structures have the prominence they do in AIDS journals, then (an apparently aberrant prominence, given the supposedly private, self-analytic function of the personal diary as a genre), because it is so vital for the text's existence, as an act of social enunciation, that it be rightly interpreted as an act of resistance. On the one hand, the writing of an AIDS diary has a prophylactic or preservative, even a decontaminatory function: it preserves the author from the temptation of suicide as the product of internalized homophobia, and after its author's death, the existence of the diary can serve as a prophylactic model for others who may be similarly situated (not that they are exhorted to write a diary, necessarily, but that they are encouraged not to yield to homophobic despair). On the other hand, the act of witness constituted by the writing of an AIDS diary functions as a statement of resistance and issues a challenge to the intolerable social forces that would rather have seen the author dead. *Redivivus,* the author's resistance lives on in the readability of the text—which is why the question of ensuring and maintaining that readability, and if possible of predetermining its quality *as* resistance is so important in these texts and, at the same time, such an object of anxiety. For on readability depends the survival of an act of witness whose very significance lies in the fact that it represents a choice to *survive:* a failure to succumb, to disappear, and to "go quietly," an option to resist, and to go on resisting.

All of which suggests the relevance, for an understanding of AIDS diaries as a genre, of the concept of "delegitimation" that is deployed to such good effect by Marie Maclean in *The Name of the Mother.* Delegitimation is the symbolic assumption, and so transvaluation, by a stigmatized subject (in Maclean's book, bastards and pseudobastards), of the stigma that brands the individual as illegitimate. "It may involve publicly laying claim to actual illegitimacy and the proud assumption of the exclusion it entails. It may, on the other hand, be the proclamation of a symbolic illegitimacy by public rejection of the father's name, the father's values, or both."[4] AIDS diaries look very like the second case: they publicly proclaim "symbolic illegitimacy" through their rejection, if not of the father's name, then of the values of a patriarchal society grounded in the assumptions of compulsory heterosexuality. In the AIDS diaries I know, I'm unaware of any examples in which delegitimation, as the rejection of the paternal, actually takes the form of assuming the name of the mother. But there are circumstances, surely, in which turning to writing *itself* is something like turning to "the mother" and all that she, as not-the-father, can symbolize. And if that is so—and if homophobia is one of the pandemic diseases of patriarchal society—then perhaps AIDS is itself the maternal name that the writers of AIDS journals turn to. In a certain situation of extremity, it offers itself as the *only alternative*—not necessarily an attractive one, although to some writers it has its seductive side—to that which makes it seem preferable: the self-destruction to which the father's *non* if not the father's name can easily reduce a gay man when his defenses are down. "Sida mon amour," writes Pascal de Duve as a recurring refrain in *Cargo Vie;* and his association of AIDS with the sea and the starlit sky, his desire for *enciêlement* or *emmerment* (consignment to the sky or the sea) as an alternative to burial does suggest quite strongly the maternal connotation his "AIDS my beloved" can be taken to imply.

But Eric Michaels would be a counterexample in this respect. AIDS, for him, is not an occasion for what he would perhaps call sentiment, but rather for the reiteration of certain "first principles." Of these, the necessity of resistance is certainly primary. But for him such resistance cannot entail anything like a pact with AIDS, because AIDS itself has the face of social repression, whose ally and instrument it is: it is cast, if you will, in the role of the father, not the mother. In refusing suicide as an option, in resisting despair and choosing to live the nightmare of his dying, Michaels thus opts for writing—including the writing of his body that is the "morphemes" of AIDS—not as an alliance with AIDS against homophobia, but as a way of mobilizing all his forces both against AIDS and against what AIDS signifies (including homophobia); and one would be quite hard pressed, I think (although it is doubtless possible), to "maternalize" the symbolic allies—chief among them aboriginality—to which, in this battle, he does turn. Certainly he has little time and not much affection for his own mother. So delegitimation here—for delegitimation it certainly is—takes another turn, one that removes us pretty much from the enchanted domain of family romance; it does so because it seeks to reinscribe resistance less as a matter of personal revolt, with psychic overtones, than as a necessary social function, a Foucauldian *discourse of resistance* of which Michaels, the author, is merely an agent.

And yet, it is not paradoxical to add that *Unbecoming* is a personally revealing text to a quite unusual degree, and that its writing is personally engaging (in all the senses of that word) in a way that few texts are. It is, precisely, through a certain performance of personality— essentially the persona of the "difficult patient"—that this text seeks to be an effective social force as an instrument of resistance. An example:

> I've been ragged and paranoid all week. Fevers and sweats coming and going and some odd lung thing that's scary. My tumours itch and seem to be developing psoriatic complications of something. It's been raining as long as I can recall; everything is mould, mould, mould. The kitchen is filled with flying weevils. The toilet is backed up. My neighbour has taken up the saxophone and tries to play hits from the *The Sound of Music* all day. I can't sleep and can't do anything but. I was up repeatedly in the middle of the night with the horrors. I don't even want to call anybody. I have no interest in working and I haven't even been pursuing my immigration business responsibly. My physician seems to have deserted me. My conviction that the world I perceive corresponds to anybody else's is slipping. Maybe I died in November and this is some awful postmodern fantasy I inhabit now? (Eric Michaels, *Unbecoming*, 118–19)

You get the picture. I don't quote this passage from *Unbecoming* as characteristic (the book is very varied in subject matter and style, containing passages of social analysis, autobiographical reflection, and academic polemic as well as—or as a part of—its reporting from the AIDS front). I quote it because it is indicative. There are no butterflies and cats in Michaels's text, and certainly no demonstrations of stoicism; he is not interested in heroism as such, or in transcendence; nor is discretion his characteristic rhetorical mode.[5] Most of these things, one suspects, he would dismiss as sentimental; and "At least one reason for publishing this journal is to counter the sentimentalised narrative that seems to be all that San Francisco has been able to produce about this sequence; and to reconfirm first principles" (144). I don't know what the specific target of the San Francisco jibe is; but my interest will be in teasing out of *Unbecoming* some sense of what these first principles might be and why the AIDS crisis requires them to be reconfirmed, as well as the way in which they are performed in the rhetoric of this text and embodied in the persona of its speaker, "ragged and paranoid" as he may be.

The first of them can be stated immediately, more or less on the basis of the quoted passage: the world is a hostile place, AIDS is a dire affliction, and there is no beyond. Any postmortem life will be figurative—"some awful . . . fantasy I inhabit now": the sense of having outlived oneself and of experiencing death while still alive that AIDS produces. Or (and we approach here the second of Michaels's

"first principles"), it will be genuinely posthumous, but in an imma-
nent sense, strictly a matter of social practices and arrangements for
dealing with the death of a member of society, including the disposi-
tion of property and (of particular interest to Michaels) of intellectual property. The point for him, then, will be so to "stagemanage his
own posthumosity" (152) that there will be some continuity—some
form of survival—between the manner of his dying—the disintegration or "unbecoming" of the man, Eric Michaels, as already a (pre-
posthumous) postmortem experience—and the unbecoming social
participant that he wants the texts signed Eric Michaels to continue,
after and beyond his death, to be. The rhetoric of the passage I just
quoted—its inspired kvetching, its performance of exasperation—is
part and parcel of the stage management of that double (present
and future) "posthumosity."

In this project, the ability to stage-manage (a recurring metaphor
in *Unbecoming*) is crucial; and the danger is that AIDS, and the order-
ing social forces with which, in Michaels's vision (perhaps a "paranoid" one, as he admits) it is aligned, will reduce the
(pre-)posthumous suffering subject to such a degree of passivity that
no spirit of resistance will survive. That is why it is important, in the
above quoted passage, to catch the *tone*—a bit campy, humorous, and
wry—that produces the persona of Michaels, through its rhetoric of
excess, as a resistant figure (if not exactly a figure of resistance), and
so anything but a defeated one, in spite of his Jobian list of ills. It is
also helpful in understanding the passage's embattled tone to have
some understanding of the circumstances that nourished Michaels's
"paranoid" vision of what anyone would agree constitutes in any case
an extremely dire situation. Michaels, a United States citizen, was
dying in semi-isolation in Brisbane (Australia), a city that came to
represent for him the worst of everything that he was facing. An
active participant in the New York gay liberation movement in 1969–
72, he was now without "direct involvement in the gay world" (79);
for five years (1982–87) he had been closely involved, as an anthropologist, in an Aboriginal community at Yuendumu (Central
Australia). The double contrast with his Brisbane life—where he felt
"comparatively alone" and "minimally connected" (55)—was thus
intense.

On the evidence of the diary itself, he had the support of numerous distant friends, but could rely on little on-the-spot help. He
seems furthermore to have been virtually estranged from his "crazy"
family in the United States and concludes bleakly, at one point, that
"if my family is to take any major responsibility for my care, we will
have to invent that family" (74). Not surprisingly, under such condi-

tions, the daily aggravations of a life in which nothing ever seems to go right—not to mention the bureaucratic harassments of an Immigration Department intent on deporting him, and the "Foucauldian horror show" (25) of the hospital—begin to loom impressively large. Not only does existence become tinged with paranoia ("My conviction that the world I perceive corresponds to anyone else's is slipping"), but the temptation to just give up becomes overwhelming: "it's the specificities that wipe us out in the end" (156). However, it is Michaels's second "first principle" that *giving up* is tantamount to being *wiped out,* and that one must therefore not give up, even if resistance is reduced to complaining about one's impotence. "Stage-managing" one's demise and one's posthumosity, even if that involves cultivating one's paranoia, is the only way not to be defeated by the whole horror show, Foucauldian or otherwise. For "I feel they can smell me now, like an injured member of the pack. And they go for me, the sons of bitches, they go for the throat!" (60).

That this is a difficult battle does not need to be underlined: "the hardest part," Michaels writes (141), "is maintaining resistance . . . so as to retain some dignity, assurance and self-definition." But in his own eyes, it's the question of paranoia ("I've been ragged and paranoid all week") that is the more troubling one (and as he notes elsewhere, the question: am I paranoid? is itself a paranoid question). To describe one's manner of death as "a way of dying which I, but maybe only I, believe has elements of murder" (53) and to write of a hospital that "I'm in a place that wants to kill me (even if my doctors—some of them—try to save me)" (147) certainly sounds paranoid enough. It becomes a major function of the diary, therefore, not only to constitute itself as a site, and a mode, of resistance, but also to do so in a way that justifies and legitimates the supposed paranoia. *Unbecoming* thus offers a specific social analysis that underpins and accounts for Michaels's vision of the world as hostile, a Foucauldian horror show, and the site of a pre-posthumous experience that can be represented, not just as a living death (which suggests passivity), but as an extended murder—the experience of being actively, if slowly, killed and of having, not only to resist, but also to keep up one's resistance over a very long period of time. And the diary's other main function will be to pursue that work of resistance into a posthumous future that has to be secured, therefore—under conditions of great difficulty—in the embattled circumstances of the pre-posthumous present.

This is as much as to say that the diary has generic elements that resemble a "position paper" (32) and other elements—"As far as I can tell, I have only intellectual property to dispense" (32)—that constitute it as a kind of will (that is, the type of document that most tangibly demonstrates a discursive authority borrowed from death). Writing in Brisbane between 9 September 1987 and 10 August 1988—a span of only eleven months (Michaels died on 26 August 1988)—Michaels found himself, with only the remotest models (Joe Orton, Anne Frank, Jean Cocteau, Anaïs Nin) as literary guides, virtually inventing the genre of the AIDS diary; and he concocted it, encouraged by his friend and publisher Paul Foss, as a capacious genre, simultaneously memoir, vehicle of informal social critique, and witnessing discourse, but one specifically oriented toward pressing present needs—its "position paper" function, as a mode of resistance and guarantee against paranoia—and an equally insistent anxiety about the posthumous future: its function as a "will." Let's consider the will first.

As a principled anthropologist, Michaels had accorded the Warlpiri among whom he worked rights of veto over the publication of his work, so that they could oversee its accuracy and appropriateness. But the Warlpiri, among whom Michaels had earned an identity as a member of the community, are like most other Aboriginal groups in that they "maintain elaborate, protracted mourning ceremonies. As dramatic as these are, they involve a contradiction in that, upon death, an individual's property, image, even name, must be obliterated. . . . Songs and designs belonging to the deceased exit the repertoire, sometimes for generations" (31). Suppose, then, that the Warlpiri insist on the diary's being destroyed on Michaels's death? (An ugly argument over the illustration of an article on Warlpiri art, which members of the community wish to censor because it includes phallic graffiti, would suggest that a Warlpiri ban on *Unbecoming* is a plausible eventuality.) This is an interesting cultural question, one of those radical contradictions between Western and Aboriginal law that are (more especially for the Aboriginal minority) a frequently lived reality in Australia. But the point of affirming *Unbecoming*'s status as a kind of will, then—a document obviously unnecessary in Warlpiri culture and so automatically subject to Western jurisdiction—is quite clearly to ensure the diary's posthumous survival in the most material sense, as the first step in its eventually reaching a readership. "I am not, nor have I ever imagined myself to be, a Warlpiri Aboriginal," Michaels carefully records (32), with an eye to future legal determinations. But of course an anxiety remains, since there is genuine ambiguity, if only because a will is meaningless in Warlpiri terms; and the ambiguity is reinforced because the Warlpiri intervention in the *Art & Text* incident shows some of them to be sensitive to what Michaels calls a Tidy Town mentality. This derives

(via Christianity) from the white Australian mentality of tidiness—
figured by Brisbane and exemplified by the hospital—that Michaels
believes is destroying him, and about which more will be said soon.
So—will or no will—there is thus some real danger of an alliance of
interests against the publication of *Unbecoming* after his death; and
that is why it becomes essential for the diary, in addition to its function as a will, to incorporate a position paper, one that identifies and
critiques, in advance, and so attempts to forestall, the dangers of the
tidying mentality.

It is fair to assume that homosexuality, and hence homophobia, lie
at the heart of this whole issue. Michaels could scarcely have been
"out" to the Warlpiri without prejudicing his work with, for, and
among them. At the same time, gayness as a social manifestation is, in
his analysis, an emancipatory movement that, since the time of Stone-
wall, has been counteracted and virtually destroyed by the repressive
social forces that are represented in his thinking not only by "tidiness" but also by the phenomenon of AIDS. He understands himself,
in this context, as a purely social "self," and to have been culturally
defined, therefore, by the appearance in 1969 on the social scene of a
"public rather than a private form" of homosexuality (28), that is, of
gayness as "liberation" as opposed to homosexuality as closeted de-
viance. And the Eric Michaels who has now contracted AIDS is similarly a social self—"this is why I have AIDS, because it is now on the
cover of *Life,* circa 1987" (29)—one whose resistance to the disease
and all it signifies (the social forces with which it is in alliance to
destroy him) is thus not a purely personal affair but also a social
resistance, something like the necessary survival into the late eighties
of the heady oppositional moment of 1969–72. At stake in the
posthumous survival of *Unbecoming* (as well as in Michaels's mainte-
nance of a resistance spirit up to his death) is therefore the social
survival—the future availability to reading—of writing that will continue to state the "first principle" of an oppositionality, signified by
gayness, that in 1987 is everywhere under the most brutal and
dangerous attack.

Tidiness, "nearly a key term" (39) in Brisbane and clearly man-
ifested in the "Foucauldian holy ground" that is the Royal Brisbane
Hospital, is one of a number of possible names for the enemy as
Michaels understands it; but it has the advantage of demonstrating
the enemy's peculiarly hypocritical structure. An AIDS patient in the
hospital needs, for survival, a clean (germ-free) environment: what
he encounters is a tidy one. The floors are kept polished, and the top
of the mobile table over Michaels's bed is cleaned twice a day: these
are surfaces that the doctors and nurses see, and it is their perspec-

tive that defines the forms of orderliness that prevail in the institution. Meanwhile, the patient is exposed to grime that gathers on the ceiling, and "the underside [of the table], with which I actually come into contact, hasn't been swabbed since 1942 as far as I can judge" (43). To place a man with AIDS in an infectious diseases ward corresponds similarly to a logic of tidiness that for the patient is potentially lethal. And the only form of resistance that is possible in the face of such practices consists of not submitting passively to being tidied away by the hospital's coercive discipline. That is, it consists of practices of noncompliance: keeping a diary certainly, but also keeping the TV poorly tuned (since it is a major instrument for inducing passivity), and—most especially—complaining, criticizing, kvetching, and the deployment of sarcasm, until it "flood[s] the room and [sweeps] the entire nursing staff into the hall" (129).

It is necessary, in short, for the AIDS patient, as part of the stage management of his dying, to do everything within his power to earn and maintain a place "at the top of the difficult patient list" (147). And—since the hospital is emblematic of the larger society—the same response can and must be extended beyond the hospital staff and beyond the Immigration Department to the full range of "specificities" that are lined up against you: the grubby landlord and the dishonest carpet cleaning company, the neighbors who play the wrong music and play it loudly, or who block access to the Hill's Hoist, but also new university colleagues and—perhaps especially— old friends, to the extent that they, too, prove (as the best-intentioned people inevitably do) inconsiderate or unempathetic or just plain irritating. The complaining passage I began with is a good example of such "difficult patient" peevishness, but the diary as a whole is an extended record of Michaels's success in keeping up this taxing performance of difficultness to the end.

It's worth pausing, though, to reflect briefly on two aspects of this difficult patient performance. The first comment must obviously be that "tidiness theory" partly obscures a personal vulnerability on Michaels's part to homophobia, a vulnerability to which being difficult is a reaction. The performance is not at all about being nasty and unhelpful, it's a prophylactic and decontaminating device, a response to the homophobic self-assessments to which gay men are susceptible at the best of times and which, in the case of the gay AIDS patient, can dangerously encourage passive submission to one's own destruction. "How have I allowed myself to internalize this guilty attitude which makes me apologize for being ill, and promise to go quietly?" Michaels asks rhetorically (76) after an interview with his dean. He has already described himself, "ashamed and cowering"

(71) at the beach, although wanting to jump in for a swim; and only two weeks later he seeks professional help because he feels "suicidal and crazy" (78). The visibility of KS lesions is part of the issue here, of course: "I can't manage my flawed countenance, and know it's only going to get worse" (80); "It's getting more and more difficult to look in the mirror" (87); "I turn myself off" (96)—until finally, under the relatively cheering stimulus of a trip to Sydney, he simply decides that "if my appearance bothered others, it should remain their problem" (106).

Beyond KS, though, there is a deeper vulnerability, suggested by Michaels's interesting analysis of the fragility of gay identity and of the role of desire and of sexual "promiscuity" in reinforcing it. The "enforced celibacy" of AIDS, he concludes (clearly generalizing from his own example, since AIDS does not of itself enforce celibacy, although it may on occasion diminish desire), is therefore a threat to gay men's sense of self: "if psychologists are right about the centrality and the fixity of identity for the human self, what terrible psychic violence something like AIDS must wreak on gays—and has perhaps done to me" (100). The psychologism of this passage, on the part of one who declares himself more indebted to Zen than to Freud and expresses elsewhere his suspicion of psychological explanations, perhaps betrays, on Michaels's part, a certain unwillingness to recognize an aspect of the "social construction" of gay men that his internalized "guilt" and willingness to "disappear quietly" nevertheless point to clearly enough: the homophobia with which it is impossible, in a homophobic social environment, not to be complicitous (even when resisting it). "Mama, you wouldn't believe how people treat you here," he wrote of the hospital on the occasion of an early visit. "It's not the rubber gloves or face masks, or bizarre plastic wrapping around everything. It's the way people address you, by gesture, by eye, by mouth" (25). The polemical construction of his difficult patient persona as an externally directed resisting response to "the way people address you, by gesture, by eye, by mouth," thus masks to some degree the sense in which the difficult patient performance also serves to bolster an internally fragile, and internally threatened, sense of identity, damaged by its own internalization of those alienating gestures, looks, and words.

That "the way people address you" implies a polemical counteraddress in the form of being difficult brings me, however, to the second aspect of the difficult patient performance, which is that it doesn't only constitute a counteraddress in the context of Michaels's dying, but also informs the structures of textual address in his writing, as part of a very carefully judged tactics designed to ensure that, having escaped the danger of obliteration, *Unbecoming* will enjoy a posthumous afterlife by finding a readership. Being difficult is essential, in other words, both to the stage management of Michaels's pre-posthumous dying (where it protects a vulnerable identity) and to the stage management of his posthumous afterlife (where it protects a social project); and in this latter respect the diary contains evidence of very careful thought regarding both the tactics of address (a stylistic matter) and the politics of publication (a more pragmatic one) that will ensure such an afterlife. Michaels understands, for example, that his lack of fame does not permit his writing to command the mass audience that Paul Foss seems to consider possible; but given his notoriety among the Sydney intelligentsia (roughly equivalent, as he amusingly puts it, to the subscription list of *Art & Text*), he might hope for a "cult" following. And, as it happens, "these may be just the folks I wanted to talk to" (153): those that the diary *can* reach are, by a fortunate dispensation, also its ideal audience, the readers who can be expected to be responsive to it. This in turn means that a provocative tactics of address, an "unbecoming" rhetoric equivalent to the performance of being a difficult patient—at the opposite pole, then, from Guibert's (1992) rhetoric of discretion—is the appropriate one: "I think now I've escaped the worst of the possible consequences of being discovered (so longed for in my youthful quest for stardom), so that even if Paul is right that these diaries get a wider than cult reading, no worries mate! And that's why Juan can paint the cover and I can call the thing *Unbecoming* (though I still like *Should Have Been A Dyke*)" (153). The thought here is condensed and allusive, but it unpacks fairly readily. The audience that a "star" might reach (imagine if Rock Hudson had left an AIDS journal) would inhibit the rhetorical practices—indicated by the title *Unbecoming* and the plan for a cover portrait by the provocative artist Juan Davila—to which Michaels is in any case drawn. An address to a cult following (whatever the actual readership might prove to be in the end) is therefore appropriate. So, no worries: "I have the satisfaction, my anger transubstantiated" (153).

What this restriction of audience means in practice is that, to our embryonic list of generic models for the AIDS journal (the position paper, the will) can now be added the posthumous revenge letter, as a vehicle simultaneously for the "transubstantiation" of the author's anger and for the recruitment of an interested (Michaels's word will be "engaged") readership. The revenge letter is a strikingly effective means of carrying on the performance of being a difficult patient—of not taking it lying down—beyond one's death; and *Unbecoming* includes (*en abyme*, as it were) three gems of the genre (66–70), addressed respectively to the sleazy landlord, an inconsiderate friend, and the offending carpet cleaning company. It also includes an example of "revenge publication," reproducing *in extenso* the hypocritical and self-contradictory letter Michaels received, a month before his death, from the Immigration Department announcing that he would be deported ("to nowhere") as soon as he was medically fit to travel. One imagines the glee with which these letters were composed, or transcribed into the diary, for later publication. But in addition to the "satisfaction" it affords the pre-posthumous author, the posthumously published revenge letter, as a denunciation of the inadequacies that have hastened a dying man to his grave, makes an irresistible appeal also to a certain kind of readership, one defined either by survivor guilt (actual in the case of those who recognize themselves in the book, symbolic in the case of those able to recognize themselves in those the book pillories), or else by curiosity and *schadenfreude* (on the part of those who enjoy watching others squirm, or who take pleasure in vicarious squirming of their own). Or, of course, by both. (That could add up to a large number of people.)

Such an intimately *involved* audience is what I understand Michaels to have in mind when he speaks of a "cult" audience as the appropriate one for his book; and it is as if he plans, therefore, to continue and extend, in the relation between his accusatory book and its readers, the fraught relation with his actual friends that is compellingly described and analyzed—sometimes with affection, self-deprecation and humor and sometimes not—at a number of points in the volume (notably 43–44, 48–49, 126, 150). It seems likely that, in this, he was guided by his perception of "the scale of Australian demography" (61), in which members of the intelligentsia, the academy, the bureaucracy, the media, and political culture all seem to know one another, and indeed, to be closely, if not intimately, interconnected: in other words, they form an extended gossip circle. Michaels, in short, is consciously relying on word-of-mouth, at least in the first instance, placing his faith in some of the more unsavory motivations humans may have for reading a book, and looking for a *succès de scandale* and a *succès de curiosité* in order to get his volume launched (this is stage-managing as one of the fine arts). But he is also, and in the long run more importantly, defining the *kind* of reading (guilty, anxious, involved, "close to") that is required by the continuation, in book form, of the performance of Michaels the difficult patient. As the hospital staff and Michaels's friends were put in a double bind by a patient who both needs their care and is never satisfied with it, so the reader of *Unbecoming* is the addressee of a Lacanian *demand* that by definition cannot be fulfilled (that's what "being difficult" means), a demand that is calculated, therefore—because it is an appeal framed as an accusation (something like: "Why don't you save me?")—to make reading an experience of disquiet, anxiety, and inadequacy.

This effort to destabilize the reader's equanimity and to produce anxiety in its place by making the unbecoming of the body the occasion of an unbecoming rhetorical performance is already visible in an astonishing predictive image that the reader encounters before even embarking on the text. It is simultaneously a frontispiece and the book's photographic *mise en abyme;* it is also one of the most remarkable representations of the AIDS body known to me; and finally, like the text itself, it stages a compelling continuity between unbecoming's two, pre-posthumous and posthumous, stages. It is the product of a photography session, reported in the journal, that took place two months before the author's death, one of a series of "shots that might serve as graphics if needed. . . . All nude to the waist down [*sic*], featuring the cancer lesions most prominently" (152). It has been taken with a flash, so that certain physical details are heightened; but it is the subject's posture that is most striking, divided between a relaxed and seemingly passive trunk and arms (not noticeably thin but spotted with lesions) and an astoundingly alive face and head with luxuriant hair and beard, intense eyes, and—the *punctum* as well as the *studium*[6]—a mouth open so that KS lesions can also be seen on the protruding tongue. In its own fashion, this image thus stages the tension, readable in the text, between the temptation of passiveness and the necessity of fierce resistance—the tension that makes the gesture of defiantly showing the body's state of unbecoming (the photo's own raison d'être) into a victory over submission to the conventions of tidiness, and over one's own complicitous willingness to go quietly or "just disappear."

But the focal point is the tongue, the flesh catching the light and its lesions visible—a tongue which, given the intensity of expression in the face and eyes (will? defiance? rage?), can be seen, in addition to displaying the ravages of cancer, to be unmistakably performing the gesture of impertinence known (in school playgrounds and elsewhere) as "sticking out one's tongue"—a singularly unbecoming gesture, its childishness (in an adult) suggestive of impotence, perhaps, but with implications of defiance and revenge as well as accusation and anger. These flash shots were intended as aids to Juan Davila's work on the portrait planned for the cover (which, in the end, this photo replaces); it is thus clear, if such corroborating evidence were needed, that the gesture of impertinence is directed into the photo's future, at us: the survivors of Michaels's death, the viewers of the photo and the readers of his text. But in addition to the book's effort to confront in this way the reader's presumed complacency, the extended tongue also figures, therefore, a certain mediatory desire: I mean the desire to bridge the space—the space of death—that separates the thin, two-dimensional plane of the photograph, in which the author is confined, from the three-dimensional world in which the viewer-reader lives and moves and, penetrating within that space, to exert an effective impact within the viewer's (survivor's) world. Poignant because it figures the picture's authority, then, and by extension that of Michaels's text, as an authority borrowed from death, the tongue also figures the power to disturb that the text thereby acquires, beyond the death of the owner of the tongue. For the tongue, qua tongue, stands, obviously enough, for language; but *this* tongue is marked by disease, by the "morphemes" of AIDS; so the message it delivers can only concern its owner's unwilling and refractory encounter with, and resistance to, the death that gives the message its power.

It would be wrong to assume, though, that there is anything ghostly or wraithlike in the image presented by Michaels's body. If the protruding tongue is accusatory, it does not threaten to "haunt" the reader-survivor, but rather to pursue, postmortem, a continuing policy of defiance and destabilization, harassment, and difficultness—a matter more of politics than of metaphysics. In the EM Press edition of *Unbecoming* there is a jacket photo of Michaels: film star handsome, well groomed, with a clipped mustache and stylish clothes (presumably an ID picture: Eric Michaels just off the plane in 1982?). This image is in striking and significant contrast to the frontispiece: the wild hair, the bushy beard, the fierce eyes, the determined facial expression, the body invaded by lesions, the extended tongue and its aggressive gesture. In this adult face with its wild features, the tongue seems to allude to a famous feature of Polynesian iconography— familiar to many from the Maori "haka" performed by New Zealand teams before football games—in which a protruding tongue is a sign of warlike fierceness. But more generally, the contrast with the jacket photo makes this an image of Michaels as *wild man*, that is, as a social persona (more than an individual), and as a figure who lives at the edge—or beyond the pale—of orderly, "civilized" society and harasses it with a kind of guerrilla warfare, even if his mission is only to offer a critical counterimage that refuses to be tidied away, or otherwise made to disappear. This portrait of the author as wild man is thus the sign of *Unbecoming*'s own mission of harassment, its ambition to function as the permanent thorn in the side of Tidy Town and the continuing Foucauldian horror show. And in this respect we might also be led to think, therefore, and again in terms of social place and function rather than of individual identity, of the aboriginality to which the image also, unmistakably, makes iconographic reference.

I'm not claiming that in *Unbecoming* Michaels is producing AIDS as a way for white people to achieve the political status of Aboriginals. That would be sentimental, and more to the point, insensitively exploitive of the shameful two-hundred-year history of Aboriginal contact with, and resistance to, the genocidal white settlement of Australia. But there is a certain structural homology between the difficult survival of aboriginality and the resistance to murderous tidiness, the struggle against the horror show that Michaels posits (it is a "first principle") as necessary. And the five or six years I assume to separate the trim Eric Michaels of the jacket photo and the "wild man" AIDS image of *Unbecoming* correspond, for Michaels, to the Yuendumu years, in the course of which—without being or imagining himself to be a Warlpiri Aboriginal—he earned an identity and a place among the Warlpiri people, who were engaged in an inspired, if "wild" (unauthorized, extralegal, *sauvage*) communicational practice of their own, an appropriation of, and so an effective intervention in, the technology, structure, and apparatus of contemporary televisual culture. They invented and operated a collectively run TV station, maneuvering in this way, from the margins, as a matter of self-defense and in their own interests: defending their culture from the destructive incursions of modernity while simultaneously giving it a "voice" within the culture of modernity, and ensuring therefore what Michaels (1988) significantly (and in the context of *Unbecoming* poignantly) called a cultural future. These years are referred to in the diary (124) as the Birth of a Station, and it is possible to think that the Warlpiri example furnished another general model—alongside the position paper, the will, and the revenge letter but (like the protruding tongue) more pragmatic than generic—for the rhetorical operation being performed in *Unbecoming*. This could be described as the birth of a "status," posthumous but effective, and hence the achievement of a cultural future, for an untidy, marginalized, "wild" subject whose body will die of AIDS.

If Michaels is careful, then, at the diary's outset, to deny any claim to an Aboriginal identity, he takes equal care, toward the end, to include, symmetrically, a thoughtfully worded statement of the reasons that underlie his affection for and affinity with the Aboriginal people: ". . . they are engaged, in a way that white Australians tend not to be. Their circumstances are interesting, to them and me. They tend to be kind. And no matter how hard they try, they mostly fail to be bourgeois. They are too familiar with poverty and suffering, perhaps. I feel a whole lot less self-conscious about the way I look and my visible marks of disease when I'm with blacks. They seem a good deal less concerned" (124–25). But here he is obviously not referring to a model of rhetorical effectiveness so much as he is defining a pre-ferred mode of reception for his own diseased self, and so, by exten-sion, for *Unbecoming*. Aboriginality is not the identity Michaels claims for himself so much as it names a certain like-mindedness and capacity for "kindness," a failure to be bourgeois that guarantees the kind of understanding—not "concern" but "engagement"—that *Unbecoming* as a rhetorical performance would like to encounter. The terminological distinction that frames the whole passage may seem subtle, though, and the terms go undefined in the text; the gloss I would offer introduces the concept of "involvement" as a mediating term. To be concerned, as in Michaels's experience white Australians tend to be, is to be interested and even sympathetic, but not involved (and so unempathetic). Perhaps, indeed, one can go so far as to say that concern is a way of disengaging oneself and one's responsibility, but without seeming to, according to a duplicitous structure that would align concern with tidiness (which pretends, for example, to be "concerned" with health when it is actually devoted to the preser-vation of a certain kind of order). The Health Minister mentioned in *Unbecoming* who, "sympathetics" notwithstanding, reassured his au-dience that "we (gays, IV drug users, haemophiliacs) are not mem-bers of the 'general public'" (181) was demonstrating concern (as politicians often do), while simultaneously tidying AIDS out of sight (and so, for his viewers, out of mind as well). Concern, then, is bourgeois because it is hegemonic, and it is a front for complacency and indifference. Engagement, on the other hand, necessarily en-tails involvement; and in Michaels's usage it seems to refer more specifically to a combination of involvement—as something akin to the phenomenological concept of "thrownness" (*Geworfenheit*): find-ing oneself caught up, willy nilly, in a situation—with a degree of disempowerment that prevents one from exerting control over it. Resistance is thus a synonym for engagement, in the cases where resistance (in de Certeau's handy metaphor) is obliged to be more tactical than strategic.[7] Engagement defines oppositional practices that are untidy, then, like the Warlpiri reinvention of TV, or the practice of noncompliance, the art of being difficult, that Michaels invents as a response to AIDS and the whole social horror show that goes with it—an art that extends to the rhetoric of *Unbecoming*. It is an anti-concern.

It is engaged readers, then (on the "Aboriginal" model), that the diary seeks: they would be understanding of, and empathetic with, the embattled situation out of which Michaels speaks. But it is a concerned readership (on the "white" model) that it is likely, as a practical matter, to reach, and which therefore inevitably becomes the prime textual addressee. And the problem of address as a rhetorical proposition then becomes one of converting readerly concern into something more like engagement—which, in the first instance, means *getting through* to concerned readers, penetrating the barrier of their disengagement, getting them involved in spite of themselves, and this across the space of death that makes the text's survival so crucially dependent on the involvement of these uninvolved survivors. Hence Michaels worrying over the "etiquette or sense of style [that] needs to be considered when agreeing to any, assumedly posthumous project" (144); hence the calculus of scandal and curiosity—of gossip—as way of engaging an audience; hence finally the protruding tongue tactics that signify so clearly the desire to break down the distance between Michaels and his posthumous audience, the text and its reception.

But it is here, perhaps, in this requirement of readerly engagement, that the textual address is most inescapably structured as Lacanian demand, so clear is it that a degree of readerly distance is definitional and so, inescapable (without a text-reader difference, reading is not reading, except in some purely mechanical sense). A concerned but scrupulous reader can make a genuine effort in the direction of involvement and engagement, but—the mechanism is relentless—the more scrupulous the effort the less easy it becomes to be sure that one has really escaped mere concern, and conversely, the more unself-conscious the concern the more easily it can mistake itself for engagement. The alternative to concern, for a reader caught in the problematics of distance that readerly difference implies, is not engagement, then, but anxiety. That is what it means, for a reader, to be separated from a text by the "death of the author" that grounds the act of reading, whether the phrase be understood in a theoretical or an actual sense; and the double bind the distance of reading enforces is similar to the double bind inflicted on Michaels's friends (as one imagines it) by his practice of difficultness: the more they try, the less they succeed. There is, in short, no escaping the fact—it's a given, a matter of *Geworfenheit*—that reading entails power, and that a text is relatively disempowered (by its author's "death" or death) with respect to its reading; which means, on the one hand, that readerly engagement is definitionally excluded (if engagement entails disempowerment) and, on the other, that the reader is always drawn in the direction of the hegemonic, enforcing norms and conventions, by way of tidying up and containing the manifestations of textual disorderliness. This is called "interpretation," and in critical circles something called "strong reading" tends to be particularly appreciated. (We might therefore try to imagine something called "weak reading," perhaps, on the analogy of Gianni Vattimo's *pensiero debole*. The problem, though, is that such reading would not be "engaged," however, but merely compliant: it would reverse the text/reader power structure rather than producing the encounter, on the plane of oppositionality—an encounter of mutual engagements—of which Michaels seems to dream.)

Engaged reading, then, is a utopia. The best a militantly uncompliant text like *Unbecoming* can expect, although it is somewhat less than it demands, is the sort of anxiously involved reading I described as scrupulous, a reading that is conscious (however hard it tries) of its own failure to be anything but concerned. This is a way of failing that is at the opposite pole from the ease with which Aboriginals, as described by Michaels, fail to be bourgeois (it's a failure not to be bourgeois, if you will). But it has something in common, perhaps—a certain desperate vigilance?—with the unremitting effort of the difficult patient to resist, and to go on resisting, despite the temptation to give in, to become passive, to go under, to disappear. The dying author's protruding tongue (which after all is a compliant medical gesture as well as an act of defiance) teaches us, perhaps, that, as readers, we *can* get some way out of our concern and into an area of anxiety; and in that area of anxiety maybe, just maybe, it might be possible to meet the tongue halfway.

NOTES

1. My corpus consists of Gilles Barbedette, *Mémoirs d'un jeune homme devenu vieux* (Paris: Gallimard, 1993); Pascal de Duve, *Cargo Vie* (Paris: Livre de Poche [Lattès], 1993); Hervé Guibert, *La Pudeur ou l'impudeur* (video, TF1, 1992); Tom Joslin and Peter Friedman, *Silverlake Life: The View from Here* (New Video, 1993); and Eric Michaels, *Unbecoming* (Sydney: EM Press, 1990) (an American edition of *Unbecoming* appeared in 1997 [Durham: Duke University Press]). For other important writing of AIDS witness, see Bertrand Duquénelle, *L'Aztèque* (Paris: Belfond, 1993); Hervé Guibert, *À l'ami qui ne m'a pas sauvé la vie* (Paris: Gallimard, 1990) and *Le Protocole compassionnel* (Paris: Gallimard, 1991); Paul Monette, *Borrowed Time* (New York: Avon, 1988) and *Last Watch of the Night* (New York: Harcourt Brace, 1994); and David Wojnarowicz, *Close to the Knives: A Memoir of Disintegration* (New York: Vintage, 1991). I wish to thank David Caron for his invaluable help in identifying and laying hands on certain of these texts, and Jean Mainil for introducing me to Pascal de Duve's *Cargo Vie*.

2. Walter Benjamin, "The Storyteller," in *Illuminations,* ed. Hannah Arendt (New York: Schocken, 1964). The verb *erzählen,* whence the *Erzähler* of Benjamin's title (storyteller or narrator), is cognate with the English "to tell."

3. See Wojnarowicz, *Close to the Knives,* 230.

4. Marie Maclean, *The Name of the Mother: Writing Illegitimacy* (London and New York: Routledge, 1994), 6.

5. This sentence refers to allusions to metempsychosis in Guibert, *La Pudeur ou l'impudeur* and Joslin and Friedman, *Silverlake Life,* and to other thematic features and rhetorical characteristics of these works.

6. See Roland Barthes, *La Chambre claire. Note sur la photographie* (Paris: Gallimard, 1980).

7. See Michel de Certeau, *Arts de faire* (Paris: 10/18, 1980).

8. A United States edition of *Unbecoming* appeared in 1997 (Durham: Duke University Press).

Notes on Contributors

PHILIP ANDERSON teaches French and Comparative Literature at Monash University. His major research interest is in contemporary French poetry. He is completing a study of Francis Ponge.

ROSS CHAMBERS teaches French and Comparative Literature at the University of Michigan (Ann Arbor). His recent publications include *Facing It: AIDS Diaries and the Death of the Author* and *Loiterature*. His current research interests concern the cultural status and generic peculiarity of witnessing literature, especially AIDS writing in Australia, France and North America.

PETER CRYLE is Professor of French at the University of Queensland. He has published a number of books on aspects of French literature, including *The Thematics of Commitment: The Tower and the Plain* and *Geometry in the Boudoir: Configurations of French Erotic Narrative*. A book on narrative and sexuality, entitled *The Telling of the Act*, is forthcoming with the University of Delaware Press.

ANNE FREADMAN is Reader in French at the University of Queensland. She has published widely on semiotics and feminist literary theory, with a focus on the articulation of genre and gender. Her articles have appeared in such journals as *Poetics, Paragraph, Sub-Stance, The Canadian Review of Comparative Literature,* as well as in collections of feminist theoretical writing.

GALE MACLACHLAN is an honorary Senior Research Fellow in the Department of European Studies at Macquarie University in Sydney. She has co-authored *Framing and Interpretation* with Ian Reid and published a number of papers on French fiction. Her essay in the present volume is related to the research for which her Ph.D. was awarded: *The Author's Others: Figures for the Author and Reader in the roman policier and related texts.*

BRIAN NELSON is Professor of French Studies at Monash University. His publications include *Zola and the Bourgeoisie* and, as editor, *Natu-*

ralism in the European Novel: New Critical Perspectives and *Forms of Commitment: Intellectuals in Contemporary France.* He has published various translations, including ones of Emile Zola's *The Ladies' Paradise* and *Pot Luck.*

GERALD PRINCE is Professor of Romance Languages at the University of Pennsylvania. He is the author of *Métaphysique et technique dans l'œuvre romanesque de Sartre, A Grammar of Stories, Narratology: The Form and Functioning of Narrative, A Dictionary of Narratology, Narrative as Theme,* and the coeditor of *Alteratives* (with Warren Motte), *Autobiography, Historiography, and Rhetoric* (with Mary Donaldson-Evans and Lucienne Frappier-Mazur), and *Corps/Décors* (with Catherine Nesci and Gretchen Van Slyke).

NAOMI SEGAL is Professor of French Studies at the University of Reading, UK. She has published numerous articles and eight books, including three coedited collections, *Freud in Exile, Scarlet Letters* and *Coming Out of Feminism?* and five monographs, most recently *Narcissus and Echo: Women and Men in the French Récit, The Adulteress's Child: Authorship and Desire in the Nineteenth-century Novel* and *André Gide: Pederasty and Pedagogy.* She is currently completing a French book of essays on Gide and a coedited interdisciplinary collection, *In/determinate Bodies.*

JULIE SOLOMON teaches French literature at Tufts University. She is the author of *Proust—lecture du narrataire* and has published articles on Proust, Baudelaire, Duras and Leiris. She is currently completing a book manuscript entitled *The Face of the Writer: Readings in Literary Self-Portraiture*

ROSEMARY SORENSEN is an editor and book reviewer. She has edited a collection of short stories, *Microstories* and coedited *The Penguin Book of Death.* Essays on love and hate have appeared in the collections *The Eleven Deadly Sins* and *The Eleven Saving Virtues.* She was editor of the *Australian Book Review* from 1989 to 1994, and is currently literary editor of the Brisbane *Courier Mail.* Her PhD thesis, supervised by Marie Maclean, was on the French nineteenth-century poet, Tristan Corbière.

NATHANIEL WING is Professor of French and a member of the Women's and Gender Studies Faculty at Louisiana State University. He is the author of *Present Appearances: Aspects of Poetic Structure in Rimbaud's "Illuminations"* and *The Limits of Narrative: Essays on*

Baudelaire, Flaubert, Rimbaud, and Mallarmé. He has published articles on nineteenth-century French writers, principally Baudelaire, Flaubert, Mallarmé, and Rimbaud in various journals including *Paragraph, Romanic Review, French Forum, Diacritics,* the *French Review, Nineteenth-Century French Studies,* and *Neophilologus.* He has recently completed a book manuscript, *Gender Divides,* on representations of gender in nineteenth-century French narratives.

CHRIS WORTH teaches English and Comparative Literature at Monash University. He coedited *Postmodern Conditions* and two volumes published by the Centre for Comparative Literature and Cultural Studies at Monash, *Discourse and Difference* and *Literature and Opposition.* He contributed a chapter on Australia and New Zealand to *The Scottish Invention of English Literature,* edited by R. Crawford, and is currently finishing a book on Sir Walter Scott and the Scottish theater.

Index

References to illustrations are in italics.